Military Strategies of India and China

Military Strategies of India and China

Col. (Retd.) S.C. Narang

PRASHANT PUBLISHING HOUSE
DELHI-110094

Published by :
Prashant Publishing House
C-34, 28 Foota Road, Gali-3,
West Karwal Nagar, Delhi-110094
Phone : 011-22963970, Mob. : 9810396373
e-mail.: prashantpublishinghouse@gmail.com

Military Strategies of India and China

First Published 2019

ISBN 978-93-88526-11-1

PRINTED IN INDIA
Published by Mr. R.K. Jha M/s Prashant Publishing House and Published at H.S. Offset House Press, Delhi.

Contents

Preface

Military strategy is a policy implemented by military organizations to pursue desired strategic goals.

In recent years, India has developed multiple strategies to deal with China's rise and threatening postures on both its land border and in the Indian Ocean. They include limited balancing based on asymmetrical arms buildups and informal coalitions with like-minded states and regular diplomatic engagement with Beijing both bilaterally and through multilateral forums. But the most significant non-traditional soft balancing efforts have been in building limited strategic partnerships with the United States and Japan as well as participation in ASEAN Forums, along with other regional groupings such as the Shanghai Cooperation Organization (SCO). The strategy is also based on institutional denial by not agreeing to China's membership in the South Asian Association for Regional Cooperation and, most prominently, refusing to join the Belt and Road Initiative (BRI). There have been some efforts at creating counter economic cooperation initiatives with regional states as alternatives to BRI. The Africa Growth Corridor with Japan was planned in 2017 as a limited alternative to BRI, although it is yet to take full shape.

India's security orientation has traditionally been continental, focused on internal unrest and external threats across contested land borders with Pakistan and China to the detriment of maritime concerns and expeditionary options. China's military expansionism, Sino-Pakistani cooperation, evolving regional nuclear dynamics, and other factors, however, are altering the strategic environment. Furthermore, India's ambitions to be a leading power on the global stage and the expectations of other international actors (not least the U.S.) for India to contribute as a regional "net security provider" impose substantial demands on Indian military capabilities. Despite its many strengths and significant potential, India will be challenged to respond to these new circumstances and objectives while still attending to its existing problems.

China's involvement in UN peacekeeping contributions has been on the rise for some time. China is also stepping up its own military and security operations abroad to protect its commercial and strategic interests, particularly in Africa. In doing so, China is exposing itself to a more complex set of issues – including international legal issues – with which it is only just starting to grapple.

China's rise and its growing military power have intensified the Sino-Indian security dilemma. For a long time after the 1962 war, India's military posture along the India–China border was mostly defensive in nature and could be characterized as imposing "deterrence by denial."

This is a reference book. All the matter is just compiled and edited in nature, taken from the various sources which are in public domain.

Military Strategy for India in the 21st Century is a comprehensive collection of high value essays defining multiple nuances of military strategy. Written by prominent military and civilian experts on essential aspects of national and military strategy, the book reflects on the need to deal with existing and potential security threats and challenges, as well as achievement of national goals and aspirations, in which the military has a role to play.

—Editor

1

India's New Military Strategy against China

Earlier this month, as a part of Exercise Bahubali, the Indian Air Force (IAF) used its C-17 Globemasters to carry, as this newspaper reported, tanks and armoured personnel carriers to Leh airport. The objective was to demonstrate capability to move men and equipment rapidly to border areas. Other than eight C-17's, IAF also deployed four IL-76's and four AN-32's to showcase its strategic lift capability.

Meanwhile The Indian Express has reported that the IAF is planning to deploy, in the eastern sector, six units of Akash missile systems along with a squadron each of Apache and Chinook helicopters and Rafale fighter aircrafts once they are inducted. An additional squadron of Sukhoi Su-30MKI may also be deployed in the eastern sector. Besides, India is speeding up its infrastructure projects in the border regions close to China.

Prompting this flurry of activity

A recent paper titled "From Denial to Punishment: The Security Dilemma and Changes in India's Military Strategy Towards China" in Asian Security by Anit Mukherjee and Yogesh Joshi may provide the answer. Before 2005, the duo argues, the power asymmetry between India and China was manageable. The terrain near the border on the Chinese side was a major barrier to offensive operations. However, now

China has not just massively improved the infrastructure in the Tibet Autonomous Region (TAR), but has also undertaken an impressive military modernisation programme and adopted a more aggressive posture on the India border. Especially after Doklam, as Colonel (retired) Vinayak Bhatt has pointed out, TAR has seen a sharp jump in Chinese air force activity and construction of new airstrips and heliports.

These developments have forced the Indian security establishment, conclude Mukherjee and Joshi, to shed its earlier 'defensive' military posture of 'deterrence by denial' to a more 'offensive' posture of 'deterrence by punishment'. According to the new strategy, India will not just confine itself to denying Chinese forces territorial gains but will actively impose costs on the adversary and may even open additional fronts. The earlier defensive posture is no longer sustainable with China possessing the capability to launch an assault without any warning leading to depletion of Indian resources in quick time.

Su-30MKI is a long range fighter aircraft that provides much deeper penetration capabilities compared to Mig-21 which provided interception ability. While C-17s, C-130 J's and Chinooks will provide strategic lift capabilities, Su-30 MKI's, Rafales and Apaches will provide the offensive firepower.

Mukherjee and Joshi also suggest that India is moulting its Pakistan-centric focus for a China-centric one. The shift actually is in line with other developments beyond the conventional realm. Most incremental additions in the nuclear domain including the induction of longer range ballistic missiles and nuclear propelled, ballistic missile-armed submarines (SSBNs) are being made with China, not Pakistan, in mind. The range of Agni series, extending till 6000 kilometres, is a clear giveaway.

In fact, India has been criticised for pursuing 'credibility' of nuclear deterrence at the cost of 'minimality' while tenuously hewing to the concept of 'credible minimum deterrence'. But as Vipin Narang of the Massachusetts Institute of Technology had elaborated in a 2013 paper titled "Five Myths about India's Nuclear Posture" in The Washington Quarterly, any 'credible' deterrence against China will easily surpass the 'minimum' for Pakistan. Narang added: "India's security managers had to choose whom they envisioned their primary deterrent adversary to be, and against whom they wanted to build and maintain a credible minimum deterrent. All the observable indicators, such as the range and numbers of their strategic missile programs, suggest unsurprisingly that they chose China."

It is true that the range of the K-15 missile that Arihant is armed with is merely 750 kilometres. However, Arihant should just be seen as a demonstrator of triad capability. India's three planned submarine-launched ballistic missiles (K-4, K-5 and K-6) will have a range upwards of 3000 kilometres.

The growing conventional asymmetry vis-à-vis China is not just prompting a rethink over conventional military strategy but also nuclear strategy. As Joshi along with Harsh Pant has argued in a recent book 'India's Nuclear Policy', the debate over India's no-first use (NFU) of nuclear weapons is partly stemming from a growing gap on the conventional front.

It is too early, however, to press the panic button and discard the NFU pledge. A review of conventional military doctrines, on the other hand, is definitely welcome. A shift from Pakistan-centric approach was also long overdue. The review process should keep in mind that internal balancing of China alone will not achieve much because: a) China is way ahead of India already, and b) India is a developing country with multiple competing demands on scarce capital, leaving little for a focused military build-up. Partnerships, especially with the US, will be key to not just providing external balancing as a complementary approach but also helping strengthen India's capabilities and boost its defence manufacturing potential.

MILITARY MODERNIZATION REFORMS IN RISING INDIA

In India, civil-military relations have focused too heavily on one side of the problem – how to ensure civilian control over the armed forces, while neglecting the other – how to build and field an effective military force. We believe that this imbalance in civil-military relations has caused military modernization and reforms to suffer from a lack of political guidance, disunity of purpose and effort, and material and intellectual corruption.

Sixty years after embarking on a rivalry with Pakistan, India has not been able to alter its strategic relationship with a country less than one fifth its size. India's many counterinsurgencies have lasted twenty years on an average, double the worldwide average, as reported by a recent RAND study. Since the 1998 nuclear tests, reports of a growing missile gap with Pakistan have called into question the quality of India's nuclear deterrent. Indeed, with the exception of nuclear weapons, sixty years of military research have not delivered one weapon to the armed forces that has altered the country's strategic position. The high point of Indian military history – the liberation of Bangladesh in 1971 – therefore, stands in sharp contrast to the persistent inability of the country to raise effective military forces.

No factor more accounts for the haphazard nature of Indian military modernization than the lack of political leadership on defence. Key political leaders rejected the use of force as an instrument of politics in favour of a policy of strategic restraint that minimized the importance of the military. Jawaharlal Nehru, for example, wrote in 1938 that he did not see any significant military challenge to an independent India; the only military role he saw for the Indian Army was in suppressing the tribes of the North West Frontier, who were, in any case, too primitive to fight a modern military outside the tribal areas.

The Government of India held to its strong anti-militarism despite the reality of conflict and war that followed independence. Much has been made of the downgrading of the service chiefs in the protocol rank, but of greater consequence was the elevation of military science and research as essential to the long-term defence of India over the armed forces themselves. Nehru invited British physicist P.M.S. Blackett to examine the relationship between science and defence. Blackett came back with a report that called for capping Indian defence spending at two per cent of GDP and limited military modernization. He also recommended state funding and ownership of military research laboratories and established his protégé, Daulat Singh Kothari, as the head of the labs. Indian defence spending decreased during the 1950s. Of the three services, the Indian Navy received greater attention. The decade saw the negotiations for the acquisition of India's first aircraft carrier. The Indian Air Force acquired World War II surplus Canberra transport. The Indian Army, the biggest service by a wide margin, went to Congo on a UN peacekeeping mission, but was neglected overall. India had its first defence procurement scandal when buying old jeeps and experienced its first civil-military crisis when army chief K.S. Thimayya threatened resignation in protest of political interference in military matters. The decade culminated in the government's 'forward policy' against China, which was foisted on an unprepared army and led to the war of 1962 with China that ended in a humiliating Indian defeat.

The foremost lesson of 1962 was that India could not afford further military retrenchment. In the aftermath of military defeat, the Indian government launched a significant military expansion programme that doubled the size of the army and raised a fighting air force. With the focus shifting North, the Indian Navy received less attention. A less recognized but close second lesson of the war was that political interference in military matters ought to be limited. The military – and especially the army – asked for and received operational and institutional autonomy, a fact most visible in the wars of 1965 and 1971. In both wars, the army chiefs explicitly asked for autonomy.

The problem, however, was that the political leadership did not suddenly become more comfortable with the military as an institution; they remained wary of the possibility of a coup d'etat and militarism more generally. Indian political leaders had been subjugating the military to effective civilian control since independence in line with standard civil-military relations practice. This process expanded. The military was further subjugated to the civilian bureaucracy.

In 1968, for example, the Indian government established the Institute of Defence Studies and Analyses (IDSA), staffed with civilian bureaucrats. IDSA clashed repeatedly with military assessments of threats and solutions. According to K. Subrahmanyam, one of the first directors, the institute survived pressure from the military due to the protection of successive defence secretaries – civilian bureaucrats serving the defence minister. The idea behind the IDSA – developing greater civilian capacity in military matters – was a laudable one, but it became part of a larger effort to control the military. In particular, the military leadership, placed in a location away from government offices, was increasingly denied political access.

The Indian civil-military relations landscape has changed marginally since. In the eighties, there was a degree of political-military confluence in the Rajiv Gandhi government: Rajiv appointed a military buff, Arun Singh, as the minister of state for defence. At the same time, Krishnaswami Sundarji, an exceptional officer, became the army chief. Together they launched an ambitious programme of military modernization in response to Pakistani rearmament and nuclearization. In the end, the move to pre-empt Pakistani rearmament and nuclearization failed. Pakistan's nuclearization allowed that country to escalate the subconventional conflict in Kashmir while stemming Indian ability to escalate to a general war, where it had superiority. India is yet to emerge from this stability-instability paradox.

We do not know why Rajiv Gandhi agreed to the specific kind of military modernization that occurred in the mid-eighties, but then stepped back from using this capacity in 1987 during the Brasstacks crisis. Sundarji later wrote in a veiled work of fiction, and told his many friends that Brasstacks was the last chance India had to coerce Pakistan to accept terms. Apart from Brasstacks, the mid-eighties saw Indian military assertion in the Siachen glacier and in Sri Lanka, both of which proved to be expensive, if not outright failures. The peacekeeping mission to Sri Lanka became India's Vietnam. Indian presence on the Siachen glacier has drained the army's resources so much so that Pakistan has found it to its advantage to reject New Delhi's efforts to negotiate an end to the issue.

The puzzle of Brasstacks stands in a line of similar decisions. In 1971, India did not push the advantage of its victory in the eastern theatre to the West. Instead, New Delhi, under uberrealist Prime Minister Indira Gandhi, signed on to an equivocal agreement at Simla that committed both sides to peaceful resolution of future disputes without any enforcement measures. India's decision to wait 24 years between its first nuclear test in 1974 and the second set of tests in 1998 is equally puzzling. Why did it not follow through after the 1974 test, and why did it test in 1998?

We have argued that underlying these puzzles is a remarkable preference for strategic restraint. Indian leaders simply have not seen the use of force as a useful instrument of politics. This foundation of ambivalence informs Indian defence policy, and consequently its military modernization and reform efforts.

To be sure, military restraint in a region as volatile as South Asia is wise and has helped persuade the great powers to accommodate India's rise, but it does not help military planning. Together with the separation of the armed forces from the government, divisions among the services and between the services and other related agencies, and the inability of the military to seek formal support for policies it deems important, India's strategic restraint has served to deny political guidance to the efforts of the armed forces to modernize. As wise as strategic restraint may be, Pakistan, India's primary rival, hardly believes it to be true. Islamabad prepares as if India were an aggressive power and that has a real impact on India's security.

What suffices for a military modernization plan is a wish list of weapon systems amounting to as much as $100 billion from the three services and announcements of coming breakthroughs from the Defence Research and Development Organization (DRDO), the premier agency for military research in India. The process of modernization is illustrative. The armed forces propose to acquire certain weapon systems. The political leadership and the civilian bureaucracy, especially the Ministry of Finance, react to these requests, agreeing on some and rejecting others. A number of dysfunctions ensue.

First, the services see things differently and their plans are essentially uncoordinated. Coming off the experience of the Kargil war and Operation Parakram, the Indian Army seems to have arrived at a Cold Start doctrine, seeking to find some fighting space between subconventional conflict and nuclear exchange in the standoff with Pakistan. The doctrine may not be official policy, but it informs the army's wish list, where attack helicopters, tanks, and long-range artillery, stand out as marquee items. The Indian Air Force, meanwhile, is the primary instrument of the country's nuclear deterrent. The IAF's close second role is air superiority and air defence. Close air support, to which the IAF has belatedly agreed and which is essential to the army's Cold Start doctrine, is a distant fourth.

The Indian Navy has been angling for a return to the Panikkar vision of the country – dominance of the Indian Ocean region. It wants to secure the country's sea lanes of communications, protect its energy supplies, and guard its trade routes. It wants further to be the vehicle of Indian naval diplomacy, not only in the region but also in the rest of the world. It sees a role in the anti-piracy efforts in the Malacca Straits and the Horn of Africa. The Indian Navy's role in India's nuclear posture, however, is unclear, though the country has launched a project to build a nuclear submarine. What is even more ambiguous is how the Indian Navy might contribute in the event of a war with Pakistan. It almost seems that the navy would like simply to brush past the problem of Pakistan and reach for the grander problems – Indian emergence as a great power, and China. Accordingly, the Indian Navy's biggest procurement order is a retrofitted aircraft carrier from Russia.

India's three services have dramatically different views of what their role in India's security should be, and there is no political effort to ensure this coordination. Cold Start remains an iffy proposition. India's nuclear deterrent remains tethered to a single delivery system: fighter aircraft. Meanwhile, the Indian Army's energies are dissipated with counterinsurgency duties, which might increase manifold if the government orders the army to enter the fight against the rising leftist insurgency, the Naxalites. And all this at a time when the primary security threat to the country has been terrorism. After the Mumbai attacks, the Indian government and the people of India are said to have resolved to tackle the problem headlong, but today the government's minister in charge of internal security, Palaniappan Chidambaram, is more under siege himself than seizing the hidden enemy.

The so-called officer shortage in the Indian Army exemplifies the lack of coordination, and indeed the failure of the country's leaders to even ask the tough questions. The Indian Army has claimed an officer shortage for three decades. The shortage, especially in the ranks of captains and majors, is reported to be as high as 30 per cent. The army has argued that the shortage is the result of tough assignments, poor pay, and falling applicant quality. Two major pay hikes in the last fifteen years have not corrected the problem – instead the pay condition has worsened since the red-hot Indian private sector offers better paying jobs.

Given this serious condition, we asked a simple question: What has been the impact of the officer shortage on the army's military effectiveness? The answer, unequivocally, is 'none at all'. The response is inexplicable. If military effectiveness has not suffered, the officer shortage is immaterial. Indeed, it goes to the Indian Army's credit that it has managed retrenchment of the officer corps so well. The army's continued insistence that it has an officer shortage, however, suggests other motives. More importantly, the persistence of officer shortage as an issue suggests that political leaders are not sufficiently tuned to military matters.

Second, despite repeated calls for and commissions into reforms in the higher defence structure, planning, intelligence, defence production, and procurement, the Indian national security establishment remains fragmented and uncoordinated. According to Anit Mukherjee, a former Indian Army officer who has studied recent defence reforms, the government and armed forces have succeeded in reforms primed by additions to the defence budget but failed to institute reforms that require reprioritization.

The Kargil Review Committee, and the Group of Ministers report that followed, for example, recommended a slew of reforms. The changes most readily implemented were those that created new commands, agencies, and task forces, essentially linear expansion backed by new budgetary allocations. The changes least likely to occur were those required changes in the hierarchy.

The most common example of tough reform is the long-standing recommendation for a chief of defence staff. A military chief, as opposed to the service chiefs, was seen as a solution to the problem that causes the army, navy, and air force not to reconcile their priorities. The government would also receive a single point of advice and have a single point of accountability for implementation of policy. However, the creation of the position of military commander-in-chief, which existed in the colonial era, has been passively rejected by the political leaders, mainly for fear of giving a military officer too much power.

The argument would be logical if political leaders stepped forward to fill the void, but they have not. To be fair, the IAF and the Indian Navy, the smaller services, have resisted the move based on their own fears that the much bigger army would return to the domination of the colonial period. Instead of a chief of defence staff, the government has tried to install an integrated defence staff that is supposed to undertake reconciliation between the services, but which really is a toothless body with little influence.

Lastly, the Ministry of Defence has a finance section deputed by the Ministry of Finance. This chapter oversees all defence expenditures, even after they have been authorized. Once the cabinet has approved a spending item. However, the finance section raises questions of propriety, wisdom, and policy that should under normal circumstances be under the purview of the defence minister. What should be an auditing function has transformed into a decision-making one, making defence spending hard to do in India.

Corruption in weapons procurement has been a political issue since the mid-1980s, when allegations of a series of paybacks in the purchase of Bofors artillery, HDW submarines, and other items mobilized an opposition that removed Rajiv Gandhi from power in 1989. Corruption scandals had erupted earlier as well, but by the mid-eighties, the problem became a central political issue and slowed down the acquisition process. Since then, Indian political leaders have tried hard not to appear to be corrupt, going out of their way to slow down new purchases.

Corruption is still a problem, as shown in the 2001 *Tehelka* expose of political leaders accepting bribes in return for defence contracts. Recently, Uday Bhaskar, the Indian Navy officer and defence analyst, wrote bitingly that for a number of years now the armed forces, which desperately need modernization, have been returning unspent funds to the treasury.

There is widespread recognition that corruption is morally venal and detrimental to the cause of Indian security. We believe, however, that the second- and third-order problems of corruption have unacknowledged impact on military modernization and capacity. The Defence Procurement Manual and Procedures on the Ministry of Defence's website are the first steps in the right direction, but the Indian government has generally failed to build a transparent and legitimate procurement process. The result has been continued corruption and delayed acquisition. Even the purchase of coffins for soldiers during the Kargil war becomes grist for the mill. This is not to say no corruption occurred in the deal, but reaching clarity and consensus on even small budget items such as coffins, is much more difficult than it should be.

The deep roots of corruption extend to military research and development and to the heart of India's foreign relations.

Given the early beliefs about science and engineering being the 'temples of modernity', military research and development has received great political attention even when the budgets have not matched ambition. Since the mid-1970s, however, the DRDO embarked on a number of ambitious and well-funded projects to build a fighter aircraft, a tank, and missiles. All three projects floundered.

While the aircraft and tank projects have largely failed, the missile programme is considered successful. The reputation of the success carried the director of the missile programme, A.P.J. Abdul Kalam, to the presidency. Yet in 2010, no Indian missile in the arsenal of the armed forces has managed to alter the strategic equation with Pakistan or China. The Prithvi short-range missile is not useful because of its range and liquid fuel needs. The longer-range Agni models have gone through numerous tests without entering the army's arsenal. Other variations, such as Nag and Akash, have limited strategic purpose.

A series of articles in *The Indian Express* in November 2006 showed that the DRDO had not produced a single weapon system capable of altering India's strategic condition. What is more, the reports said, the Indian government was unwilling to subject the organization to public scrutiny. An official investigation, called the Rama Rao Report, suggested reorganization of DRDO's labs and facilities, but that is only the superficial problem.The virtual monopoly over military research in state-owned labs has meant that the abundant energies of the Indian private sector have remained outside the defence industry. Where in the United States, small and medium-sized defence contractors form the backbone of the research complex, India is far from thinking along those lines. Despite recent efforts to include the private sector through various schemes, there continues to be distrust of private industry in the Indian defence establishment. We believe it is easier for a private foreign supplier to win a contract with the Ministry of Defence than it is for a small private Indian company to do so.

The problem with the DRDO is ideological corruption. For decades, the Indian government has accepted dishonest promises made by DRDO as the basis for providing billions of dollars of support because of the persisting ideology of autarky. The greatest success of military research in India comes not from the DRDO, but from the Atomic Energy Commission, which built the nuclear devices. But the government has been unwilling to subject DRDO to public accountability – claims of military secrets are disingenuous because the organization is not developing a weapon as yet uninvented; most of its work is reverse engineering. Instead, the head of DRDO serves as the defence minister's scientific adviser. The two positions – of supplier and adviser – bring inherent conflict of interest, but this has not been an issue in India at all.

The second pattern of systemic corruption comes from the inability of the Indian defence system to wean itself from the supply of Soviet/Russian equipment. The reasons why India initially went to the Soviet Union for weapons are well-known. The United States chose Pakistan, India went to the Soviet Union. But that political decision was reinforced by ideas about the corruption-free nature of the state-owned Soviet defence industry and the profit-mindedness of western, and especially American, firms.

This characterization has always been untrue. Soviet/Russian suppliers have engaged in as much corruption as western firms, but because the Soviet Union was a closed system, the corruption – which was inevitably reported first in the press in the supplier countries – was never really reported in the Soviet Union. This tradition continues, though the Russian free press has been more critical of the country's defence deals. Indeed, those who served as Indian 'agents' for the Soviet firms have highlighted the better business practice of Russians, a laughable matter in light of India's recent travails with the retrofit and sale of the Russian aircraft carrier, Admiral Gorshkov. The tendency is reiterated in Indian preferences in dealing with the West as well. New Delhi seems to prefer government-to-government foreign military sales, which are in turn causing some degree of protest from users who want longer-term maintenance arrangements with suppliers.

In contrast, western firms have always been seen as money-grubbing, an opinion that exists across the political spectrum and is prevalent in the civilian bureaucracy. When the armed forces stuff their wish lists with western, not Russian, weapons, these elements of the system become suspicious. Fears of corruption surface, the DRDO promises to produce the system at home, and the acquisition process is held up.

The political rapprochement between India and the United States has not yet filtered into the system for attitudes to change dramatically. India's growing military supply relationship with Israel is instructive. The most successful Israeli firm in the Indian market is Israel Aerospace Industries (IAI), a state-owned company. IAI was quick to adopt the Russian model of operation in India: offering the DRDO co-development opportunities to win contracts. In contrast, American firms are reluctant to work with, let alone transfer high-end technology to a state owned enterprise. They would prefer to set up a subsidiary in India which could retain control of the technology. Given the civil-military arrangement, however, the debate in India does not hinge on these issues, American firms continue to have a disadvantage, and the Indian military wish list remains unfulfilled.

India has been one of the biggest importers of advanced conventional weapons in the last thirty years, but this sustained rearmament has not altered India's strategic position. The armed forces push for modernization, but do not have the authority to mount the national campaign necessary for transforming the security condition of the country. Budget increases delivered by a rapidly expanding economy and access to western technology previously denied to India have led to optimism about Indian military power, but the dysfunction in India's civil-military relations reduces the impact of rearmament. Arming without aiming has some purpose in persuading other great powers of India's benign rise, but it cannot be the basis of military planning.

Without real change in the defence system, bigger budgets and newer weapons are unlikely to alter the political position of the armed forces within the Indian defence establishment. The armed forces are likely to be increasingly dissatisfied, especially with growing exposure to the operational cultures of western armies and defence corporations, but rebalancing India's civil-military relations will require major institutional and attitudinal changes. Apart from the problems we have highlighted above, the Indian government will need to transform the way it thinks of defence. On the one hand, bring in the military to serve as a full-fledged arm of the government and, on the other, invite genuine public participation in everything from the security debate to military research and development, and not use secrecy as an excuse to hide failures.

EXAMINING MILITARY POWER PROJECTION

To some, the phrase "power projection" suggests imposing regime change on a state far away from home for strategic gain. In this view, a prototypical example might be Operation Iraqi Freedom, the 2003 U.S.-led invasion of Iraq. While such a conceptualization captures some key elements of power projection, it is far too narrow.

The U.S. Department of Defense (DoD) defines power projection much more broadly as being "[t]he ability of a nation to apply all or some of its elements of national power—political, economic, informational, or military—to rapidly and effectively deploy and sustain forces in and from multiple dispersed locations to respond to crises, to contribute to deterrence, and to enhance regional stability."

Focusing specifically on the final element of national power in the DoD's definition—the use of military tools—it is possible to disaggregate military power projection into nine different aspects based on the political goals being sought and the level of force employed. Four of these relate to the employment of "soft" military power (securing sea lanes of communication, non-combatant evacuation operations, humanitarian relief, and peacekeeping), and five are primarily concerned with "hard" military power (showing the flag, compellence/deterrence, punishment, armed intervention, and conquest).

Soft Military Power Projection

Securing Sea Lanes of Communication. The protection of shipping lanes from attack by hostile states or irregular threats. As the Indian Navy's maritime doctrine notes, trade is increasingly critical to the Indian economy, which makes the protection of the sea lanes transiting the Indian Ocean a significant priority. Following the attacks of September 11, 2001, the Indian Navy played a high-profile role in escorting U.S. shipping through the Straits of Malacca.

More recently, Indian naval vessels have been deployed to the Gulf of Aden, where they have thwarted several attempted hijackings by pirates.

Non-combatant Evacuation Operations. The evacuation of Indian or friendly third country civilians from a foreign country when they are endangered by war or civil unrest. For example, during Operation Sukoon (Urdu: Relief) the navy evacuated 2,280 Indian, Sri Lankan, and Nepalese civilians from Lebanon ahead of the 2006 Israeli-Hizbollah War. Several orders of magnitude larger was the airlift of over 100,000 Indians from Iraq and Kuwait ahead of the 1991 Gulf War.

Humanitarian Relief. The use of military forces abroad to assist in the aftermath of a natural disaster. Following the 2004 Asian tsunami, the Indian Navy mobilized 32 ships and over 20,000 naval personnel to evacuate casualties, as well as provide emergency sources of power and water to the peoples of Sri Lanka, the Maldives, Indonesia, Thailand, and Malaysia.

Peacekeeping. Military operations designed to support diplomatic efforts to reach a long-term political settlement to an ongoing dispute. India has been one of the most significant contributors to U.N. peacekeeping missions. As of 2009, the Indian Army had roughly 8,000 personnel deployed in the Democratic Republic of Congo, Lebanon, East Timor, the Ivory Coast, and the Golan Heights.

Hard Military Power Projection

Showing the Flag. The symbolic deployment of military forces to a region to demonstrate political interest, resolve, or willingness to take more forceful military action. For example, in June 1987 the Indian Air Force violated Sri Lankan airspace when it undertook Operation Poomalai (Tamil: Garland), the forced airdrop of relief supplies to ethnic Tamils during the siege of Jaffna. This action sent a clear message to the government in Colombo about New Delhi's desire to see a negotiated end to the conflict and helped lead to the signing of the Indo-Sri Lankan accord. More recently, the Indian Navy has undertaken several high-profile deployments to the South China Sea and the Persian Gulf, which have been interpreted as important signals of Indian interest in these regions.

Compellence and Deterrence. The use or the threat of military force against another state to induce it into or dissuade it from pursuing a given policy.

In this form, power projection acts as a diplomatic tool, attempting to influence the decision-making process and calculus of foreign actors. For example, the governor of East Pakistan's decision to surrender to India in 1971 has been attributed to the compellence effect of well-timed air strikes on his residence in Dhaka at the very moment he was conducting a crisis response meeting. In the same conflict, the destruction of East Pakistani airfields after the air force in the territory had been attritted was an exercise in deterrence by denial that sought to preclude intervention by an outside power.

Punishment. The punitive use of force against another state in response to its pursuit of a given policy. Aside from limited punitive strikes on Pakistani posts across the Line of Control in Kashmir in response to militant activity (not an expeditionary use of force), punishment has not been widely employed by the Indian military.

Armed Intervention. The forcible movement of military units into another nation's territory to influence the internal affairs of the target country, short of outright conquest. Historical examples in India's immediate neighborhood range in size from the 1988 deployment of a parachute battalion to the Maldives (Operation Cactus) to put down a coup to the 1971 intervention in East Pakistan by three corps of the Indian Army to assist guerillas fighting for independence.

Conquest. The offensive use of military assets to forcibly occupy non-contiguous territory controlled or claimed by another state. This has not been an aspect of power projection pursued by independent India, although at the time some observers believed that the use of military forces in Hyderabad (Operation Polo), Goa (Operation Vijay), and elsewhere as part of the post-Independence consolidation of the Indian Union was "an act of military aggression and conquest."

Given this disaggregation, it is clear that power projection is a much broader concept than mere invasion seeking regime change. Military assets, depending on how they are employed, can advance a state's foreign policy goals by facilitating the projection of either hard or soft forms of military power. Moreover, since Independence, India has employed at least seven, and perhaps eight, of the nine aspects of military power projection.

INDIA'S CONVENTIONAL MILITARY AND POWER PROJECTION

The three varieties of conventional military power—sea power, air power, and land power—all contribute to power projection in different ways. As Table 1 indicates, sea power has a high degree of fungibility across various power projection missions and will likely form the foundation of India's global reach in coming years. This is particularly true in India's "extended neighborhood," since the region stretching "across [Asia's] sub-regions—be it East Asia, West Asia, Central Asia, South Asia or Southeast Asia" is largely a maritime domain. In contrast, air and land power play more limited, but nonetheless important, roles in India's power projection capabilities.

Sea Power

In light of the fact that roughly 90% of India's external trade by volume and 77% by value is seaborne, Indian maritime power has a role to play in sustaining domestic economic development. Indeed, a host of observers dating back to the pre-Independence period has argued that India's economy is "at the mercy of the power which controls the sea." In the northern Indian Ocean, securing sea lanes of communication will be facilitated by the Indian Navy's ability to exercise "sea denial" (negating an enemy's ability to use the sea but at the same time making no attempt to control the sea itself) in a region stretching from the Arabian Sea in the west to the Straits of Malacca in the east. Moreover, as India looks farther away for energy resources, its political and military leaders are explicitly linking this effort with the need for the Indian military, particularly the navy, to be able to "protect the country's economic and energy interests" in key parts of the Indian Ocean.

Aircraft carriers, surface ships and submarines equipped with land-attack cruise missiles, and amphibious landing ships—the latter of which are discussed with land power below—are the key maritime power projection platforms that can influence events on land from the sea. While submarines can rely on stealth to approach an enemy coastline, task forces of cruisemissile-armed surface platforms, amphibious assault ships, and aircraft carriers require the assistance of attack submarines, maritime patrol aircraft, and modern destroyers to protect them from hostile submarines, aircraft, and anti-ship cruise missiles. Tankers and supply ships sustain maritime forces with food, fuel, and ammunition when operating a significant distance from friendly ports.

In 2008, then-Chief of Naval Staff Admiral Sureesh Mehta foresaw that the navy of 2020 would be "capable of influencing the outcome of land battles and performing a constabulary role in the Indian Ocean region." Achieving this will require a significant upgrade in capabilities. Naval planners envision a three-carrier fleet as the cornerstone of India's future blue-water navy: the 44,500-ton, Russian-built INS *Vikramaditya* (Sanskrit: Brave as the Sun) which is expected to join the fleet after 2012, and two domestically built aircraft carriers of the Vikrant class weighing in at 40,000 tons (INS *Vikrant*) (Sanskrit: Powerful) and 64,000 tons (INS *Vishal*) (Sanskrit: Great), scheduled to enter service in 2015 and 2018, respectively. At the same time, the introduction of the fourth-generation supersonic MiG-29K Fulcrum provides India with the most powerful naval strike aircraft in the region and increases its force projection capacity by an order of magnitude.

However, these optimistic projections mask a dark reality: at present India's existing 28,000-ton aircraft carrier, launched in 1953, is on its last legs. Should the induction of the *Vikramaditya* or the *Vikrant* be delayed beyond the middle of the decade, as some informed observers speculate, the navy could find itself without a carrier for several years. At the same time, only 11 of the 30 Mk. 51 Sea Harrier fighters that were in service in the 1980s remain, and at the time of this writing, there is yet to be a test flight of the naval version of Hindustan Aeronautics Limited's domestically designed Tejas lightweight fighter, which is supposed to replace the Harriers in providing air defense to the carriers.

Furthermore, the *Vikramaditya* and the *Vikrant* will carry only 16 fighters each. Assuming that the bigger *Vishal* will accommodate a larger complement of aircraft (50–60), analysts say it would have to operate in tandem with one of the 40,000-ton carriers to produce "as much striking power as a single U.S. Nimitz-class carrier. Even armed with precision-guided munitions, a contingent of this size could sustain only a modest land bombardment, and only for a modest time." Moreover, a three-carrier fleet will only ensure that the navy has at least one carrier at sea at all times, given the repair, training, and deployment cycles for modern naval vessels. To be able to implement Admiral Mehta's constabulary role in the Indian Ocean, the navy would need to have the ability to maintain two carriers at sea at all times, which would suggest a need for twice as many flattops. With an estimated unit cost of $1.5

billion, against an annual naval procurement budget of $2.3 billion, building each additional carrier over six or seven years could easily tie up 9% to 11% of the acquisition budget per platform, making a rapid expansion of the fleet unlikely.

The Indian Navy's surface-strike capability centers on the 290-kilometerrange supersonic BraMos cruise missile. A joint venture between Russia and India, the BraMos can achieve Mach 2.5 speed, which is three times faster than the U.S. Tomahawk cruise missile. While highly effective in an anti-shipping role, the BraMos is less useful as a land-attack weapon because it possesses only one-tenth the range of the U.S. Tomahawk.

This latter characteristic is also true of the land-attack variants of the Russian-designed 3M-54 Klub cruise missile (275 kilometer range) also in service with the Indian Navy. The relatively short range of these missiles would render surface-launched cruise missile strikes against a state with even modest anti-access capability (attack submarines, anti-ship missiles, or supporting surveillance systems) a risky proposition. According to published reports, the Defence Research and Development Organization is currently developing a subsonic cruise missile with a reported range of 1,000 kilometres. Code named *Nirbhay* (Sanskrit: Fearless), it could fill an important gap in the navy's land-attack capability. However, test flights of the missile have been repeatedly delayed.

Finally, the Indian Navy's ability to project maritime power in the Indian Ocean and beyond is constrained by the fact that it is currently decommissioning surface ships faster than it is adding them. At present, large portions of India's fleet of 57 surface combatants, including five of its eight destroyers and seven of its 11 frigates, are approaching the end of their service life. The navy requires these types of platforms, equipped with advanced anti-aircraft and anti-submarine systems, to operate in hostile littorals. Moreover, to achieve a real power projection capability, the navy will require several additional fleet replenishment tankers and modern replacements for its cadre of Soviet-era minesweepers.

Air Power

Air power projection comes mainly in two forms: strikes against ground-based targets and the transport of ground troops. Since the latter role is primarily a supporting one, it is taken up in the discussion of land power below.

As a tool for power projection, the use or threat of air power is primarily used for compellence/deterrence or to punish another state, should the initial efforts fail to bring about a desired policy change. Affecting targets at a range beyond a few hundred miles requires advanced strike aircraft (typically operating in conjunction with refueling tanker aircraft) capable of penetrating enemy air defenses, longer-range cruise missiles, or ballistic missiles.

The chief of the Air Staff, Air Chief Marshal F. H. Major, has argued that Indian air power needs "a strategic reach to safeguard our national interests," which requires a "long-range presence, persistence and 'forward-basing arrangements'." In this vein, the IAF's revised war doctrine is reportedly structured around "both pre-emptive action and swift retaliation" across a region stretching from the Persian Gulf to the Straits of Malacca. However, the air force has long suffered from the piecemeal acquisition of aircraft, and much of its fleet is facing obsolescence—raising questions about future combat power.

Nonetheless, the IAF has pushed for an independent strategic role in future conflict, arguing that air power can influence the battle space through deep-strike missions. The air force "aims to achieve this objective by operating advanced, long-range platforms with air-to-air refueling capability" and "must be equipped for long-reach, persistence, all-weather, precision, air dominance, networked, and space-enabled force capabilities." Most notable in this regard are efforts to induct long-range strike aircraft—particularly 272 fourth-generation Sukhoi Su-30s. The combination of SU-30s with precision-guided munitions, such as the AS-14 air-to-surface missile, would produce a significant ability to strike targets across the immediate neighborhood. Even though long-range strike Sukhoi aircraft are quite capable, their ability to operate at a significant distance depends on the IAF's in-flight refueling capability. Although the IAF does have six IL-78MKI Midas tanker aircraft (which doubles the Sukhoi's range to 6,000 kilometres), this only amounts to, in the words of one retired air marshal, "baby steps towards acquiring the capability of projecting combat power in the region.

At this point in time, the capability is limited to a token force and cannot be described as significant." In this regard, the IAF's hope to acquire an additional six new Airbus Military A330 Multi-Role Tanker Transports is a positive step. However, to support an expeditionary strike package of 60 aircraft, which would provide a modest ground-attack capability against multiple targets, at least 15 IL-78/A330 tankers would be required, notwithstanding the need for reserves or simultaneous capability in other areas. If the entire fleet of Sukhois were to be so supported, the IAF would require nearly 60 tanker aircraft. Beyond existing procurement plans, achieving the capability to support 60 Sukhois with tankers would require an additional \$1.13 billion, while equipping the entire fleet would cost \$11.7 billion, against an annual IAF procurement budget of \$4.19 billion.

Strike aircraft are not the only way that offensive air power can contribute to compellence/deterrence or punishment type power projection missions. Given the simultaneously increasing lethality of air defense systems and the cost of combat aircraft, India may instead increasingly rely on surface-tosurface missiles for "deep strike against heavily defended targets in depth, such as airfields."

This could presage an increased role for India's ballistic missile forces, which just saw the 3,000-kilometer range Agni III approved for induction into the army. The follow-on 6,000-kilometer range Agni V intercontinental ballistic missile is expected to be tested in 2011. While these missiles are commonly associated with India's strategic nuclear program, they could be employed in a conventional role if necessary, thus having potentially coercive effects on neighboring powers.

Land Power

The employment of expeditionary land power requires the facilitation of airlift or sealift capabilities, as well as specially trained forces (such as airborne troops or marines), long-range command and control capabilities, and a significant logistical ability to support and sustain troops once an initial landing has been made. The chief of Army Staff, General Deepak Kapoor, had argued that "in keeping with our growing regional aspirations," the army needed to develop the capability to deploy ground forces for an out of area operation. In that vein, at a 2009 infantry commanders' conference, the army's senior leadership explored the idea of transforming into an "expeditionary force" capable of responding to an overseas contingency on short notice.

Although such capability may be required to fulfil U.N. peacekeeping obligations, there is some evidence that senior army leaders have been pressing for an increased overseas presence, "even outside the U.N. banner." "Given its emerging regional power status," one former Indian flag officer contends, "India may be called upon to project power in the region, which may involve airlift of large military forces to areas of interest . . . outside of our borders and [the capability] to provide sustained logistic support." This would, in turn, require a substantial expansion of the country's strategic airlift capability, which some argue is virtually nonexistent. Lacking sufficient assets to suppress air defenses, some analysts believe that India's transports lack the ability to operate in hostile air environments. However, other observers contend that India has sufficient civilian airlift capacity to move and sustain up to a brigade of troops in a permissive environment—provided there is access to secure airfields.

The strategic reach provided by heavy airlift also has utility in noncombatant evacuation operations and humanitarian relief missions. In 1991 the IAF, along with civil air assets, played a key role in evacuating 100,000 Indian nationals from the Persian Gulf ahead of the Gulf War. More recently, India's airlift capabilities have reached across the extended neighborhood to ferry supplies and humanitarian aid during crises in venues from Lebanon to China.

For future power projection, Brigadier Gurmeet Kanwal (Retd.), the head of the Indian Army's principal think tank, the Centre for Land Warfare Studies, argues that India requires a dedicated air assault brigade by early 2012. The Agra-based 50th (Independent) Parachute Brigade might form the core of an air assault capability. But such a unit would require extensive organic fire support in the form of Lancer and Hind attack helicopters, to compensate for the lack of artillery possessed by such highly mobile troops. Moreover, the ability to move such a force in a rapid reaction scenario would require a significant increase of airlift capability. The IAF is rumored to be interested in buying 10 Boeing C-17s for heavy lift. However, moving a single battalion 2,000 kilometres in one day to respond to a crisis in the immediate neighborhood, as was done during the 1988 coup in the Maldives, would necessitate a lift capacity of 19 C-17 equivalents. Furthermore, the ability to do so with an entire brigade would require 55 C-17 equivalents. Although the former is notionally within the capacity of present airlift assets, questions persist about the condition of these aircraft, raising doubts about the military's capacity in an emergency. Achieving the latter target by 2012 appears unrealistic because acquiring the equivalent of 55 C-17s would cost an estimated $9.1 billion, not including spare parts and maintenance. Against an IAF procurement budget of $4.19 billion, even if these aircraft were phased in over the next decade, it would still tie up 20% of the IAF's annual budget for new transport aircraft for the period.

In terms of amphibious lift, the navy's present ability to move 3,000 troops plus vehicles and equipment is centered on the INS *Jalashva* (Sanskrit: Sea Horse), a 16,900-ton, American-built Landing Platform Dock (LPD) that can transport nearly 1,000 soldiers and six medium helicopters. Acquired in 2007, the *Jalashva* addresses India's lack of heavy sea-lift and mass-landing capability, while also providing a potential command-and control platform for fleet operations in an amphibious landing or emergency response scenario. There is great interest in acquiring more LPDs through a combination of foreign acquisition and indigenous development. The present complement of Magar-class Landing Ship Tanks—which can transport 500 men or 15 armored vehicles—will be supplemented by four new amphibious assault ships.

In line with these developments, a joint doctrine for amphibious warfare was developed by the tri-service Integrated Defence Staff and tested in exercises in 2005 and 2007. Earlier this year, the army formally stood up a dedicated amphibious brigade, the 3,000-man 91 Infantry Brigade based at Thiruvananthapuram, which is expected to form the core of a larger amphibious force in the future. The navy has expressed a desire to double the size of its own Marine Commando Force, which focuses on maritime counterterrorism operations and offshore raids, from its present strength of 2,000. Yet, such efforts will likely be hindered by budgetary constraints.

The *Jalashva*, operating together with one of the new carriers and a pair of Landing Ship Tanks, provides roughly the same size amphibious force as a typical U.S. Marine Expeditionary Unit in terms of deployable troops, armored vehicles, fighter aircraft, and helicopters.

With proper logistical support and training, this force could provide India with an expeditionary intervention force that could respond to contingencies or crises of limited scope or duration in its "extended neighborhood." As with the carrier battle groups, the ability to operate close to hostile shores requires assistance from surface vessels with advanced anti-submarine and anti-aircraft capabilities.

Should the Indian military reach its target amphibious lift capacity of 10,000 personnel, which would require both new amphibious platforms and more amphibious-ready troops, New Delhi would notionally be able to mount an operation like the 1983 U.S. intervention in Grenada. Similarly, it could respond to a major humanitarian crisis or non-combatant evacuation mission. This would go a long way toward Admiral Mehta's stated goal of playing a constabulary role in the Indian Ocean littoral region.

The army's ability to conduct expeditionary operations is no doubt enhanced by its long history of involvement in U.N. peacekeeping missions, which provides practical experience in small-unit operations as well as support functions: intelligence, medical, logistics, transportation, and engineering. However, one should not take the parallel too far because traditional peacekeeping operations are conducted in more-benign environments— which makes deployment, logistical support, and intelligence gathering significantly easier.

CHINA'S STRATEGIC FORCES TODAY

China does not publish information about the size of its nuclear weapons arsenal. The United States intelligence community, however, has released considerable amounts of information. Although some of this information is contradictory—the intelligence community is certainly not a monolith—some assessments can be made by comparing quantitative assessments from the intelligence community with qualitative descriptions provided by authoritative Chinese sources.

China appears to maintain the smallest operationally deployed nuclear force (and perhaps the smallest stockpile) of any of the five nuclear weapon states party to the Treaty on the Non-Proliferation of Nuclear Weapons. According to unclassified U.S. intelligence assessments, China "has over 100 warheads deployed operationally on ballistic missiles. Additional warheads are in storage." Declassified documents from the 1990s place classified estimates of the total stockpile, including a small stockpile of aircraft-delivered gravity bombs, between 200 and 250 warheads.

The majority of these missiles were developed in the 1960s and 1970s, beginning with the 1965 *banian sidan* plan ("eight years, four missiles") to develop medium-, intermediate-, and intercontinental-range ballistic missiles by 1972. As it turns out, China did not complete deployment of its first-generation large liquid-fuelled ballistic missiles until the deployment of the first DF-5 intercontinental ballistic missiles (ICBMs) in silos beginning in 1981. In the 1980s, China focused on developing solid-fuelled, mobile ballistic missiles to replace its first generation of ballistic missiles. Although China deployed the first of these new missiles, the DF-21, beginning in the early 1990s, flight-testing of the DF-21 continued through the 1990s, and China did not begin large-scale deployments in earnest until around 2000. China is just now beginning deployments of the DF-31 and DF-31A, which will replace China's DF-4 and DF-5 missiles.

China is also developing a submarine-launched variant of the DF-31, called the JL-2. China has built at least two new ballistic missile submarines since 2007. The Office of Naval Intelligence believes China may build as many as five of the new submarines to replace China's lone Xia-class nuclear-powered ballistic missile submarine, which is not believed to be operational. Although the JL-2 may become operational as soon as 2010, China appears to have rather limited capabilities for communicating with submarines at sea and probably has not established operational practices for conducting deterrent patrols.

The growth in China's ballistic missile arsenal is not confined to China's nuclear forces. China has also developed new conventionally armed solid-fuel short-range ballistic missiles, the DF-11 and DF-15, which it deploys in very large numbers near Taiwan. China has also deployed a conventional variant of the DF-21, the DF-21C, and is further developing a fourth modification to serve as an anti-ship ballistic missile. Finally, China has deployed a new land-attack cruise missile—the ground-launched DH-10—as part of a broad effort to acquire ground-, air-, and sea-launched cruise missiles.

This process of replacing liquid-fuelled ballistic missiles with solid-fuelled ballistic and cruise missiles underpins China's ongoing strategic modernization. Although many observers have linked the deployment of the DF-31 and DF-31A to recent U.S. missile defence deployments, it is important to keep in mind that these programs date to the mid-1980s and were supposed to have been completed many years ago.

China is not developing new warheads for its new ballistic missiles. The warheads for the new nuclear delivery systems—the DF-31, DF-31A and JL-2—were tested during the 1990s, before China signed the CTBT in August 1996. Since that time, China has observed a moratorium on nuclear tests. Without resuming yield testing, China would have significant difficulty in designing and certifying a new design, such as those incorporating insensitive high explosives. China does appear to have a significant stockpile stewardship program that may make use of hydro-dynamic experiments at the Lop Nor Test Site.

China may also have a small stockpile of gravity bombs for delivery by aircraft, but no aircraft appear to have the primary mission of nuclear warhead delivery, and nuclear warheads do not appear to be deployed at Chinese airbases. Before permanently moving its nuclear testing underground in the 1980s, China tested numerous nuclear weapons by dropping them from aircraft; however, Chinese officials have stated that the purpose of "airdrop" tests was to reduce test debris that would assist foreign intelligence agencies in analysing the test results.

China probably does not deploy tactical nuclear weapons, although it has the capability to do so and successfully tested an enhanced radiation weapon or "neutron bomb" in 1988.

If China's modernization seems unusual, perhaps it is because China is only now completing the deployment capabilities that other countries have possessed for decades. This is not to suggest that missile defence and other aspects of U.S. strategic modernization have no effect on Chinese decisions. China has developed and flight-tested a sophisticated suite of penetration aids for the DF-21 and DF-31 family of ballistic missiles. Some Chinese specialists have argued that China may increase the number of nuclear warheads capable of reaching the United States, rather than simply replacing the DF-4 and DF-5 on a one-to-one basis.

It remains to be seen whether China will increase its number of nuclear warheads as much as current U.S. intelligence community predictions, which anticipate very large increases in Chinese nuclear forces to respond to U.S. missile defence efforts. In 2001, the U.S. intelligence community asserted that the number of Chinese warheads capable of reaching the United States could grow to 75–100 by 2015. In 2006, the National Air and Space Intelligence Centre warned that the number of Chinese nuclear warheads that could reach the United States "could expand to well over 100 in the next 15 years."

Although such increases are within China's economic and industrial capabilities, especially if China were to deploy as many as five new ballistic missile submarines, it is also possible that China's modernization will occur within the general parameters of its overall force posture, characterized by keeping warheads in storage and a restrictive nuclear no-first-use declaratory policy.

China's nuclear arsenal also stands out from the other nuclear powers not merely due to its small size, but also because China keeps its nuclear forces off alert and under the strictures of a no-first use pledge.

By all indications, Chinese nuclear warheads are not normally mated to their missiles. Robert Walpole, then national intelligence officer for strategic and nuclear programs at the CIA, stated in 1998 that "China keeps its missiles unfueled and without warheads mated." The warheads are stored at nearby, but separate, bases. Press reports of Chinese mobile ballistic missile exercises published by the state-run Xinhua News Agency indicate that nuclear warheads would be mated in the field to mobile ballistic missiles before launch, similar to the procedure used by Soviet Mobile Technical Rocket Bases (PRTB, in Russian) stationed in East Germany and elsewhere during the Cold War.

Anecdotal evidence from public descriptions of Chinese exercises and doctrinal materials suggest that Chinese forces expend considerable effort training to conduct retaliatory missions in the harsh environment after a nuclear strike. One Chinese textbook that is used to train cadres is forthright about the difficulty of maintaining a survivable retaliatory capability under a no-first-use doctrine. "According to our principle of no first-use of nuclear weapons," the text *Zhanyi Xue* (Operational Studies) warns future commanders, "the nuclear retaliation campaign of the Second Artillery will be conducted under the circumstances when [the] enemy has launched a nuclear attack on us. ... The personnel, position equipment, weapons equipment, command telecommunication system and the roads and bridges in the battlefield will be seriously hurt and damaged."

Whether Chinese leaders will change these features of their nuclear posture is difficult to predict. Western analysts have long predicted, for example, that China would eventually move away from a no-first-use posture—yet China's political leaders continue to appear committed to the policy.

In part, the judgment that China would dump no-first-use has been based on voluminous criticisms of no-first-use in Chinese military writings. The considerable ink spilled in Chinese military publications complaining about "no-first-use" is probably the best evidence that the policy remains in place. Dissatisfaction among some Second Artillery commanders with no-first-use might also explain the growing deployments of conventionally armed ballistic missiles, which are presumably subject to less doctrinal interference from senior leaders and Chinese nuclear weapons scientists.

Fundamental changes are more likely to result from ongoing changes in China's domestic politics, rather than as a mechanistic response to changes in U.S. strategic capabilities such as missile defence or conventional strike. China's small cadre of scientists and engineers continue to play a significant role in matters relating to nuclear policy—but today, unlike in Nie's era, they are no longer the only voices on nuclear policy. As part of an effort to ensure that military priorities are better reflected in defence science and technology investment, the General Armaments Department replaced the Commission on Science and Technology for National Defence, which was run by Nie's son-in-law as late as the mid-1990s. Although the GAD itself may be a distinct interest group, relative to the Second

Artillery or the Navy, it is presumably much less independent than in Nie's day.

Moreover, the Second Artillery and the Navy are vastly more professional today than even ten years ago. In the past it would have been difficult to imagine the parochial service interests overriding a desire for central control over China's nuclear forces—as embodied in aphorisms such as "the party must control the gun, the gun must never control the party." But today China is very different: the PLA is far more professional than ever before, and China's leaders were children when the United States subjected China to nuclear threats.

MILITARY MODERNIZATION OF CHINA

The military modernization begun in the late 1970s had three major focuses. First, under the political leadership of Deng Xiaoping, the military became disengaged from civilian politics and, for the most part, resumed the political quiescence that characterized its pre-Cultural Revolution role. Deng reestablished civilian control over the military by appointing his supporters to key military leadership positions, by reducing the scope of the PLA's domestic nonmilitary role, and by revitalizing the party political structure and ideological control system within the PLA. Second, modernization required the reform of military organization, doctrine, education and training, and personnel policies to improve combat effectiveness in combined-arms warfare. Among the organizational reforms that were undertaken were the creation of the state Central Military Commission, the streamlining and reduction of superfluous PLA forces, civilianization of many PLA units, reorganization of military regions, formation of group armies, and enactment of the new Military Service Law in 1984.

Doctrine, strategy, and tactics were revised under the rubric of "people's war under modern conditions," which envisaged a forward defence at selected locations near China's borders, to prevent attack on Chinese cities and industrial sites, and emphasized operations using combined-arms tactics. Reforms in education and training emphasized improving the military skills and raising the education levels of officers and troops and conducting combinedarms operations. New personnel policies required upgrading the quality of PLA recruits and officer candidates, improving conditions of service, changing promotion practices to stress professional competence, and providing new uniforms and insignia. The third focus of military modernization was the transformation of the defence establishment into a system capable of independently maintaining a modern military force. As military expenditures remained relatively constant, reforms concentrated on reorganizing the defence research-and-development and industrial base to integrate civilian and military science and industry more closely. Foreign technology was used selectively to upgrade weapons. Defence industry reforms also resulted in China's entry into the international arms market and the increased production of civilian goods by defence industries. The scope of PLA economic activities was reduced, but the military continued to participate in infrastructure development projects and initiated a program to provide demobilized soldiers with skills useful in the civilian economy.

INDIA'S RISE AS A GREAT POWER

In considering India's rise as a great power, this chapter focuses specifically on India's relations with its strategically significant neighbours, Pakistan and China. Though India's increasing projection of influence may change the regional dynamics, the fundamental balance of power among India and its neighbours will not change dramatically in the near future. Pakistan is already overwhelmed by the military strength of India, thus its strategic outlook will remain unchanged, while China and India have increasingly intertwined relations and evenly-matched conventional and nuclear forces, ensuring relative regional stability.

Analysis – The Problem of Pakistan

India's geographically closest and most frequently problematic relationship is with its neighbour and prodigal twin, Pakistan. India's rise as a great power will have its most immediate impact on the extremely dangerous stalemate which exists between the two states. Many security concerns converge in Pakistan, as: the state has been a key supporter of the Taliban in Afghanistan, factions of which the Pakistani Army is now fighting in a de facto civil war; elements within the state support Islamic terrorist organisations that periodically attack India, provoking regional crises; and, the Pakistani Army has a growing nuclear arsenal, which could be vulnerable to misuse by malicious elements within the state.

India and Pakistan engaged in wars in 1965 and 1971, with crises about continuing Pakistani support for insurgents in the disputed Indian state of Jammu and Kashmir erupting periodically, and threatening war in 1990. Following Indian and Pakistani nuclear tests in May 1998, Pakistani incursions across the Line of Control in the Kargil region of Kashmir led to another limited war, and the veiled nuclear threat by Pakistani Foreign Secretary Shamshad Ahmed that, 'We will not hesitate to use any weapon in our arsenal to defend our territorial integrity.'

Major terrorist attacks in Jammu and Kashmir on 1 October 2001 and in the Indian capital Delhi on 13 December 2001 again threatened war, though merely resulted in major military manoeuvres by India, code-named *Operation Parakram*. The lack of military retaliation by India despite grave provocation seems to suggest that India is successfully deterred by Pakistan's nuclear capability, and this in turn only fuels the eagerness of some elements within Pakistan to provoke India.

Pakistan has adopted an "asymmetric nuclear escalation posture", which has deterred Indian conventional military power and thus enabled Pakistan's 'aggressive strategy of bleeding India by a "thousand cuts" with little fear of significant retaliation.'

India is four times larger and seven times more populated than Pakistan. As Pakistan averages only 300 miles in width, it is susceptible to a central assault that would split the country in two. A number of important Pakistani cities also lie close to the international border in the Indus River basin.

As Pakistan is thus extremely vulnerable to conventional attack by India's larger military, it defines such an attack as an existential threat to the Pakistani state. Pakistani Lt. Gen. Khalid Kidwai thus outlined that Pakistan would use its nuclear weapons if: India attacks Pakistan and conquers a large part of its territory; India destroys a large part of Pakistan's land or air forces; India blockades Pakistan in an effort to strangle it economically; or, India pushes Pakistan into a state of political destabilisation.

This asymmetric escalation posture is designed for a rapid first use of nuclear weapons against conventional attacks, thus leaving India without the ability to punish terrorist attacks through conventional retaliation. As elements within Pakistan continue to provoke India, this creates an extremely dangerous imbalance reliant on India's restraint to maintain peace.

India and Pakistan escalating to the use of nuclear weapons within the first 12 days. New analyses of this eventuality reveal that a conflict between India and Pakistan, in which 100 nuclear bombs were dropped on cities and industrial areas within the two countries, would kill more than 20 million people from the blasts, fires and radioactivity. In addition, the explosions could produce enough smoke to cripple global agriculture. Smoke generated by burning cities could create a climatic response that immediately reduces sunlight, cools the planet, and reduces precipitation worldwide. This "nuclear winter" would reduce or eliminate agricultural production over vast areas, simultaneously decreasing crop yields nearly everywhere. Approximately one billion people worldwide today live on marginal food supplies and would be directly threatened with starvation.

While some analysts maintain that nuclear weapons would be used in only a measured way, the chaos, fear and interruption of communications that would follow nuclear war's commencement leads some to doubt that attacks would be limited in any rational manner. Additionally, Pakistan could face a decision to use its entire nuclear arsenal quickly or lose it to Indian forces which seize its military bases. Thus, unrestrained nuclear war in South Asia potentially has cataclysmic regional and global consequences.

Following the terrorist attack by Kashmiri militants in December 2001 and the subsequent military standoff with Pakistan in *Operation Parakram*, the Indian Army announced a new limited war doctrine in April 2004 called the Cold Start doctrine, which aims to allow conventional retaliation without posing an existential threat to Pakistan. Under Cold Start, the Indian army would avoid delivering a catastrophic blow to Pakistan, and instead make shallow territorial gains, 50-80 kilometres deep, that could be used in post-conflict negotiations.

This doctrine aims to deny Pakistan the justification of "regime survival" for employing nuclear weapons in response to a conventional Indian attack. However, Walter C. Ladwig III foresees that, 'An operational Cold Start capability could lead Pakistan to lower its nuclear red line, put its nuclear weapons on a higher state of readiness, develop tactical nuclear weapons, or undertake some equally destabilising course of action.'

The danger of escalation is further compounded by the relatively immature "command and control" and early warning systems of both the Indian and Pakistani nuclear arsenals. There also remains the danger of nuclear accident as, if one nation accidentally detonates a nuclear warhead on one of its own military bases, it probably will not have adequate surveillance intelligence to know that it has not been attacked by its enemy, and thus may falsely "retaliate" against the other country.

Meanwhile, in the context of the continuing conflict in Afghanistan, Pakistan believes that the United States would intervene to prevent war, as it relies on Pakistani troops along the Afghan border and supplies for American forces are transported through Pakistan.

Thus, Pakistan believes the only potential military action available to India is air-strikes against Islamist training camps, which itself is not a serious problem, and may actually help Islamabad by killing destabilising jihadists while generating massive support among Pakistanis for their government.

The dual problems of nuclear escalation and American reliance on Pakistan for counter-insurgency meant that following terrorist attacks in Mumbai by Pakistani group Lashkar-e-Taiba on 26 November 2008, which killed 163 people, India was unable to respond with conventional military strikes. Any attack by India might either destabilise the Pakistani Government, or escalate the conflict to nuclear exchange. In the event of state disintegration, Pakistani nuclear weapons could fall into the hands of militant elements who would attempt to use those weapons against India or the West.

Unfortunately, there is no easy path to stabilising reform within Pakistan. Pakistan essentially has a feudal political establishment, run by a civilian aristocracy of wealthy agricultural landowners and industrialists, and the Army.

The civilian political parties primarily function as patronage networks, without deep-seated ideological differences, and merely struggle to control state resources. As a key aim of the agricultural and industrial élites is to avoiding paying income taxes, the Pakistani Government is also chronically in debt. The Army is seen by most Pakistanis as the primary defender of the nation and the ultimate guarantor of domestic stability. The ever-present threat of India is used to justify the Army's disproportionate share of national resources, and the Army itself also owns and manages a large agricultural and industrial empire. Domestically, the Army is the ultimate power-broker between the political parties, and has acted on several occasions to remove the party in power. As successive governments have received bailouts from international financial institutions, neither the civilian political élites nor the Army have felt any real incentive to institute fundamental change.

For the time-being, the Army is objectively the most stable and responsible force to control the country. The Pakistani military is the only state institution that works effectively, and without it Pakistan would probably have disintegrated long ago.

The dire alternatives are representatives of the rising wave of radical Islam who arose from the madrassas under the patronage of General Zia ul-Haq, and gained their training in the US-backed *mujahedeen* struggle against the Soviet occupation of Afghanistan. These elements, and more recent jihadist recruits, are currently involved in Kashmiri terrorist organisations like Jaysh-e-Mohammad, and Lashkar-e-Taiba, as well as in the Afghani and Pakistani Taliban which occupy Pakistan's border provinces.

While the Pakistani Army and intelligence services are often unwilling to directly challenge these forces (and, indeed, currently cultivate relations with the Kashmiri groups and the Afghani Taliban), and external (and, particularly, American) attempts to move forces into Pakistani territory would almost certainly make things worse, this unstable situation is likely to continue.

As India's power increases, so will its ability to strategically encircle Pakistan, through relations with Iran and Afghanistan, and via naval power.

At the same time, India's patience for Pakistan's continuing terrorist provocations will probably lessen. Nevertheless, Pakistan's deterrent capabilities remain, as attacks on the Pakistani state – either unsuccessful or successful – are likely to result in either nuclear exchange or widespread chaos and bloodshed. If India continues restraint, however, and reaches out to more moderate elements within the military and civilian political parties, it could leverage its growing economic strength to gradually help a more moderate Pakistani state develop.

The Challenge of China

On a grander strategic level, relations between India and China will be highly significant as India emerges as a great power. There is a growing interdependence between the two Asian giants, as China is now India's number-one trading partner, with more than $52 billion in bilateral trade, and estimates are that China-India trade will surpass US-China trade by 2020. China's powerful manufacturing sector complements India's combination of a raw materials and cutting-edge technology economy. Strategically, a strong and influential India helps to create a more multipolar world, consistent with Chinese interests, although China increasingly regards India as its main Asian rival.

China is thus involved in a complex game of encirclement with India. China has armed Pakistan with nuclear weapons and ballistic missile technology, and has built 'strong military-to-military ties with Burma, Pakistan, Nepal, Bangladesh, and Sri Lanka as part of what Indians see as a strategy to tie India down, Gulliver-like, in its region.' China is also developing deep-water ports throughout the Indian Ocean to support its projected blue-water naval capacity.

Meanwhile, on the border, China continues to press its claims to vast tracts of Indian territory. Over the past years, increased friction in the border area between India and China has led to incursions by Chinese troops, the wounding of several Indian border police, and a build-up of military forces on both sides, as Beijing has been uncharacteristically assertive in its claims to sections of India's Arunachal Pradesh state. The Indians responded by moving 30,000 troops and their latest warplanes into the area, leading some analysts to predict a China-India war within five years.

China rejects the McMahon Line that forms the border, and places the traditional Sino-Indian border at the base of the Himalayan foothills. Stratfor's George Friedman argues that, for China, control of Tibet is of vital strategic importance, providing a barrier against its populous and economically and militarily-advancing neighbour. The high mountain passes of Tibet provide virtually impenetrable terrain which is easy to protect militarily. Along the frontier directly south of this border, in India, is one of the largest population concentrations in the world. If China were to withdraw, Beijing fears that this population could migrate into Tibet, and Tibet could gradually turn into a beachhead for Indian power that would directly abut Sichuan and Yunnan provinces. The Chinese thus see control of Tibet as a matter of fundamental national security.

They also see the 1959 decision by Indian Prime Minister Jawaharlal Nehru to give asylum to the Dalai Lama, and the continuing support for the Tibetan government-in-exile, as perpetuating this threat. Thus, 'Beijing's price for a border settlement and for normalisation of ties with India, appears to be that India dismantle the Tibetan settlement in Dharamshala and request the Dalai Lama take up residence in another country.'

On a broader front, 80 per cent of China's oil and gas supplies transit the Indian Ocean and South China Sea, so the Chinese navy is increasingly making its presence felt in the area in order to secure its lines of supply. For China, like India, the steady flow of imported resources is not just an issue of economic growth, but also of the longevity of the Chinese Communist Party. Chinese leaders increasingly fear that adversaries could blockade sea lanes and strategic bottlenecks such as the Strait of Malacca, and are thus moving to an offshore defence policy that will include "distant ocean defence". China's actions, however, may impinge upon India's interests and destabilise relations.

Jason Blazevic argues that, following "defensive realist" strategies, each nation will attempt to gain power for self-preservation and other nations will see this move as a strategic threat, thus decreasing collective security. As part of this competition, China has been developing a so-called "string-of-pearls" strategy, expanding influence into ports in Burma, Sri Lanka and Pakistan.

According to a report by US defence contractor Booz Allen Hamilton, 'China is building strategic relationships along the sea lanes from the Middle East to the South China Sea in a way that suggests defensive and offensive positioning to protect China's energy interests.' China emerged as the biggest military spender in the Asia-Pacific in 2006, and now has the fourth-largest defence expenditure in the world. Its navy is also considered the third-largest in the world behind only the US and Russia, and is superior to the Indian Navy.

In this context, India perceives Chinese actions as power maximisation, and fears that China's forward-basing strategy will be used to contain India and rapidly achieve hegemony in the Indian Ocean.

Meanwhile, China and India have adopted nuclear "assured retaliation" postures (what they sometimes refer to as "credible minimum deterrence"), which rely on a small but secure and survivable nuclear force that assures a retaliatory strike against a primary opponent.

In many ways, this seems like the most stable aspect of the competition between India and China, though it is yet to be seen what reaction a new generation of *Surya* missiles might provoke in China. Meanwhile, analysts like Stephen Walt expect that China will follow a consistent but non-provocative build-up of its military capabilities and diplomatic alliances over the long-term, aiming to gradually edge the United States out of a hegemonic position.

India is likely to mirror this build-up and thus tension, and possible low-level confrontation, may result on the India-China border and in the Indian Ocean region.

INDIA'S PATH TOWARD GREAT-POWER STATUS

Indian leaders have pursued power and influence in a variety of ways. Like the heads of most emerging states, Indian officials have sought to build their country's material self-help capabilities via economic and military expansion, albeit in various ways. India has also followed a longstanding strategy of using multilateral institutional venues and weak-state ententes to project a louder political voice than India's capabilities would otherwise permit. Third, Indian officials have often sought to position their state between the existing great powers to seek triangular leverage—i.e., the influence that comes from being closer to two stronger rivals than they are to one another.

India has not followed all of these strategies—building capabilities, using institutional channels for influence, and cultivating triangular leverage—all of the time or with consistent success. The road has been bumpy, India's progress was slow during the decades following independence. Conditions over the past two decades have been more favourable, enabling and encouraging India to revitalize its economy, expand its leadership in selected forums, mend fences with the United States, and establish new leverage as a "swing state."

Guarding Independence Without Might, 1948-1970

In the decades immediately following independence, India pursued great-power status primarily in the three ways. Building material might was one consideration. The relations among states depend heavily on perceptions, but underlying "objective" military and economic might provides much of the basis for those perceptions and the ordered social relations that flow from them. India's first foreign secretary, Gijra Shankar Bajpai, made this point in a 1952 essay, declaring, "armed power supported by industrial power...constitutes the only safeguard against a threat to a country's independence."

India was materially weak, however, and needed to prioritize domestic regime consolidation. Nehru thus sought to compensate through an active and moralistic form of diplomacy, particularly in multilateral forums. Nehru lamented in 1946 that the postwar settlement smacked of "a continuation of power politics on a vaster scale." He thus declared, "there really seems no alternative between world conquest and world association; there is no choice of a middle course." Beneath such poetic pronouncements, however, Indian leaders understood institutions to be both venues for fostering cooperation and crucial arenas for power politics. In practice, that meant charting precisely the "middle course" to which Nehru alluded: steering between the advancement of specific state interests and the development of broader normative frameworks and institutional arrangements within which those interests could be achieved. India's diplomatic approach was thus a kind of "institutional realpolitik." Without enough guns or butter to qualify as a major power, it used multilateral venues to level the playing field, promote desired norms, and boost its influence in world politics. Indian leaders subscribed to the view that skillful and assertive diplomacy can help a state punch above its weight, that their own rigorously selected civil servants had the skills to do so, and that their experience as anti-colonial vanguards put them in a position to lead the Global South.

Officials in New Delhi saw institutions as important spaces for norm incubation but were well aware that the norms that hatched and took flight depended largely on a competitive political process. India thus used—and has continued to use—liberal institutional venues, norms, and rhetoric in the service of a foreign policy rooted largely in national interests.

India also tried to use triangular leverage to guard its independence and improve its standing. Adopting a relatively neutral position among stronger powers was one way that India—like many developing countries—sought to avoid subservience to a superpower patron, maintain relative autonomy, and increase diplomatic and economic leverage by playing off the superpowers.

This strategy merged to a considerable extent with India's institutional agenda, as Nehru spearheaded initiatives to advance the political and economic interests of developing countries. These include the Non-Aligned Movement (NAM), which Nehru helped to establish in 1955, and the G-77, founded in 1964 to influence UN policies.

Nehru expected that non-alignment would deliver material benefits to India by helping the country avoid exploitation and by prompting rival great powers to vie for influence on the subcontinent. He also believed that Third World solidarity would help the country enjoy secure relations with neighbours and enable it to devote resources to national development strategies instead of military uses. Indeed, India enjoyed economic support from both Washington and Moscow during the early years, and China and India had something of a honeymoon period in the 1950s. As strategic divides hardened, however, India's refusal to take sides and reap the military rewards of an alliance left it acutely vulnerable. India's policies under Nehru tended to emphasize norms over firepower. They raised India's international profile but did little to address the country's hard power deficit.

The humiliating 1962 defeat in the war against China shattered Nehru's faith inThirdWorld cohesion and encouraged India to refocus attention on military capabilities and increase reliance on the USSR. China's nuclear tests and the 1965 war against Pakistan—a friend of the PRC and a treaty ally of the United States—drew further attention to India's military weakness. The looming threat of another war with Pakistan in 1971 finally pushed India decidedly away from its avowed policy of non-alignment and into an informal alliance with the USSR, a relationship fortified by the clear American "tilt toward Pakistan" during the Indo-Pakistani conflict.

Suffering Sluggish Growth, 1971-1990

As Indo-Soviet ties solidified, officials in New Delhi redoubled their efforts to build military strength through the development of nuclear weapons. For some, the nuclear program was a means to counterbalance the Chinese bomb. Nehru's daughter,"Prime Minister Indira Gandhi, also believed nuclear weapons were the key to achieving great-power status.

The 1974 "Smiling Buddha" test at Pokhran—India's first test explosion of a nuclear device—certainly helped, but it did not catapult India onto the world stage as officials in New Delhi might have hoped. Rather, it resulted in ostracism, as the United States led the establishment of a forty-five member Nuclear Suppliers Group for legitimized nuclear powers and pointedly excluded India.

India's conventional armed forces developed only sluggishly during the period. The breakup of Pakistan (and birth of Bangladesh) in 1971 had left India the dominant military force in South Asia, and Soviet arms helped India sustain its lead over Pakistan and likely helped to deter further Chinese advances. However, India's resources remained limited, and many of the weapons sent by the USSR were outdated. Consequently, India was able to maintain an army that could defeat Pakistan but had little strategic reach and influence beyond its immediate borders, and it would be no match for China.

Although close ties to Moscow helped fortify India's external security, they did little for India's stunted economy, which would likely have been better served by orienting toward the West and plugging more fully into capitalist channels of trade and finance. In that sense, a pro-Soviet tilt frustrated India's great-power aspirations over the medium term. An autarkic economic model and "license raj"—the pejorative label applied to India's heavy-handed bureaucracy—severely constrained the country's growth. The interests of a powerful civil service were partly responsible, but a desire to avoid dependency on Western capitalist powers also helps explain why Indian leaders allowed statist principles and red tape to suffocate the economy. The Indian government began to liberalize and boost growth in the late 1980s, but dire poverty and industrial weakness remained albatrosses to the government's foreign policy aspirations.

Politically, India continued to emphasize anti-imperialism in the NAM and other forums. Severe economic problems in India and other parts of the Third World during the 1970s led to an increasing focus on principles of distributive justice as the "north" raced ahead economically, leaving developing states even further behind. India was a leading member of the G-24—set up in 1971 as an unofficial shadow IMF board for developing countries—and a key driver of the movement for a "New International Economic Order" in the 1970s and 1980s. Naturally, India's anti-imperial push and pro-Soviet tilt had political drawbacks as well, contributing to India's second-class status in Western-led institutions and clubs. In short, India's Cold War experience showed the difficulty of pursuing several strategic goals—autonomy, security, development, and status—in a dangerous and polarized international environment. It also reinforced the difficulty of achieving any of those aims without the benefit of strong raw capabilities.

Repositioning and Revitalizing, 1991-2000

The end of the Cold War brought about a profound shift in Indian domestic and foreign policy. The economic reforms that began under then Finance Minister Manmohan Singh in 1991 were the most decisive turning point in the country's effort to build great-power capabilities. The end of the Cold War brought serious economic and security challenges to India and essentially shocked the country into liberalization. Economically, the 1991 Gulf War led to a spike in oil prices and led India's fragile economy into a balance-of-payments crisis. At the same time, the loss of Soviet military support left India vulnerable from a security standpoint. To secure an IMF rescue package, repair relations with Washington, and plug into a globalizing economy that was leaving it behind, India undertook a series of economic reforms that began to unlock the country's potential. The decision to plug into the global economy indeed helped India begin to mend fences with the United States after decades of relative estrangement. Growth during the 1990s also put India in a position to devote more resources to defense. This was crucial to India's emergence as a great-power candidate, because a great power cannot be built easily on the back of a frail economy.

Regionally, India worked during the 1990s to develop leadership in South Asia. That effort was best encapsulated in the "Gujral Doctrine" developed by Prime Minister Inder Kumar Gujral in the 1990s, which laid out a series of core principles for South Asian regional relations, including accommodative Indian policy toward much smaller states, non-interference in neighbours' political affairs, a respect for territorial integrity, and a commitment to peaceful dispute resolution. Indian leaders also sought with limited success to exercise leadership by promoting trade liberalization and confidence-building measures through the South Asian Association for Regional Cooperation (SAARC), a regional institution founded in 1985.

In multilateral diplomacy, India remained broadly committed to multilateralism and the interests of the Global South. Its leaders continued to work assiduously to develop institutional clout at the United Nations, largely by mobilizing diplomatic coalitions in the General Assembly, often to oppose or counteract Western initiatives and to make up for India's lack of a vote on the Security Council.

In fact, even in the decade following the end of *leaders continued to position* the Cold War, India voted against the United States in the General Assembly more often than Cuba. Indian leaders continued to position themselves as chiefs of the "outsiders." Thus, even when India has not had direct interests at stake, it has often sought to mobilize "Third World" coalitions. Its opposition to Western-led interventions in Iraq, Kosovo, East Timor, and elsewhere can be viewed partly through this lens.

Despite stronger growth and a thawing relationship with the United States, India's aspirations for recognition as a major power continued to be frustrated. New Delhi's "Pokhran II tests" of nuclear weapons in 1998 were a turning point in the country's effort to gain that recognition. More about demanding attention and respect than meeting any military necessity, they reflected both India's mounting aspirations and a continuing streak of defiant independence in its foreign policy. Foreign Minister Jaswant Singh referred to the tests as an escape from "nuclear apartheid."

The Pokhran II episode quickly resulted in a new wave of sanctions—which temporarily set back India's great-power quest—but ultimately appears to have had the desired effect. As India awoke economically and as Cold War tensions receded into history, New Delhi began to draw more serious attention from major capitals—especially Washington. The relatively even-handed U.S. response to the 1999 Kargil crisis, in which Pakistani forces moved across the Line of Control in Kashmir, was a key pivot in Indo-U.S. relations. President Bill Clinton demanded a Pakistani withdrawal and helped broker an end to the fighting, suggesting to Indian officials that the United States was not irrevocably committed to siding with Islamabad in a crisis.

Becoming a Key "Swing State," 2001-2010

Over the past decade, India has arguably made better progress on its great-power quest than in any previous period and has been better able to advance its core foreign policy objectives. It has done so by continuing to grow its economy, pursuing rapprochement with the United States, and keeping ties open to other major powers, which enables New Delhi to reap the rewards of status as a key swing state.

Enhancing Capabilities

Perhaps the leading driver of India's progress toward great-power status this decade has been its robust economic growth; a general consensus exists across Indian political parties on the centrality of economic growth to the country's great-power aspirations. Former Finance Minister P. Chidambaram said in 2007 that, "India is not respected because it has acquired the capacity to launch rockets or satellites, or because of the size of its population...The world respects India because of its capacity to emerge as an economic powerhouse." Since 2002, India has enjoyed an average annual real GDP growth of roughly 8 percent, one of the highest in the world. The country's dynamic high-tech sector and entrepreneurial successes have also encouraged investment and fed expectations of future growth. The vestiges of India's state-controlled economy were blessings in disguise during the Asian financial crisis in the late 1990s, and although India suffered in the crisis of 2007-2009, it has rebounded well.

After decades of a relatively closed economy, India still lacks global economic impact commensurate with its size. For example, its total external trade still falls well short of Taiwan's—a country with roughly one-fiftieth its population.

Infrastructure bottlenecks also threaten to choke off future growth. As the poverty and inequality remain major problems, challenging the credibility of India's great-power aspirations at home and abroad. India's economy has not arrived at the great-power level yet, though its trajectory is broadly positive.

The same can be said of India's military. The challenges it faces are considerable. Tensions with China and Pakistan continue to simmer on land and at sea.

India's efforts to cultivate influence in Kabul to contain Pakistani influence have generated an uptick in tensions between the old adversaries, and the possibility of a U.S. withdrawal from Afghanistan could further complicate India's regional relations.

However, greater aggregate wealth has helped India build its hardpower capabilities, with military expenditures rising by approximately 350 percent in nominal terms between 1999 and 2009 and including purchases of more high-end systems. India has long had one of the world's largest armed forces in terms of personnel; in recent years its quality has also improved.

Economic openness and a stronger military have helped India develop triangular leverage more effectively. During the Cold War, India lacked the independent power capabilities to make a decisive difference in the systemic balance of power at that stage.

As growing capabilities put it on the map as a major power, its influence as a potential swing state has risen. Further, financial and trade ties have facilitated rapprochement with the United States and, to a lesser extent, with China. India's two-way trade with the United States has grown from less than USD 15 billion in 2000 to a projected USD 50 billion in 2010, and its trade with China has exploded from a mere USD 2 billion to nearly USD 60 billion over the same period.

Mending Ties with the United States

Rapprochement with the United States has been at the centre of India's recent approach to building capabilities and clout. Shared counterterrorism concerns after September 11 helped solidify the new Indo-U.S. partnership. The United States dropped the post-Pokhran sanctions, and India entered into more substantial defense arrangements with the United States and its Asia-Pacific allies. The expanded annual *Malabar* naval exercises are perhaps the most noteworthy indication.

They began bilaterally in 1992 in the western Indian Ocean but now include Australia, Japan, and Singapore, and feature war games in the Bay of Bengal, closer to the crucial Straits of Malacca. They constitute a major way in which India is trying to secure its own naval environs as China develops a blue-water fleet.

Indo-U.S. rapprochement also paved the way toward a series of arms deals and the headline civil-nuclear agreement. U.S. officials came to see India as a key swing state in the international system and hoped that it would become an informal ally vis-à-vis China, a stalwart supporter of the campaign against terrorism, and a possible partner in advancing the spread of democracy. Indian leaders used that perception to their advantage, especially after the start of George W. Bush's second term in 2005. The civil-nuclear deal arguably knocked down one of the most salient impediments to India's accession to great-power status.

The deal was not easily sold in India given the country's longstanding commitment to an autonomous foreign policy. After decades of mutual estrangement, Indian parties on both the left and right raised significant domestic political resistance to what Jaswant Singh called "strategic subservience" to the United States. Nevertheless, the deal survived, and India was the primary immediate beneficiary. It helped usher India into the club of legitimate nuclear powers (albeit through the back door), it led to similar pacts with other states to develop civil nuclear technology, and it helped quench some of the Indian economy's growing appetite for energy. India's tilt toward the United States has not revolutionized its raw capabilities, but it has helped at the margins and has increased expectations about India's potential for future economic and military expansion.

The desire for autonomy remains a core Indian priority, however, and New Delhi has by no means pursued ties with the United States alone. Instead, it has returned to the policy Nehru advocated in the early Cold War era of seeking triangular leverage through multidirectional partnerships. Thus, as it became closer to the United States on issues related to defense and counterterrorism, India was also able to strengthen bonds elsewhere.

Indo-Russian ties have rebounded since the conclusion of a "strategic partnership" in 2000. Moscow is again India's dominant arms supplier, swapping obsolete Soviet-era hardware for modern equipment, and in recent years the two countries have concluded a number of pacts for military, technical, and economic cooperation.

India's trade with China is booming despite residual distrust in the New Delhi defense establishment. In 2005, India became an observer to the Shanghai Cooperation Organization, a group led by China and Russia that is focused on transnational threats in Central Asia.

India's loose alignment with the United States has not come entirely without constraints on policy autonomy. For example, India's relative restraint in opposing the U.S.-led war in Iraq reflected a degree of accommodation of U.S. interests. India has also taken a more neutral line on Iran's nuclear program.

New Delhi originally opposed sanctions, but its cordial ties with Tehran—fostered largely to secure energy resources and reduce reliance on pipelines through Pakistan—have ruffled feathers in Washington. It is unclear whether India will support the U.S. position when it assumes a rotating Security Council seat in January 2011.

On other issues, India has shown a clearer willingness to assert its autonomy from Washington. For example, seeing economic opportunities and fearing instability or excessive Chinese influence in neighboring Myanmar, India has resisted U.S. calls for tighter sanctions. India has also refused periodic U.S. requests that it sign the Nuclear Non-Proliferation and Comprehensive Test Ban treaties.

Pursuing Reforms in International Institutions

India's independent streak has been even more manifest in its continued approach to international institutions, and a stronger economy has supported a larger role for India in multilateral talks. India was the leading champion of the poor-country cause in the World Trade Organization (WTO), it spearheaded opposition to wealthy states' agricultural subsidies during the Doha Round, and it has been perhaps the most important state in resisting the Western trade liberalization agenda.

Its role has been much maligned in first-world capitals—Commerce Minister Kamal Nath is often accused of sinking the Doha Round—but India was able to cast a large shadow by leading the emerging world opposition. India has also remained a strident critic of the governance of the IMF and multilateral development banks (although it is a major customer of the latter) and a loud proponent of the need for UN Security Council reform.

India's positions are partly attributable to normative convictions but also reflect an effort to maintain credibility as a leader of the NAM and the Global South. By speaking for developing countries, India can enjoy importance vis-à-vis the great powers that it lacks in the context of unequal bilateral relationships. India can become something of an alternative power centre in negotiations.

Multilateral groups and institutions also offer a way for India to amass influence even before it achieves bona fide great-power capabilities. India's greatest recent success in building multilateral clout has come through the G-20, which has emerged from its humble 1999 beginnings as the G-7's weaker sibling to play a more central role in the international economic system.

Indian leaders have also been invited as guests to some recent G-8 meetings and have risen in the unofficial pecking order that determines the meeting calendars of senior great-power officials on the sidelines of major multilateral gatherings. India has also had recent success building clout at the Bretton Woods institutions. India has long been underrepresented at the IMF, World Bank, and Asian Development Bank (ADB) in terms of its capital contribution (and thus voting power). Its capital share at the IMF actually dipped from 1.95 percent to 1.91 percent—a share smaller than Belgium's—in the 2006 round of IMF quota reform, which then Finance Minister P. Chidambaram called "hopelessly flawed."

However, in October 2010, the G-20 reached agreement on major reforms to the IMF's governance structure. In November, the IMF announced that it will give emerging powers greater weight and make India the Fund's eighth-largest shareholder, with 2.75 percent. This change, which could presage similar reforms in the World Bank and ADB, represents a significant institutional step for India, marking it more clearly as a major power.

Permanent membership on the UN Security Council—which one scholar calls "the holy grail of Indian foreign policy"—remains elusive. It would require amending the UN Charter, which would mean winning a two-thirds vote in the General Assembly and the approval of all five permanent members.

India received a much-coveted U.S. endorsement *"the* in November 2010, when President Barack Obama visited the Indian parliament and said: "in the years ahead, I look forward to a reformed United Nations Security Council that includes India as a permanent member."

The United Kingdom, France, and Russia have also supported New Delhi. China has been the most wary permanent member, but took a cautious half-step toward supporting India's bid in May 2010 when Chinese Premier Wen Jiabao said that he "supports India's aspiration for a greater role in the UN, particularly the [Security Council]." Foreign Ministry spokesman Hong Lei repeated similar language in response to questions about President Obama's statement of support in November, leaving China's exact position unclear.

Despite recent progress, India faces an uphill climb for a permanent seat. Reform will require difficult deal-making that involves the G-4 candidates (India, Germany, Japan, and Brazil) and aspirants from Africa and elsewhere. Any proposals for change will likely face considerable opposition. Pakistan has already sought to block India's bid, working with large countries such as Italy, South Korea, and Argentina under the rubric of "Uniting for Consensus" to oppose a deal that would empower their respective G-4 neighbours.

In addition to concerns about specific candidates and regional representation, at least a few members have expressed fears about lost efficiency and effectiveness if the Council becomes too large. Given these concerns, Indian accession to the permanent members' club seems relatively unlikely in the short term.

At the regional level, India has also made some progress. It is the natural leader of SAARC, but that organization continues to underperform in the context of the ongoing feud between its two largest members (India and Pakistan). India has plugged eagerly into Asian institutions, joining the ASEAN Regional Forum in 1996 and the East Asia Summit in 2006, and has launched a bid to join the Asia-Pacific Economic Cooperation (APEC) forum, thus far without success.

As in global institutions, India is encountering some regional headwinds despite its rising capabilities, as existing regional leaders—especially China—remain cautious about welcoming New Delhi into the fold.

In sum, India has pursued its three basic strategies quite effectively over the past ten years. In a period of relative peace among the great powers, it has been able to diversify its defense linkages as well as economic and diplomatic linkages.

Doing so has helped India build capabilities and establish itself as a key "swing state" in the eyes of the U.S. government and others.

Identification as a pivotal state helped admission to one of the key clubs that defines great-power status: the club of legitimate nuclear powers. At the same time, India has managed to pursue an international agenda that often runs directly counter to U.S. preferences in the WTO, the Bretton Woods institutions, the United Nations, and elsewhere.

Looking Forward

India's recent policy approach has performed well at building capabilities and influence and at advancing the country's core foreign policy goals. For the first period since early in its independent history, India enjoys friendly relations with almost all major powers.

By trading on its potential as a swing state, India has obtained significant gains in status and security from the United States without major concessions in autonomy. It has also lifted millions out of poverty and raised its international profile. Nevertheless, India's road to great-power status is not complete. The country's significant challenges have been noted. Growth has not ended the problem of poverty; military modernization has occurred in the context of new security challenges; New Delhi faces new constraints on its policy choices; and India has not been granted full admission to the inner institutional sanctums of the great-power club.

2

China's Military Strategy: Implications for India

On May 26th, China released its white paper on military strategy, emphasizing a shift from "offshore water defence" to "open seas protection". The white paper focuses on the current predicament in South China Sea. Otherwise, it contains the usual rhetoric of Taiwan's unification, Tibetan independence, and makes thinly veiled references to outside powers perceived to be meddling in China's domestic affairs, namely United States and Japan.

The paper mentions that while China has long followed the policy of defensive restraint, it will now follow a policy of "active defence". Specifically, it means that China is going to be more involved in securing its interest abroad and participating in "regional and international security cooperation exercises actively". However, the interpretation of "active defence" is that it is of defensive nature only in words, and can be used by party cadres to justify a military action. This means that if China initiates a military attack, then it will be interpreted as only defending itself and its interests against belligerent "expansionists".

The armed forces of China are entrusted to adhere to the CPC's leadership and take part in the dream of Chinese rejuvenation. This is being repeated in all propaganda campaigns across China, in light of the recent anti-corruption drive and arrest of certain high profile military leaders. Civil-

Military Integration (CMI) is also being strengthened under Xi Jinping. It is further entrusted to build up strategic capability to counter threats in new domains, such as cyber-counterattacks and fighting off local wars within a limited timeframe. Chinese defence policy is highly influenced by the Gulf War of 1991 and the United States military complete dominance in bringing the war to a swift end.

The PLAAF will also expand on its defensive and offensive capabilities. PLA will be built into flexible and mobile units, capable of switching between theatres at short notice. This is important for India to ponder over because it shares a long border with China, divided into three sectors. China does not face any major land based threat in the region as much as it faces from India and this policy maybe directed at India. A rather proactive strategy is also being adopted for outer space security and cyber strategy.

Regarding its nuclear strategy, the paper notes that nuclear force will continue to be the centrepiece of national security and sovereignty. And it will continue to pursue a policy of no-first use.

The greatest emphasis has been laid down on the maritime domain. The paper states, "The traditional mentality that land outweighs sea must be abandoned, and great importance has to be attached to managing the seas and oceans and protecting maritime rights and interests." China has actively studied the role of sea-lanes and their independence in securing a strong domestic front, both from history and United States dominance of open seas. "Far Seas" concept would see a rise in offensive capabilities of the PLAN centred on aircraft carriers.

Days of Deng Xiaoping's dictum of "keeping a low profile" are over. The military strategy paper clearly demonstrates China's changing priorities and strategies. A blue water navy is surely up on the cards.

Even though the primary focus of the white paper is power projection in the Pacific sector, PLAN is bound to enter into the Indian Ocean.

India, does not feature prominently in the white paper, apart from obscure references, such as "Some external countries are also busy meddling in South China Sea affairs", in an apparent reference to India's deal with Vietnam for oil exploration in South China Sea. Implications of the white paper for India are that the land border is not as much a focus for China as the maritime domain is.

India should expect greater involvement of the PLAN in the Indian Ocean Region (IOR), on the pretext of anti-piracy operations and naval exercises. As the Maritime Silk Road gets momentum, China will be actively be involved in protecting its interests in the region. China will also expand its capabilities to protect SLOC's passing through Malacca Straits. Stand-offs in the regions could be expected.

India, has clearly not appreciated China's involvement in Pakistan and Sri Lanka. Selling of 2 diesel submarines to Bangladesh again questions China's true intention in the region. The paper talks about fostering peace and development in the region, however its actions prove otherwise.

As a response, greater cooperation with the Australian and other regional powers is necessary for India. Furthermore, India should also deepen its relationships with its friends in the South China Sea. India's 5-year defence agreement with Vietnam is likely to ruffle some Chinese feathers, and will surely see some counter action in coming days.

THE CATALYSTS FOR REFORM

The Gulf War stimulated deep introspection and analysis in the PLA about the nature of contemporary warfare and the reforms necessary to ready the Chinese armed forces to wage it. In the wake of the Gulf War, PLA strategy was revised to focus on "limited wars under high-technology conditions." Evidence of new defense policy and doctrinal initiatives, structural changes, altered training regimen, new weapons procurement programs, and other changes became noticeable during 1995-96. These reforms had some continuity with previous programs and reforms undertaken in the late 1980s and early 1990s, but others were entirely new and could be traced to the lessons learned from the Gulf War.

Then, in March 1996, another event jarred the PLA, provoking further reflection, rethinking, and readjustment. The PLA's strategic rocket forces, the Second Artillery, began to practice coercive "missile diplomacy" in the Taiwan Strait—firing M-9 missiles within miles of the entrances to Kaohsiung and Chi'lung harbors—and the United States dispatched two aircraft carrier battle groups, centered on the USS *Independence* and *Nimitz,* to the vicinity. With their deployment, the powerful American task forces displayed the greatest show of strength directed at China since the Sino-American rapprochement of 1971. From positions in the waters east and north of Taiwan, the small armada flew combat exercises and monitored the PLA's own live-fire "exercises" in the Strait. Washington, Beijing, and Taipei all drew different lessons from the U.S. deployment, but for the PLA it meant only one thing: to expect American military involvement should the PLA use force against Taiwan. PLA leaders had long wondered whether they would have to confront the vaunted U.S. military in a Taiwan crisis—now they could assume so.

The 1996 "Taiwan Crisis" added new urgency to China's military modernization and reform program, focusing some of the lessons of the Gulf War. But it also diverted broader efforts to create a more comprehensive force structure and a balanced military modernization program. Since then many elements of PLA planning, training, and procurement have become contingency-driven, dominated by the specter of a military conflict with the United States over Taiwan. Exercises, force deployments, and weapons procurement (particularly from Russia) are preparing the PLA for such a conflict. Hard allocation choices channeled resources into services, programs, and weapons thought necessary to fight not only Taiwan's military but the United States as well.

Resources that might have contributed to a broad-based and systematic military modernization have instead gone into the purchase of expensive Sovremmeny-class destroyers from

Russia, built principally to counter Aegis-equipped destroyers and cruisers (which escort aircraft carriers) and the on-board defenses of American carriers, as well into the procurement of Su-27 and Su-30 fighters, Kilo-class submarines, and other equipment intended to plug critical gaps in PLA capabilities against Taiwanese and U.S. forces. China pursued the acquisition of Israel's Phalcon airborne early-warning and control systems—a sale aborted by the Israeli government in July 2000 under considerable pressure from Washington—as a key to controlling the skies in the Taiwan theater. (Chinese pilots currently only have ground control links and no aerial multiple-tracking capability). PLA marines and ground forces practice beach assaults and amphibious landings in mock invasions of Taiwan or the offshore islands and increasingly train with air and naval units in joint-force exercises. Knowing that Taiwan currently has no effective defenses against short-range ballistic missiles, the PLA is embarked on a major and rapid buildup of these weapons opposite the island (approximately 300 by 2000 and increasing by about 50 per year). Also, the steady program to modernize and deploy more nuclear-capable intercontinental ballistic missiles is in large part driven by the need to have a bona fide second-strike minimum deterrent against the United States.

Just as the PLA was adapting to the new military challenges posed by the Taiwan situation, the third rude shock of the 1990s struck: the Kosovo crisis and NATO's war against Serbia in 1999. This time the jarring effect on the PLA was both political and military.

On the political level, Beijing perceived NATO's actions as illustrating a new propensity on the part of the United States (which China's media always dubbed "U.S.-led NATO") to intervene in regional conflicts, under the pretext of "humanitarian intervention," for the purpose of extending and consolidating American global "hegemony" and domination. During and after the war, the Chinese media (including the military media) unleashed a barrage of invective against the United States unequaled since the Cultural Revolution and the

Vietnam War. NATO and American actions forced Chinese analysts to question the core assumptions about international relations and the global strategic landscape that had guided their worldview since the late Deng Xiaoping's 1985 pronouncement, that the threat of war was on the decline, that the global system of power relations was inexorably moving toward multipolarity, and that all countries sought "peace and development." Instead of sinking into relative, if not absolute, decline, as Chinese analysts had predicted just a few years earlier, the unrivaled strength and unipolar power of the United States now seemed to be growing significantly. Furthermore, contrary to the touted thesis of "peace and development," regional conflicts, and the American propensity to intervene in them, were seen as increasing. Moreover, American military deployment around the world remained at high, even expanded, levels. Although Chinese strategic theology predicted, and the Chinese government had officially called for, the abrogation of alliances and withdrawal of forces from foreign soil, Washington had in fact strengthened and broadened its network of global alliances in the aftermath of the Cold War.

Thus the U.S. role in the Balkan war had a profoundly disturbing and dissonant effect on Chinese military and strategic thinkers as well as on national leaders. When the NATO intervention was considered in the context of the 1991 Gulf War and 1996 Taiwan crisis, China perceived itself to be facing a United States bent on global dominance and the permanent separation of Taiwan from China. The possibility of U.S. intervention in China's ethnic troubles in Xinjiang and Tibet as a result of the "Clinton Doctrine" of humanitarian intervention added to Beijing's sense of urgency.

On a military level, too, the Yugoslav campaign jolted PLA analysts, who paid close attention to how NATO prosecuted the war. They set up two 24-hour centers to monitor the military dimensions of the conflict—one in the General Staff Department's intelligence "Watch Center" and the other at the Academy of Military Sciences. They witnessed tactics, technology, and weaponry similar to those used in the Gulf War eight years earlier, but they also observed a number of new features. Information and electronic warfare appeared to play a more important role in disabling enemy command infrastructure and defenses. Cruise missiles had improved accuracy. NATO suppressed Serbian air defenses in the early stages of the conflict and gained complete command of the skies; aerial bombardment was significantly more intense (in operational tempo, if not in tonnage of ordnance). With the use of in-flight refueling, bombing raids using the newly deployed B-2 strategic bomber were initiated half a world away instead of within theater. One such bombing raid tragically and mistakenly targeted the Chinese Embassy in Belgrade. The bombs themselves were equipped with new satellite and laser guidance systems. Perhaps most important, PLA analysts watched a war prosecuted from great distances—where the Serbs could not see, hear, or reach their attackers. With all of the high-tech weaponry deployed, not a single allied soldier was lost to hostile fire.

The 2001-2 U.S. military campaign against the Taliban regime and al-Qaeda terrorists in Afghanistan was also carefully studied by PLA analysts, although the lessons derived remain unclear at this time. As in the case of the war against the Serbs in Bosnia, PLA analysts were alarmed on both the political and military levels.

Politically, they were quite uncomfortable with the prospect of U.S. and allied military forces deployed in Pakistan and particularly in Central Asian countries on China's northwestern periphery. The prospect of a long-term American military presence in the Central Asian republics is particularly unsettling to Chinese national security planners, as it represents (in their somewhat paranoid view) a major new step in what is perceived as an American strategy of encircling China. From this perspective, only the direct northern frontier, where China borders Russia, is free from a U.S. military presence.

At the outset of the Afghanistan conflict in October 2001, PLA officers at the PLA National Defense University in Beijing warned, mistakenly, that like the British in the nineteenth century and the Soviet Union, the United States would become bogged down in an Afghan quagmire. They warned that this was a different kind of enemy, which could not be subdued by aerial bombing, and doubted whether America was prepared to insert ground troops and risk casualties (arguing that the United States continued to suffer from a "Somalia syndrome"). If the United States did deploy ground troops, PLA analysts warned, they would be consumed in a quagmire of guerrilla war, which they were not prepared to fight, and U.S. helicopters and aircraft would be shot down by Stinger missiles in possession of the Taliban and al-Qaeda. Similar prognoses had been offered by PLA analysts at the outset of the Gulf War and the Bosnian bombing. They were proven wrong each time, reflecting fundamental misunderstandings of U.S. military strategy and tactics.

Militarily, in Afghanistan, PLA analysts witnessed displays of high-technology warfare similar to those seen in the Gulf War and the Serbian conflict, as well as some new techniques and ordnance. Long-range strategic bombing with extremely sophisticated precision-guided munitions (PGMs) played a key role. During ninety days of bombing, the United States dropped a total of nearly 13,000 bombs on Afghanistan, of which 9,000 were PGMs. The accuracy and lethality of these weapons proved far more advanced than had been witnessed in Iraq or Bosnia. In addition to sustained precision bombing, and early suppression of Afghan defenses, PLA analysts also noted the key role played by real-time allied intelligence. In addition to the kinds of sensors and satellites previously seen, two new elements appeared in Afghanistan that did much to provide instantaneous intelligence: special operations forces on the ground and aerial unmanned drones. Other new factors noted by PLA analysts included AH-64 attack helicopters and A-130 airborne gunships. These and other new capabilities attracted the attention of PLA analysts. As was the case with the Iraq, Taiwan, and Bosnian conflicts, the Afghan war will be intensively studied for some time in the PLA, with alternations in doctrine, tactics, and training subsequently becoming apparent over time.

The lessons the PLA drew from these conflicts are discussed at much greater length in chapters 3 and 7; suffice it to note here that it increased the Chinese leaders' sense of the urgent need for military modernization, and, particularly, of a looming threat from the United States. Funds for the military continued to rise, on average by 15 percent, in fiscal years 1999-2002. Certainly, popular sentiment against the United States peaked following the Chinese embassy bombing, and there were public calls in China for a reordering of modernization priorities with increased emphasis on the military.

Throughout the 1990s, the PLA was reading and hearing about the "revolution in military affairs" (*xin junshi geming*) that was evolving in the United States. As if the Chinese military was not humbled enough by the impressive display of firepower and electronic wizardry on display in the 1991, 1996, and 1999 and 2001-2 conflicts, PLA strategists were led to believe that the U.S. military was entering one of those periods of technological advance that come along every few generations, when there is a quantum leap in a family of technologies and operational concepts that push warfare into completely new realms. Such technological advances stimulate concomitant changes in the way forces are structured and deployed, how logistics are managed, and how force is used. Not only was the PLA High Command thus obliged to witness a series of powerful demonstrations of modern military prowess, but it also had to reflect on the prospect that, while it was trying to upgrade its equipment from the 1960s to the 1970s, and its doctrine from the 1980s to the 1990s, the already impressive American military of the late twentieth century was on the verge of a significant leap forward into the twenty-first century.

CHINESE ARMY MODERNIZATION

The Chinese People's Liberation Army (PLA) is in the third decade of a comprehensive program of modernization and transformation that began in 1979 after the PLA's last major campaign against a foreign enemy, its "self-defensive counterattack" against Vietnam. The program continues with renewed vigor into the new century. Chinese military modernization encompasses all four services with priority of effort directed toward the PLA Navy (PLAN), the PLA Air Force (PLAAF), and the strategic missile force (known as the Second Artillery). The ground army, which previously had been the centre of gravity of the Chinese Armed Forces, remains the largest service and still provides the bulk of senior leadership for the military, but it has felt the brunt of force reductions as the PLA's mission emphasis has shifted. U.S. Army personnel who served in the post-Vietnam and post-Gulf War military should be able to appreciate the scope of what the Chinese are attempting and understand the time period required to achieve their goals.

The strategic underpinning for a long-term military modernization process was set in 1985 when China's supreme military command, the Central Military Commission (CMC), headed by paramount leader Deng Xiaoping, declared the most likely military contingency China faced to be "local, limited war" (replacing the threat of the "early, major, and nuclear war" foreseen by Mao Tse-tung).

Because the threat of major war was deemed low, senior Chinese leaders made the critical strategic decision to subordinate military modernization to other aspects of national economic development, such as agriculture, industry, and science and technology. Thus, in the 1980s and early 1990s, the Chinese Government did not spend vast sums of money and national resources to rapidly modernize the PLA. The "bloated" PLA could take its time to reform, focusing first on downsizing its 4-million-plus force.

For the first 10 years of modernization, China perceived its major potential foe to be the Soviet Union. Using force to reunify Taiwan with the mainland was low on the list of China's military priorities. By the mid-1990s, the situation between the mainland and Taiwan had changed considerably.

A multiparty democratic form of government was taking hold on the island, and voices for independence had risen. After the 1995-1996 crisis in the Taiwan Strait, China's leaders decided they needed to develop military capabilities more rapidly to prevent what Beijing perceived as further steps toward Taiwanese independence.

Although Chinese leaders preferred peaceful reunification of the island with the mainland, they knew Taiwan and its supporters in the United States had to see China's military power as credible. As a result, after 1999 the intensity of the PLA's modernization process increased, focusing principally on the goal of deterring Taiwan's independence and, if necessary, on imposing the will of Chinese leaders by force. Although the Taiwanese scenario became the top planning priority, training for a variety of military missions continued throughout the country and in all PLA units.

The acceleration of PLA modernization after 1999 became possible to a large extent because of the confluence of a more specifically defined mission, the availability of increased resources, a smaller force, and 20 years of previous effort that had laid the groundwork for what was to follow. In particular, many advances in the PLA since 1999 have taken advantage of the Nation's impressive economic growth during the 1990s, especially developments in the Chinese electronics industry. The end of the Soviet threat, along with the availability of advanced military weapons from a cash-strapped Russian Government, also contributed to changes in China's strategic posture in the late 1990s. Still, despite some marked improvements in China's military capabilities, the effectiveness of PLA modernization has yet to be proven in battle against a hostile force.

Elements of Modernization

By the turn of the 21st century, several distinct but interrelated elements have been seen in the PLA's modernization program. The following components of modernization were directly linked to developments of the previous two decades and enhanced by increased resources available since 1995:

* Reduction in force size.
* Changes in force structure.

* Reform of the structure and missions of the reserves and militia.
* Changes in the personnel system.
* An influx of new equipment.
* Doctrinal revision to prepare the PLA to fight and win Local Wars Under Modern High-Technology Conditions or Local Wars Under Informationalization Conditions.
* Improvements in the frequency, content, and methods of military training, with emphasis on joint operations.
* Transformation of the PLA logistics system.
* Enhancement of all soldiers' standard of living, pay, and lifestyle.
* Modification of the professional military education system.

Members of the U.S. Army will appreciate the complexity of the PLA's transformation, its long-term nature, and the difficulty of the tasks Chinese military leaders face. The PLA is also pursuing modernization with a much smaller resource and combat experience base than did the U.S. Army in the 1970s and 1990s. On the positive side, the PLA's modernization goals are more manageable because, unlike the U.S. Army, the PLA does not seek to project force across oceans, and it limits its scope of operations to what it considers protection of Chinese sovereignty (which, by definition, includes Taiwan and much of the South China Sea). The PLA does not have to man foreign bases and respond to a web of defence commitments throughout the world. Moreover, unlike the U.S. Army, the PLA remains a party-army bonded by loyalty to the Chinese Communist Party.

Security apparatus. The PLA is one of three elements of the Chinese Armed Forces, each of which is a separate, distinct organization, although all are closely related. According to China's National Defence Law of March 1997, Chinese Armed Forces are composed of the—

* PLA, both active and reserve units.
* People's Armed Police (PAP) Force.

* People's militia (ordinary and primary units).

The PLA is primarily responsible for defending China from external threats, with the secondary mission of domestic security in accordance with the law; that is, when requested by local authorities and approved by the central leadership. The ultimate command authority for the PLA is the CMC, with command running through four general headquarters departments in Beijing to the forces deployed in seven military regions throughout the country. The PLA, PAP, and militia wear similar but distinct uniforms, have similar organizational and rank structures, and undergo similar basic training, but they have separate systems for command and control, funding, promotion, education, and training. All three support national economic development with labour and service projects and can be mobilized to provide rescue and relief support in the event of floods, earthquakes, and other natural disasters. The PAP and militia are paramilitary organizations. By law and in practice, the PAP is not part of the PLA, although it is sometimes mistakenly called military police by Chinese and foreign sources alike. The PAP's primary mission, worked in conjunction with the Ministry of Public Security police force, is internal security. The PAP has a dual command structure that includes the CMC and the State Council through the Ministry of Public Security. Its secondary mission is to help the PLA in local defence against external enemies.

The militia supports the PLA in time of war and also helps maintain public order when necessary. The PLA chain of command and local civilian governments are in the militia's command structure. They cooperate through established joint civilian-military organizational mechanisms.

The 1.7-million-person civilian Ministry of Public Security police force is primarily responsible for law enforcement and domestic security. It and the Ministry of State Security, with the missions of counterespionage and domestic and foreign intelligence, respond to the State Council and are not part of the Chinese Armed Forces. However, in its annual human fights reports, the U.S. Department of State (DOS) includes the

Ministry of Public Safety with the PLA, the PAP, the Ministry of State Security, and "the state judicial, procuratorial, and penal systems" as part of the Chinese Government's security apparatus.

According to a recent DOS report, "[c]ivilian authorities generally maintained effective control of the security forces." What kind of control they exercised is not altogether clear because "[s]ecurity policy and personnel were responsible for numerous human rights abuses.... At times, police used excessive force against demonstrators." There is no recent confirmed evidence of the PLA being used routinely to control domestic demonstrations or dots, although that could change if the civilian police force and PAP fail in their missions.

The PLA is also distinct from the civilian-run (but mostly government-owned) defence industrial sector composed of some 2 million workers and thousands of enterprises that produce and sell military equipment and civilian goods and services.

Reductions in force. The PLA has undergone two large reductions in force in the past decade, starting with about 3 million people in 1995 and losing 500,000 people from 1997 to 2000 and another 200,000 from 2003 to 2005. By the end of 2005 the PLA have about 2.3 million people on its active duty roster. As the largest component of the PLA with the lowest priority in modernization, army ground forces suffered the largest proportion of cuts. Current estimates put the number at 1.6 million—town about 500,000 from 1995. Reserve personnel, most of whom are in reserve army units, number about 800,000. The PAP might have up to 1.5 million in its ranks. The primary militia, according to a 2004 defence white paper, has 10 million members, but the number of ordinary militia, presumably a larger force, was not announced.

While PLA active duty forces have been cut by approximately 23 percent over the past 10 years, the officially announced defence budget has nearly quadrupled from about 64 billion yuan in 1995 to 248 billion yuan in 2005. Yet these figures do not account for the total funds available to the PLA from extra-budgetary sources, such as support from local governments and special budgets for the purchase of foreign weapons. The PLA-watching community has debated exactly what should be included in estimates of actual Chinese defence expenditures and what factor should be applied to announced budget numbers to arrive at true defence spending. Estimates range from about 1.5 to 3 times (or greater) the announced figure. Whatever the true amount of funds available, such a large force is still relatively resource-constrained; thus, PLA leaders constantly look for ways to save money as new equipment enters the force and training opportunities increase. Future personnel reductions with increased defence budgets would not be surprising.

CHINA'S GROWING MILITARY

China's defence budget rose 10.7% this year to USD114.3 billion. The White Paper claims, "Over the years, the PLA has been proactively and steadily pushing forward its reforms in line with the requirements of performing its missions and tasks,and building an informationised military."

The PLA is becoming more mobile with smaller modular units, yet it has also shrunk dramatically after undergoing progressive downsizing in 1985, 1997 and 2003. These programmes reduced the armed forces by one million, 500,000 and 200,000 personnel respectively. In other words, the PLA cut its size by 40+% over a ten-year period! Today the army service of the PLA has total manpower of 850,000. The PLA Navy (PLAN) is a major beneficiary of new equipment under China's offshore defence strategy; a blue-water capability is necessary to conduct mobile operations, cooperate internationally and counter non-traditional security threats. The PLAN has 235,000 personnel and the PLA Air Force (PLAAF) 398,000 people.

Modernisation of the armed forces cannot be separated from the transformation of Chinese society in general. The PLA was a very late starter in terms of modernisation. In the 1980s, expenditure was static so the defence budget started from a very low baseline. Since then the budget has grown in parallel with the economy as a whole. Rather than raw figures, the percentage of GDP is a better indicator of defence spending levels. In the past decade it has varied from 1.22% to 1.42%, which is not outlandish. In contrast, the USA averaged 4.7% in 2010-11. Furthermore, unlike Europe and the USA, China does not have a network of alliances and international technological partners with which it can jointly develop weaponry. China is not pursuing a sudden arms race, but it is gradually upgrading a hopelessly obsolete force. Much spending goes to improving pay and living conditions – for example, in 2011 salaries and benefits for non-commissioned officers (NCO) increased 40%.

Despite new equipment reaching the PLA, older weapon systems predominate. For instance, only a third of in-service ground systems can be considered modern. Similarly, just 25% of naval surface vessels and aircraft are modern. Comparing raw numbers of weapons on paper does not reflect just how outdated PLA equipment in China's inventory actually is. China recognises its equipment cannot compete directly with that of the USA, for instance. Additionally, the aircraft and amphibious vessels necessary to project power from Chinese shores are also lacking. Most analysts agree that the PLAN's capability still falls behind that of Japan's navy.

China has no recent combat experience either. Our recently commissioned Liaoning aircraft carrier is an all-new capability and it will take years to master its use. In comparison, the US Navy has a wealth of accumulated wisdom after operating carriers for 91 years. It is inevitable a nation will develop its military as its economic power rises. During the Cold War, the Soviet Union was launching a new submarine every month. In comparison, China's build-up has been measured and unhurried.

Defence Minister Liang Guanglie told US Defence Secretary Robert Gates in January 2011, "I also firmly believe that in terms of the level of modernisation of the PLA, we can by no means call ourselves an advanced military force. The gap between us and that of advanced countries is at least two to three decades." It is true there are maritime territorial disputes in the East China and South China Seas. However, the PLA has been careful not to get involved. These are the domain of the China Marine Surveillance (CMS) agency. It is hoped these disputes can be solved diplomatically, as China has strong historical claims on these territories.

Another half-baked idea thrown around, particularly by Indian media, is the 'string of pearls' notion of Chinese naval ports stretching across the Indian Ocean. This theory has no truth, something confirmed by Jane's Intelligence Review in an article entitled 'Harbouring Ambitions' published in November 2009. China contributed financially to build commercial ports in Myanmar (Sittwe), Bangladesh (Chittagong), Sri Lanka (Hambantota) and Pakistan (Gwadar), but these are not used for naval purposes. Conversely, the USA maintains bases or has access to facilities in Japan, South Korea, the Philippines, Guam, Australia and Singapore. This is the equivalent of China possessing naval bases in Canada, Mexico, Cuba and Greenland to surround the North American continent. Such an action would doubtlessly make Americans feel uncomfortable. The Chinese people feel the same way about this robust US presence. To date, China has made no effort to establish overseas bases, and it even declined an offer from the Seychelles Islands.

Painful History

The USA complains the PLA is "not transparent". It must be remembered that China is emerging from a very turbulent past. While the military may not yet have attained the standards of US or European openness, it is making progress. A series of White Papers has given progressively more information as the country moves towards greater transparency. Since 2002, the PLA has held 28 joint exercises and 34 joint training sessions with 31 different countries as it opens up. Indeed, on 6 September three PLAN warships sailed into Hawaii to begin a three-day search-and-rescue exercise with the US Navy. The last such visit to US territory was seven years ago.

Remember, too, that history has scarred the Chinese psyche. European nations invaded and imposed unfair treaties on China (e.g. the opium wars). Japan's invasion from 1937-45 caused terrible suffering and resulted in numerous atrocities. That conflict left 20 million dead and 100 million internal refugees.

Japan has not fully admitted to many atrocities (e.g. the Nanjing Massacre), and this is a deep-seated irritant in Sino-Japanese relations. An increasingly nationalistic Japan is thus a great source of concern. Prime Minister Shinzo Abe's promise to restore his country's "greatness" is like a red rag to our nation. China has already suffered from Japanese nationalism, and we remain mistrustful of European, US and Japanese intentions based on past injustices.

Multiple Tasks

In fact, the PLA has little time for 'regional or global domination'! Common threats frequently highlighted by the Chinese government are terrorism, separatism and extremism. Uygur separatists in Xinjiang Province, for example, are constantly fomenting trouble. The country has 22,000km of land borders with 14 neighbours, plus an 18,000km coastline. Safeguarding these borders is difficult and arduous, and it occupies a good proportion of the country's manpower.

The PLA is also responsible for providing support in cases of natural disaster and public-health outbreaks (e.g. SARS). For example, in 2008, the armed forces/ militia contributed 1.26 million members to combat snowstorms in southern China. Another 221,000 mobilised after the deadly Sichuan earthquake that year. In 2011-12, the PLA contributed 370,000 servicemen, 197,000 vehicles/pieces of equipment, obilised 870,000 militiamen/reservists and flew 225 sorties to support rescue operations.

The PLA is constitutionally required to support national and local plans for economic and social development too. It commits personnel and assets to key infrastructure projects, environmental protection and poverty alleviation measures. The PLA does much more than defend the country, for it is an integral component of societal development and improving people's livelihood.

Greater Reach

Fuelled by a booming economy, the PRC needs to import a continuous stream of raw materials. It must then send its commodities to export markets, primarily by sea. Last year, China's imports and exports were worth USD3.87 trillion, surpassing the USA for the first time and making China the globe's largest trader. The country thus needs to protect its sea lines of communication (SLOC), and non-traditional security threats such as piracy in the Gulf of Aden have demonstrated the need for countries to protect domestic shipping. China, as a responsible global player, has worked closely with other nations to successfully thwart would-be pirates. Since the first naval task force was despatched to the Gulf of Aden on 26 December 2008, the PLAN had escorted 4,984 ships till the end of last year.

Some say China does not contribute enough to international alliances, but the facts reveal otherwise. The PLA has despatched 22,000 personnel to 23 United Nations (UN) peacekeeping missions to date. As at July 2013, 1,703 officers and soldiers were deployed on UN missions. Of the five permanent members of the UN Security Council, China supplies more personnel than any other. The USA, for instance, had a mere 24 servicemen on UN missions, and the UK just 278. Furthermore, since 2002, the PLA has conducted 36 international humanitarian-aid missions to 27 disaster-struck countries.

The PLAN conducted a landmark evacuation of nationals from Libya in 2011. In the PRC's largest ever overseas evacuation, the rescue of 35,860 nationals was assisted by a frigate (on a Gulf of Aden escort mission at the time) and four aircraft. Such crises demonstrate the need for a capable navy, as China does not wish to rely on external powers like the USA to protect its people and interests.

CHINA'S MILITARY CAPABILITIES

As highlighted by its white paper conclusions, China's main pre-occupations are first and foremost with internal security, its regional neighbours and in maintaining its strategic position within the balance of power in Asia. This is subsequently reflected in the configuration of China's conventional military forces. Its forces are extensive, consisting of approximately 2.1 million active personnel, 1.5 million paramilitary forces and a further 800,000 reserves. Land and air forces are largely structured for territorial defence and only limited regional offensives, potentially against Taiwan. Paramilitary forces are configured for maintaining internal security and border defence; while China's significant surface and tactical submarine fleet is also deployed with offensive military contingencies across the Taiwan Strait in mind. The Navy's current lack of aircraft carriers severely limits its expeditionary capability. It also has no overseas bases and no forces permanently based in other countries. As such China's ability to project military power beyond its immediate sphere of influence is limited to its nuclear capabilities and requisite delivery systems.

China's pre-occupation with the regional balance of power has also had an impact on the development of its indigenous defence industrial base. Although China's military-industrial complex is vast, since the late 1940s it has been a centralised, state-owned operation beset by inefficient practices and with investment largely channelled into those niche capabilities considered a priority for maintaining regional influence and any potential offensive against Taiwan. China's missile industry was, for example, one such niche. Even then the industrial success of those prioritised sectors has varied. As Shun Zhenhuan points out in his discussion of the Chinese defence industry for the US Institute for National Strategic Studies: Under the circumstances of a weak economic base, then, this system played an important role in concentrating abilities on those priority projects in the defence industry [...]

China devoted major efforts to developing the A-bomb, the H-bomb, satellites, and nuclear-powered submarines with limited funds and an inadequate technical force. While some areas in the defence industry came up to advanced world standards, much of our general mode of production lagged.

Shortcomings such as high consumption, high cost, inefficiency, and low quality were present everywhere, and some advanced defence technologies were set aside for years. In order to make up for this domestic shortfall, since the 1950s the Soviet Union, and now Russia, has traditionally been China's main source of military technology and military assistance. That relationship was strengthened after the Tiananmen Square massacre in 1989 when the US and EU unilaterally imposed arms embargoes on China, both of which remain in force. Between 2002 and 2006, therefore, China accounted for 45% of Russia's military exports. On a more general level SIPRI has estimated that China was the largest recipient of international transfers of major conventional weapons in the world during the same period, importing an estimated $14.6bn worth of equipment. Consequently the majority of China's current assets have either been procured directly from the Soviet Union or Russia; have been built under licence in China or are second and third generation capabilities that have been reverse-engineered from original Soviet and Russian designs.

In the last few years China has, however, been attempting to reduce its reliance on foreign military imports and shore up the capabilities and competitiveness of its own domestic manufacturing base. The government's main motivation is to meet the future manufacturing requirements of the PLA indigenously. A secondary objective has been to improve China's share of the global defence market. China's relationship with Russia has been particularly instrumental in the level of success achieved thus far as technology transfer from foreign purchases and licensed production agreements have allowed the defence industry to advance its own knowledge and skills base, particularly through the process of reverse engineering.

In addition, significant private investment, some rationalisation of state-owned enterprises, measures to stamp out corruption and inefficiency in the defence procurement process, and the introduction of liberal working practices, including open contract bidding, have improved the efficiency and quality of indigenous defence products. In June 2007 the

Chinese state media also reported that the Chinese government would, in the future, allow foreign private investment in certain areas of the defence sector as part of broader plans for shareholder reform. Although those reforms will not apply directly to key military enterprises that design and manufacture major weapons systems or have a direct impact on national security, those companies are nonetheless likely to indirectly benefit from reforms introduced both lower down the supply chain and in the commercial sector, particularly with respect to dual-use technologies that could have military applications. The potential transfer of knowledge and skills gained in China's commercial aviation sector for example, has been raised as a concern. Despite the progress that has been achieved so far in improving China's defence industries, China's dependency on overseas military suppliers is considered likely to continue for the foreseeable future. China's military modernisation plans for the next 20 years, for example, envisage the procurement of a range of technologically advanced weaponry that are arguably way beyond the capabilities of China's existing domestic manufacturing base. As RAND noted in its 2005 report *Modernizing China's Military:*

As with most aspects of modernization in China, reform of the defence industry has been uneven. We find that in each of these sectors [aviation, shipbuilding, information technology and defence electronics, and missiles] the capabilities of manufacturers to design and produce key systems are improving, but weaknesses and limitations persist. Some sectors have been more successful than others: Improvements in information technology and shipbuilding have been very impressive whereas aviation has lagged. Yet there is also some debate as to whether China will continue to enjoy exactly the same level of access to advanced technologies in the future, including Russian-sourced capabilities. As RAND has noted:

Western countries, with some exceptions, are not willing to transfer technologies to China that have direct military applications. Few, if any, foreign companies are willing to provide China with their most advanced "core" technologies, although

Russian and Israeli companies appear to be willing to provide China with some advanced military technologies that U.S. or French companies would not.

However the report went on to state: It is unclear whether the Russian aviation industry, one of China's key suppliers, will have the technological capability and resources to create and manufacture significantly more sophisticated designs in the future. Indeed the Russian newspaper *Nezavisimaya Gazeta* reported at the end of January 2008 that the Russian government was currently undecided about what type of future technologies China should have access to. According to that chapter "the main issue is indecision over which technology can safely be sold to China, as well as Beijing's desire to receive licences to do the work itself".

Were Russian attitudes to exporting advanced technologies to China to change in the future, China may subsequently find itself in somewhat of a dilemma. Access to Western technologies is currently limited and its domestic manufacturing base continues to fall short. Efforts by China to diversify its suppliers by opening up the European market could consequently result in greater diplomatic pressure being put on EU member States to abolish the EU-China arms embargo that was imposed in 1989.

People's Liberation Army Ground Forces

The PLA Ground Force is extensive in terms of both manpower and capabilities. It consists of 800,000 regular personnel in addition to 800,000 conscripts, although reductions in the number of conscripted personnel continue to be made. Total ground forces account for 76% of the whole of the armed forces. Land forces are configured for territorial defence, internal order, border and coastal security and limited forays into the region, potentially against Taiwan. Those forces are organised into 18 group armies (GA), each with a manpower strength of between 30,000 and 65,000 personnel. The structure, size and combat readiness of those GA varies according to its role and geographical location. The 18 GA are organised among the seven regional military commands.

Infantry, armour, artillery and missile units are also organised into a combination of divisions and brigades which are deployed throughout the seven military commands. In addition the PLA has a number of forces configured specifically for border and coastal security, more specialist roles such as mountain combat, aviation and logistics support such as engineering and signals. In reserve there are approximately 30 infantry divisions, each with three infantry and one artillery regiment, 12 air defence divisions and seven logistics support brigades.

The Pentagon has estimated that 400,000 personnel are currently deployed in the Taiwan Strait area, and specifically in the Nanjing, Guangzhou, and Jinan military regions. This equates to approximately 19% of China's overall ground forces. The Pentagon's latest assessment of deployed ground forces is as follows:

Due to decades of reliance on the Soviet Union for its military capabilities, most of the PLA's current ground force capabilities are second or even third generation domestically manufactured technologies, based on original Soviet designs from the 1950s, 60s and 70s. Overall the PLA deploys approximately 7,660 main battle tanks (MBT) (largely T-59, T-79, T-88, T-96 and T-99), 1,000 light tanks (Type 62-I and Type 63A), 3,500 armoured vehicles (variants of the Type 63, T-77, T-89 and WZ-523) and in excess of 17,700 artillery pieces. Of significance was the first delivery in 2006 of theType-99 (ZTZ-99) MBT to the PLA's elite armoured divisions in the Beijing and Shenyang military regions. The PLA's aviation regiments are also equipped with a range of attack (Z-9), assault (Gazelle), support and utility (Z-11) helicopters and an unspecified number of unmanned aerial vehicles (UAV). The PLA is also currently flight testing the Z-10 attack helicopter, which is China's first indigenously produced helicopter of this type and is expected to enter service in 2008 or 2009.

The upgrade and modernisation of land forces with the T-99 MBT and Z-10 attack helicopter, particularly those deployed in the three military commands closest to Taiwan, is expected to continue. How far modernisation of the PLA's ground forces will extend beyond these new capabilities, however, is the subject of some debate.

The 2006 white paper, for example, put emphasis on developing trans-regional mobility and rapid assault capabilities, as opposed to those configured for territorial/regional defence. In addition PLA modernisation funding has, thus far, been largely channelled into the navy and the air force. The PLA ground forces are making steady if painstakingly slow progress to recapitalise their combat capabilities in the face of limited acquisition funds and sharply rising personnel welfare costs. Consequently, army chiefs have held back on undertaking an extensive army-wide rearmament effort and are instead concentrating on incremental improvements in selected areas, such as the development of special operations forces and beefing up dedicated amphibious and army aviation units.

People's Liberation Army Navy (PLAN)

Although not on a par with the manpower strength of the PLA's ground forces, the personnel strength of the PLAN is still considerable. It consists of 215,000 personnel, 40,000 of whom are conscripts and includes 26,000 naval aviation personnel and 10,000 marines.

The Navy is divided into three fleets, each covering a specific geographic region and consisting of a number of surface ship, submarine, naval air force, coastal defence, and marine units:

North Sea Fleet – operates in the Yellow Sea and seaward and largely in line with the coastal defence of the Shenyang, Beijing and Jinan military regions. The naval headquarters of the fleet is based at Qingdao, which is also a major naval base for both the surface and nuclear submarine fleet and a naval dockyard capable of undertaking repairs on any class of vessel in the Chinese fleet. Major naval bases are also located at Lushun and at Xiaopingdao. The Lushun naval base in particular is considered to be of strategic importance, primarily because of its location but also the fact that it is the home base of some of the navy's most advanced submarine and surface fleet capabilities. The primary tasks of the fleet are protecting China's northern coasts and the capital Beijing. In the event of an offensive against Taiwan the fleet could provide critical support capabilities to the other two fleets.

East Sea Fleet – operates in the most southern parts of the Yellow Sea and the East China Sea and seaward and equates to the coastal defence of Nanjing military region. The naval HQ is based at Ningbo which is largely a commercial sea port, although the Zhousnan naval base is adjacent. Other major naval bases of the fleet are located at Shanghai and Fujian. The principal mission of the East Sea Fleet would be a key role in any offensive against Taiwan.

South Sea Fleet – operates in the South China Sea, including the Paracel and Spratley Islands and seaward and has responsibility for the coastal defence of Guangzhou military region. The naval HQ is based at Zhanjiang which is also a major naval base incorporating most of the surface fleet of the South Sea Fleet. Major bases are also located at Yulin (one of China's three major submarine bases) and Guangzhou. As with the East Sea Fleet, the principal mission of the fleet would be in any amphibious offensive against Taiwan.

From a capabilities perspective the PLAN has a significant surface and tactical submarine fleet, both of which have been the subject of significant investment and modernisation in the last few years to turn it from a largely coastal force into a truly 'blue water' navy.

Overall the surface fleet currently comprises 75 principal surface combatants. Of these 29 are destroyers, principally variants of the Luda-class which entered service between 1971 and 1991. In the last few years, however, investment in the surface fleet has seen the introduction of several, more advanced, destroyer capabilities.

Specifically the PLAN has been augmented by two Guangzhou-class multi-role destroyers which entered service in 2004; four Sovremenny-class destroyers equipped with SS-N-22 Sunburn anti-ship cruise missiles which have entered service since 2002; two Lanzhou-class; and the newest ships of the fleet: two Luzhou-class, the first of which was launched in 2005. All four classes of vessel have introduced greater stealth, advanced weaponry and vastly improved air defence capabilities, areas that had been considered major weaknesses in previous Chinese warships as they imposed geographical limitations on the activities of the fleet.

The deployment of the Luzhou-class destroyer reportedly equipped with the Russian SA-N-20 surface-to-air missile system, which has a range of approximately 150km, for example, more than doubles the range of previous PLAN air defence systems.

In addition to its destroyer fleet, the PLAN also includes 46 frigates. Primarily comprised of variants of the Jianghu-class the fleet has benefited from recent additions: the Jiangwei-I and II classes (four and 10 vessels respectively) and two vessels of the Jiangkai-class, which only began entering service in 2007 and is the PLAN's first guided-missile frigate. As with the newly acquired destroyers, these latter classes of frigate have provided the PLAN's surface fleet with significantly improved air defence capabilities. The PLAN also has 233 patrol and coastal combatants including 63 fast patrol craft equipped with surface-to-surface missiles; 65 mine warfare vessels; approximately 234 amphibious landing ships of various designations, including 74 medium and heavy landing ships; and 160 logistic and transport vessels. In September 2007 sea trials of thc new Type-71 Yuzhao-class amphibious landing platform dock began. Although it is unclear when the ship will enter operational service, it is widely acknowledged that it will represent a major improvement in the PLAN's ability to support amphibious operations.

According to the Pentagon's 2007 assessment of China's military power, approximately 64% of the destroyer fleet and 85% of the PLAN's frigates are deployed in the East and South Sea Fleets for use in any potential offensive operation across the Taiwan Strait.

The conventional submarine fleet comprises 59 tactical subs, including its ageing Ming and Romeo-class vessels; four

Han-class nuclear powered attack submarines; 12 Kilo-class (the newest of which are equipped with SS-N-27B anti-ship cruise missiles and could possibly be equipped with the 3M-14 land-attack cruise missile (LACM)); 10 Song-class and two Yuan-class patrol submarines.

The latter is the newest class of diesel-electric submarine to enter service in the PLAN and are currently undergoing sea trials. Two vessels of the second generation Shang-class nuclear-powered attack submarine, which is earmarked to replace the Han-class, also entered service in 2007. The new Shang-class submarine is also thought to have been deployed with an LACM capability. The Kilo, Yuan and Shang classes of vessel are all considered to constitute major technological advancements over previous generations of submarine and particularly in relation to stealth, sonar, propulsion, command and control, and weapon systems, most of which are advanced capabilities procured from Russia. In contrast to the surface fleet, less than half of the submarine fleet is reportedly deployed in the East and South China Seas, while the SSBN and nuclear powered vessels are located in the North.

The PLAN also has a sizeable naval aviation arm which consists of 792 combat capable aircraft deployed among the HQ of each sea fleet. Of those aircraft, 346 are fighter interceptor aircraft (J-8 Finback variants and J-7/MiG-21F); 296 are ground attack aircraft (JH-7, Su 30-Mk2 and J-6/MiG 19S), in addition to 130 bomber aircraft (H-5 and H-6) and a number of reconnaissance, maritime patrol, tanker and transport aircraft. The naval aviation arm also operates a number of anti-surface warfare, support and search and rescue helicopters.

The majority of China's major combat ships have been constructed domestically, albeit with considerable assistance from Russia and equipped with imported key technologies, including sonar, propulsion technologies, and air defence systems. The only major exceptions to this domestic procurement approach in the last few years has been the Kilo-class submarine and the Sovremenny-class destroyer, both of which were purchased directly from Russia. Despite claims to the contrary

Russia has, however, denied assisting China with the construction of its new Jin-class SSBN.

China's nuclear-powered attack and ballistic missile submarines are built at the Bohai/Huladao shipyard on the coast of the Bohai Gulf in close geographical proximity to the Dalian shipyards and the Lushun and Xiaopingdao naval bases. China's conventional submarines, in contrast, have been largely constructed at the Wuhan shipyard in Hubei Province in inland China, although in 2003 construction of the Song-class submarine also began at a second conventional submarine yard at the Jiangnan Shipyards in Shanghai. On that basis the chapter suggested that if this rate is sustained then China could produce and/or purchase about 40 new submarines by the end of this decade.

China's major surface combatants are predominantly constructed at shipyards in Dalian, Shanghai, and Guangzhou. Over the last 20 years an extensive programme of expansion has been undertaken at Dalian, which now consists of two shipyards and is the main focus of China's naval modernisation shipbuilding programme, reportedly incurring investment of $1.25bn per year and responsible for around 25% of ship production in China.

By 2015 China's shipbuilding capacity is forecast to exceed 50 million deadweight tons (DWT), a rate of expansion which has raised concerns among several analysts given the naval focus of much of the PLA's modernisation plans. Indeed it has been suggested that future extensions of the fleet could, by 2010, provide the PLAN with a naval area denial capability up to 400 miles from its eastern and southern coastlines.

Despite the extensive capabilities of the PLAN, the recent attempts to modernise the fleet and the capacity of the domestic manufacturing base to support it, analysts have continued to question the credibility and effectiveness of the Chinese navy. Many, including the Pentagon, consider it largely untested in the skills of modern naval warfare. The PLAN also continues to lack key capabilities. The fleet's expeditionary capability is currently limited by the lack of any aircraft carriers; while the manufacture of many of the PLAN's newest acquisitions has relied heavily on the import of key foreign technologies including power plants, navigation and key weapons systems.

As RAND point out in their report: This high degree of reliance on foreign subsystems creates challenges for systems integration and complicates serial production of some platforms because of the potentially uncertain availability of certain subsystems [...] In short, Chinese shipbuilders have been able to produce better designed and better-fabricated warships in less time than previously, but these new platforms lack the advanced weapons, electronics, and propulsion subsystems needed to properly outfit these vessels. It is these technologies (and their integration) that will ultimately determine the PLAN's military efficacy.

People's Liberation Army Air Force (PLAAF)

The Chinese Air Force comprises approximately 250,000 personnel. Conscripts make up approximately 37% of the total force, although in line with the PLA's overall policies on conscription that proportion is being steadily reduced.

From an equipment perspective, the PLAAF has approximately 1,762 combat capable aircraft in its inventory. Of those aircraft, 1,179 are fighter/interceptor aircraft, largely variants of the J-7 and J-8 aircraft which entered service in the 1970s and 1980s, although the most recent variant of the J-7, the J-7G only entered service with the PLAAF in 2003; and the Su-27 SK/J-11B. Since 2004 the PLAAF has also augmented its fleet with the introduction of the J-10, a multi-role fighter with sophisticated avionics and more advanced weaponry which has been considered the first Chinese-developed fighter aircraft to meet the performance and capabilities benchmark provided by Western fighter aircraft. The third regiment to have received the J-10 was identified in 2007 under the 2nd Air Division in Guangdong Province. Some analysts have suggested that the PLAAF will have acquired 300 J-10 aircraft by 2010, although US Defence Intelligence has reportedly estimated the PLAAF's overall J-10 requirement to be up to 1,200 aircraft.

At present it is unclear whether the PLAAF will acquire the JF-17/FC-1 multi-role fighter that China is currently developing in conjunction with Pakistan and which entered serial production in 2007. The aircraft is considered a less capable, albeit less expensive aircraft compared to some of the aircraft that China is currently procuring, including the J-10. China has also reportedly begun development on its fourth-generation fighter, the J-X (or J-XX/J-14). China's fighter/ interceptor aircraft are equipped with AA-12, P-27/AA-10, P-37/AA-11, PL-2B, PL-5B and PL-8 air-to-air missiles, in addition to the new PL-12 beyond-visual-range-air-to-air-missile (BVRAAM) which is deployed on the J-10 and J-11B aircraft.

In addition to its interceptor aircraft, the PLAAF also has 551 ground attack (FGA) aircraft. The FGA fleet consists primarily of the Q5-C and Q5-D aircraft, although since the 1990s significant capability improvements to the fleet have been made with the addition of the JH-7, the improved JH-7A variant which entered service in late 2004, and the Su-30 MKK. Aircraft are equipped with AS-14, AS-17 and AS-18 air-to-surface missiles. The Q5 is also believed to be nuclear capable.

The PLAAF's bomber divisions consist of approximately 82 aircraft comprising the H-6 and more recent upgraded variants of that aircraft including the H-6E/ F and H. The newest variants of the H-6 have recently been equipped with the YJ-63 which is the air force's first air-launched land-attack cruise missile (LACM). Up to 20 H-6 bomber aircraft are believed to be nuclear-ready.

Supplementing the PLAAF's fast jet and bomber aircraft are 183 reconnaissance (the ageing MiG-19 and MiG-21 and the JZ-6 and JZ-8) and airborne early warning aircraft; an unspecified number of UAV; 314 tanker and transport aircraft and in excess of 522 training aircraft. The PLAAF also has a small support and utility helicopter fleet. In order to supplement and modernise its airborne early warning fleet, the PLAAF is currently developing a number of AEW platforms including the KJ-200 which is based on the Y-8 transport aircraft and is being configured for an AEW role as well as intelligence and maritime surveillance; and the KJ-2000 airborne warning and control system which is based on the Russian A-50 AWACS aircraft.

Overall these forces are organised into 32 air divisions (22 fighter, 3 bomber, 5 attack and 2 transport divisions) and are deployed among the PLA's seven military commands. The majority of forces are, however, located in the eastern part of the country, a reflection of the priority given to any potential offensive against Taiwan. The exact nature of the infrastructure supporting PLAAF operations is, however, the subject of debate. According to the Federation of American Scientists those 32 divisions are located across 37 military air bases and four airfields which may be capable of supporting both civilian and military operations. Six of those airbases are considered to be within short range of Taiwan (<400km); whilst 11 are within medium range (400-600km). The organisation Global Security has suggested, however, that the number of Chinese air bases or airfields/airports capable of supporting military operations is in the region of 150.

The PLAAF also has a dedicated air defence force equipped over 1,578 surface-to-air missiles. The manufacture of most of China's combat aircraft has been undertaken domestically. However, China's aviation industry has its limitations, particularly its ability to successfully manufacture Turbofan engines for its combat and heavy aircraft. Like most of China's naval vessels, therefore, China's air forces have benefited significantly from the incorporation of foreign technology and other assistance, particularly from the Soviet Union/Russia.

A significant number of Soviet and Russian fighter aircraft have, for example been reverse engineered by Chinese industry over the years (with varying degrees of success) and then upgraded into second and third generation variants.

The J-7 was, for example, initially copied from the Soviet MiG-21 and then upgraded domestically. More recently China has also indicated that it will attempt to reverse engineer the Russian turbofan engine which has been incorporated into its J-10 for use in future variants of the aircraft. China's H-6 bomber is also a domestic copy of the Russian Tupolev Tu-16, while its HY-6 tanker aircraft is a copy of a converted Tu-16. The majority of China's transport aircraft are also based on the Antonov AN-2 (Y-5), the AN-12 (Y-8), the AN-24 (Y-7) and the AN-26 (Y-7H).

China has also established a number of licensed production agreements with Russia including an agreement for the domestic production of the Su-27Sk/J-11B aircraft. On occasion China has also directly purchased aircraft from overseas in order to supplement its fleet. The PLAAF operates, for example, several variants of the Il-76 transport aircraft purchased from the Soviet Union and Russia in the 1990s. In 2005 China ordered a further 38 Il-76MD long-range transport aircraft and Il-78 tanker-transport aircraft from Russia in a deal reportedly worth $1bn.

China has also taken a similar procurement approach to some, although not all of the PLAAF's missile capabilities. The PL-2B and PL-5B missiles, for example, are upgraded versions of the PL-2 which was produced under licence in China and based on the Soviet K-13 air-to-air missile. China also acquired a number of its missile technologies from Israel during the 1980s, including the PL-8 which is produced under licence and based upon the Israeli Python-3 air-to-air missile. Israel has also been an important source of unmanned aerial vehicle (UAV) and unmanned combat aerial vehicle (UCAV) technologies. Despite improvements in China's aviation industry it has been pointed out that even with the potential indigenous production of a fourth generation fighter aircraft, China will still be a generation behind the technological capabilities of the US.

People's Armed Police (Paramilitary Forces)

The People's Armed Police, in its current configuration, was established in the 1980s following a decision by the Chinese government to re-establish a dedicated force for internal security and law enforcement purposes. The force comprises 1.5 million active personnel broken down into 45 divisions and deployed across China's 22 provinces and four autonomous regions. During peacetime, the PAP is responsible for guarding key targets, including personnel and key economic and industrial installations; dealing with emergency crises including riots, insurgency and other mass incidents; anti-terrorism, including anti-hijacking and bomb disposal; and assisting in the economic development of the country, including mining and taking part in large transportation and energy construction projects.

In a situation of conflict the PAP could also be used for the purposes of territorial defence and in support of regular ground forces.

3

India Will React to the Rise of China: The Soft-balancing Strategy

Recent developments in China-India ties have suggested two potential future pathways for the bilateral relationship. First, from June to August 2017, China and India were embroiled in an intense militarized standoff in Doklam, a disputed area at the tri-junction of Bhutanese, Chinese, and Indian territories. Though the countries ultimately found an "off-ramp" from the immediate crisis, ongoing military activity in the tri-junction's vicinity and lingering misperceptions among Beijing, New Delhi, and Thimphu suggest future clashes are possible. Second, in April 2018, Chinese President Xi Jinping and Indian Prime Minister Narendra Modi attempted to put Doklam in the rearview mirror and "reset" the Sino-Indian relationship at the Wuhan Summit. The critical question going forward is whether a managed relationship will become an intense Sino-Indian rivalry akin to the one between India and Pakistan — with more militarized conflicts and crises like Doklam — or will the two rising powers manage and transform their rivalry into friendly competition and mutual accommodation?

China's provocative behavior in the South China Sea and increasing economic and naval presence in the Indo-Pacific are among the reasons the United States has recently characterized China as a "strategic competitor." Some analysts seem to assume

New Delhi is a natural partner and will join the United Statesin this struggle as China becomes more powerful and threatening. However, while these analysts do acknowledge the constraints, they nonetheless tend to overestimate India's willingness to serve as a counterweight to China, while underestimating internal and external constraints on such explicit balancing behavior. My contention is that India is likely to form both a soft-balancing coalition, relying on diplomacy and institutional cooperation, and a limited hard-balancing coalition, that is, strategic partnerships short of formal alliances. But an outright alliance with the United States is very improbable. The recently concluded U.S.-India "two-plus-two" meeting of foreign and defense ministers and secretaries suggests that the path toward a limited hard-balancing coalition may be opening despite many remaining hurdles. Whether a limited U.S.-India hard-balancing coalition progresses toward an outright hard-balancing alliance will depend heavily on China's behavior, especially the threat level it poses to India in the years to come.

A Widening Yet Managed Rivalry

It may well be possible to manage the China-India rivalry, but with each passing year, India's challenges vis-a-vis China are becoming more intractable. Until recently, the rivalry centered on the territorial conflict over the un-demarcated Himalayan border. But there has been relative calm since Indian Prime Minister Rajiv Gandhi's visit to Beijing in 1988, when both sides agreed to set up a joint working group to settle the border dispute. The mechanism of regular border talks resulted in some level of pacification until the Doklam standoff in 2017. Although war was averted, the crisis continued for 73 days.

Beyond the territorial dispute, today the rivalry encompasses competition over water sharing (especially due to China's efforts to dam the water that flows from Tibet into the Brahmaputra River), trade imbalance, membership in international institutions, and China's foray into India's traditional sphere of influence in the Indian Ocean as well as India's own increasing interests in the Asia-Pacific and Africa.

As discussed in my new volume *The China-India Rivalry in the Globalization Era*, crisis escalation has been averted in recent years thanks to the willingness of political leadership in both countries to pull back. However, the continued buildup of forces by both sides near the border as well as in the Indian Oceansignify that they have not yet fully made the compromises necessary to avert a future conflict from erupting.

Meanwhile, the smaller states of South Asia are increasingly playing smart games to hedge between China and India: They obtain high levels of economic and military assistance from China, forcing India to offer them increased aid as well. But the amount of Indian economic and infrastructure aid is nowhere near China offers. The Indian Ocean littoral is fast emerging as China's ocean too, with a military base operational in Djibouti and one planned in Pakistan, and commercial ports under construction or planned in Sri Lanka, the Maldives, Bangladesh, and Myanmar. Small dependent states such as the Maldives are breaking away from India in a rare display of independence. China's Belt and Road Initiative, although largely built around economic and infrastructure development, has immense geopolitical significance. India is one of the most affected countries, especially given its unwillingness to join as a junior partner.

In the face of these challenges, India appears to have devised multiple strategies toward China, some ad hoc and others more long-term and deliberate. As outlined in my new book, *Restraining Great Powers: Soft Balancing from Empires to the Global Era*, the Indian strategy has been to engage in limited hard balancing by obtaining asymmetrical military capabilities, as well as soft balancing by forming limited coalitions with the United States, Japan, Australia, and some ASEAN countries. These informal coalitions of like-minded states have pressured China to respond more aggressively. Its intermittent belligerence and occasional olive branches toward India are partly an effort to forestall more active Indian efforts at soft balancing and to prevent even limited efforts to form hard-balancing coalitions. At the same time, in response to U.S. President Donald Trump's maverick policies, India is currently seeking to "reset" relations with China.

It is unclear what India's strategic options are if the U.S.-China rivalry becomes too intense. There are already signs of this happening with increasing trade tension and military activism in the South China Sea as well as the Indian Ocean. More importantly, if China engages in higher levels of hostility, what kind of response can India afford to make without provoking war?

A New Non-Alignment Plus?

One option is to develop a reformulated nonalignment policy, something a group of experts proposed in 2012 as a way of maximizing Indian strategic autonomy. However, some policymakers feared this would preclude India from seizing strategic and economic opportunities and responding to an unpredictable security environment characterized by an increasingly powerful China. Today, might India rethink the non-alignment strategy in a different format, given America's turbulent relationship with allies and adversaries, including India?

The history of nonalignment as a soft-balancing mechanism is relevant here. In the 1950s, facing the intense Cold War rivalry between the two superpower-led blocs, India, under its first prime minister, Jawaharlal Nehru, took the lead in organizing the Asian-African nations. The Non-Aligned Movement and its precursor, the Afro-Asian conference in Bandung in 1955, were examples of materially weaker states using institutional cooperation and diplomacy to soft-balance great powers immersed in rivalry.

The Non-Aligned Movement attempted to delegitimize the threatening behavior of the two superpowers and other imperial powers, particularly through their activism in the United Nations and other forums. They worked as promoters of new norms in the areas of decolonization and nuclear arms control and disarmament. In particular, the nonaligned declarations on nuclear testing and nuclear nonproliferation helped to concretize the Partial Test Ban Treaty, several nuclear weapons-free zones and, most importantly, the Nuclear Non-Proliferation Treaty. The tradition of the non-use of nuclear weapons or the nuclear taboo, as some would call it, was strengthened partially due to the efforts of the nonaligned countries' activism at the United Nations.

With great power rivalry once again heating up, renewed activism by leading global south countries seems a possible way to prevent intensified competition and even military conflict. Non-great power states could be the first victims if war between China and the United States breaks out.

Theoretically, India could support smaller states in their refusal to make formal alliances with China or the United States, as it did during the early Cold War era, although changing strategic circumstances and India's own great power ambitions make that only a remote possibility. In this scenario, regional states could work to develop a code of conduct vis-a-vis the two rival powers stating that they would not offer military support to or permit the use of military bases by either the United States or China in the event of a conflict. They have an interest in making sure the support for economic and infrastructure development from China and its competitors does not lead to excessive debt traps and new forms of imperialism. ASEAN is spearheading this movement toward a code of conduct in the security arena, but Chinese responses have been slow, although negotiations are continuing.

The small states can also demand that China and the United States abide by fair trade practices and support the creation of regional free trade mechanisms and security institutions. India could join the ASEAN states in their efforts to negotiate a code of conduct with China in the South China Sea and extend that to the Indian Ocean. All these points are contained in India's occasional statements on regional and world order, but they have yet to be codified or articulated as Nehru did in the 1950s.

The challenge will be to confront the wedge strategies China employs to divide the ASEAN states and its use of salami tactics to gradually gain territorial control in the South China Sea. China's deep pockets and India's limited economic support have made many small states hesitate to join any coalitions yet. This could change if China's strong-arm tactics and the potential high debt burden become too unbearable . A few, such as Malaysia, have already shown willingness to cancel infrastructure contracts with China that they consider against their national interests.

New Delhi's non-alignment option is constrained by its desire to become an independent center of power with military and economic heft, including nuclear weapons and naval capabilities. It has unsteadily played limited balance-of-power games to hedge against both Beijing and Washington, notwithstanding recent signs that it is forming a limited hard-balancing coalition with the United States. These policies have not done much to reassure potential partners in the developing world about following a non-aligned path. For these reasons, India is unlikely to lead a new non-aligned movementagainst the United States and China, as some have suggested.

ALIGNMENT AS A STRATEGIC OPTION

The opposite of non-alignment is alignment. In the face of intense rivalry with China, India could opt for a quasi-military alliance with the United States and Japan, as it did with the Soviet Union during the 1970s.. Indeed, some who are skeptical of soft balancing would like India to cooperate more actively with the United States, Japan, and Australia, in addition to building its own military capabilities. This possibility is the one China dreads the most, as such a coalition would form a powerful counterweight to Beijing in the Indo-Pacific region. This could occur if China raises the level of the rivalry to unacceptably high levels and begins to encroach more directly on India's strategic and economic interests as well as territorial boundaries.

India and the United States are already showing some signs of limited hard balancing, and there probably would be more if not for the careless policies of the United States under Trump. Using each other's naval facilities for repair work of naval craft, the transfer of high-tech weapons, the Communications Compatibility and Security Agreement (COMCASA), and the number of joint naval exercises such as Malabar all suggest greater military cooperation is taking place.

However, for India to seriously consider a formal alliance like the one the United States has with Australia or South Korea, China would have to seriously threaten India's core security both on land and at sea. Such an alliance isn't likely unless some major crisis occurs such as the 1970-71 East Pakistan/Bangladesh conflict: A border clash in which India faces an imminent defeat could be the watershed moment that leads to a formal alliance. That same possibility forced Nehru to consider alignment with the United States during the 1962 war with China, although he quickly abandoned the idea as the China threat receded. Similarly, if China engages in naval clashes with Indian naval forces in the Indian Ocean or in an encirclement operation with the help of Pakistan, it could push India into the arms of the United States. But the chances of these scenarios developing in the foreseeable future are low, partly because Chinese naval capabilities are limited in the Indian Ocean and India can offer a strong defense against any Chinese naval attack. Also, India's possession of nuclear weapons could reduce the possibility of a massive defeat — and therefore of an alignment with the United States, assuming India is willing to assume the risks of escalating conflict to a nuclear level.

Still, a manifold increase in China's regional naval presence or even a simultaneous two-front war with China and Pakistan are not beyond the pale of imagination. In this way, it is up to China to prevent India from opting for a formal military alliance. Any major military escalation on the border or in the Indian Ocean would put tremendous pressure on New Delhi to join a counter-coalition. It will not be a repeat of 1962 as India has sufficient asymmetrical military capabilities, but short of nuclear escalation, China can indeed threaten India with much damage, especially if Pakistan opens up a second front in Kashmir. The deepening strategic and economic relationship between Pakistan and China suggests that a balancing coalition already exists on India's western front.

Outright alignment with the United States is further constrained — at least for now — by India's longstanding strategic partnership and arms relationship with Russia. According to the 2018 SIPRI report, during the past five years, nearly 62 percent of India's weapons imports were from Russia. This historical relationship has proven to be in India's interests. Moscow rarely imposes the same stringent conditions that Washington does, especially on end-user controls and technology co-production. India has, in fact, diversified its weapons import sources — the United States and Israel are now more important suppliers — but the chances of abandoning Russia in the near future seem quite low.

RISING MILITARY POWER OF INDIA

China has taken serious note of India's growing military power over the last decade. India, which has traditionally talked of the power of argument began to talk of the argument of power. In fact, the 1998 nuclear tests themselves were indicative of the fact that India had begun to realize the role of hard power in securing its national interests and also in making her voice heard in international politics.

India's growing military profile is especially evident in the maritime domain. The Indian navy has emerged as the net security provider in the Indian Ocean over the last decade. In 2004, it unveiled its first-ever naval doctrine that defined India's legitimate areas of interest stretching from the Persian Gulf to the Malacca Straits.

It released its updated version in 2009, incorporating the rapid changes in the geo-strategic environment involving India. India's defense ties with the US have developed at a frenetic pace, which has played the central role in India's military modernization. For example, recent defense contracts signed with the US include US$ 1.1 billion for C-130J Super Hercules transport planes and US$2.4 billion for 10 Globemasters airlifters. In January 2009, the Indian Navy signed an agreement with the U. S. to buy eight P-8I planes worth nearly US$2.1 billion, so as to replace the aging long range aerial reconnaissance fleet of eight Russian-made Tu-142s and five IL-38 planes.

The tests of its China-centric Agni series missile systems and the development of a Ballistic Missile Defense system. India's future military plans are even more ambitious, which further complicates China's strategic calculations. For example, the Indian Ministry of Defense in late 2011 announced its biggest expansion package to date, a US$13 billion military modernization plan. Under this plan within next five years, the Indian army is set to deploy 90,000 more soldiers and raise four new divisions along India's border with China, the largest such mobilization since the Sino-Indian border clashes of 1962.

INDIA AND THE BALANCE OF POWER

After disappointing itself for decades, India is now on the verge of becoming a great power. The world started to take notice of India's rise when New Delhi signed a nuclear pact with President George W. Bush in July 2005, but that breakthrough is only one dimension of the dramatic transformation of Indian foreign policy that has taken place since the end of the Cold War. After more than a half century of false starts and unrealized potential, India is now emerging as the swing state in the global balance of power. In the coming years, it will have an opportunity to shape outcomes on the most critical issues of the twenty-first century: the construction of Asian stability, the political modernization of the greater Middle East, and the management of globalization.

Although India's economic growth, its new foreign policy has been less noted. Unlike their U.S. counterparts, Indian leaders do not announce new foreign policy doctrines. Nonetheless, in recent years, they have worked relentlessly to elevate India's regional and international standing and to increase its power. New Delhi has made concerted efforts to reshape its immediate neighborhood, find a modus vivendi with China and Pakistan (its two regional rivals), and reclaim its standing in the "near abroad": parts of Africa, the Persian Gulf, Central and Southeast Asia, and the Indian Ocean region. At the same time, it has expanded relations with the existing great powers — especially the United States.

India is arriving on the world stage as the first large, economically powerful, culturally vibrant, multiethnic, multireligious democracy outside of the geographic West. As it rises, India has the potential to become a leading member of the "political West" and to play a key role in the great political struggles of the next decades. Whether it will, and how soon, depends above all on the readiness of the Western powers to engage India on its own terms.

THREE STRATEGIC CIRCLES

India's grand strategy divides the world into three concentric circles. In the first, which encompasses the immediate neighborhood, India has sought primacy and a veto over the actions of outside powers. In the second, which encompasses the so-called extended neighborhood stretching across Asia and the Indian Ocean littoral, India has sought to balance the influence of other powers and prevent them from undercutting its interests. In the third, which includes the entire global stage, India has tried to take its place as one of the great powers, a key player in international peace and security.

Three things have historically prevented India from realizing these grand strategic goals. First, the partition of the South Asian subcontinent along religious lines (first into India and Pakistan, in 1947, then into India, Pakistan, and Bangladesh, in 1971) left India with a persistent conflict with Pakistan and an internal Hindu-Muslim divide. It also physically separated India from historically linked states such as Afghanistan, Iran, and the nations of Southeast Asia. The creation of an avowedly Islamic state in Pakistan caused especially profound problems for India's engagement with the Middle East. Such tensions intertwined with regional and global great-power rivalries to severely constrict India's room for maneuver in all three concentric circles. The second obstacle was the Indian socialist system, which caused a steady relative economic decline and a consequent loss of influence in the years after independence. The state-socialist model led India to shun commercial engagement with the outside world. As a result, India was disconnected from its natural markets and culturally akin areas in the extended neighborhood.

Finally, the Cold War, the onset of which quickly followed India's independence, pushed India into the arms of the Soviet Union in response to Washington's support for Pakistan and China — and thus put the country on the losing side of the great political contest of the second half of the twentieth century. Despite being the largest democracy in the world, India ended up siding with the opposite camp on most global issues.

The last decade of the twentieth century liberated India from at least two of these constraints; state socialism gave way to economic liberalization and openness to globalization, and the Cold War ended. Suddenly, New Delhi was free to reinvent its foreign policy — positioning itself to face the rise of China, shifting its strategic approach to its other neighbours, and beginning to work closely with the world's existing great powers.

VARIETIES OF INFLUENCE

India's recent embrace of openness and globalization has had an especially dramatic effect on the country's role in the region. As the nations of the subcontinent jettison their old socialist agendas, India is well positioned to promote economic integration. Although the pace has been relatively slow, the process has begun to gain traction. The planned implementation of the South Asian Free Trade Agreement this summer signals the coming reintegration of the subcontinent's markets, which constituted a single economic space until 1947.

At the same time, optimism on the economic front must be tempered by an awareness of the problematic political developments in India's smaller neighbours. The struggle for democracy and social justice in Nepal, interminable political violence and the rise of Islamic extremism in Bangladesh, and the simmering civil war in Sri Lanka underscore the potential dangers of failing states on the subcontinent. There are also the uncertain futures of Pakistan and Afghanistan: defeating religious extremism and creating modern and moderate states in both countries is of paramount importance to India. A successful Indian strategy for promoting peace and prosperity within the region would require preventing internal conflicts from undermining regional security, as well as resolving India's own conflicts with its neighbours. In the past, great-power rivalries, as well as India's own tensions with Pakistan and China, have complicated New Delhi's effort to maintain order in the region. Today, all of the great powers, including the United States and China, support the Indian objective of promoting regional economic integration. The Bush administration has also started to defer to Indian leadership on regional security issues. Given the new convergence of U.S. and Indian interests in promoting democracy and countering extremism and terrorism, New Delhi no longer suspects Washington of trying to undercut its influence in the region. As a result, it is more prepared than ever to work with the United States and other Western powers to pursue regional goals.

Meanwhile, the external environment has never been as conducive as it is today to the resolution of the Indo-Pakistani conflict over Kashmir. The conflict has become less and less relevant to India's relations with the great powers, which has meant a corresponding willingness on New Delhi's part to work toward a solution. Of particular importance has been the steady evolution of the U.S. position on Kashmir since the late 1990s.

The support extended by President Bill Clinton to India in its limited war with Pakistan in 1999 removed the perception that Washington would inevitably align with Islamabad in regional conflicts. But India remained distrustful of the Clinton administration's hyperactive, prescriptive approach to Kashmir. It has been more comfortable with the low-key methods of the Bush administration, which has avoided injecting itself directly into the conflict. The Bush administration has also publicly held Pakistan responsible for cross-border terrorism and has extracted the first-ever assurances from Pakistan to put an end to the attacks. New Delhi does not entirely believe these promises, but it has nonetheless come to trust Washington as a source of positive of influence on Islamabad.

These developments have opened the way for a peace process between the two governments. With the growing awareness that the normalization of relations with Pakistan would end a debilitating conflict and help India's regional and global standing, New Delhi has begun to negotiate seriously for the first time in decades.

Although the pace of talks has not satisfied Pakistan, the two sides have agreed on a range of confidence-building measures. Indian Prime Minister Manmohan Singh has rejected the idea of giving up territory, but he has often called for innovative solutions that would improve living conditions and for common institutions that would connect Kashmiris across the Line of Control. Singh has made clear that the Indian leadership is ready to risk political capital on finding a diplomatic solution to Kashmir.

India's recent effort to resolve its long-standing border dispute with China has been just as bold. New Delhi decided in 2003 to seek a settlement with Beijing on a political basis, rather than on the basis of legal or historical claims. As a result, during Chinese Premier Wen Jiabao's visit to New Delhi in April 2005, India and China agreed on a set of principles to guide the final settlement. The two governments are now exploring the contours of mutually satisfactory territorial compromises.

India's search for practical solutions to the disputes over Kashmir and its border with China suggests that the country has finally begun to overcome the obsession with territoriality that has consumed it since its formation. Ironically, the nuclearization of India and Pakistan in 1998 may have helped in this regard: although nuclearization initially sharpened New

Delhi's conflicts with both Islamabad and Beijing, it also allowed India to approach its territorial problems with greater self-assurance and pragmatism.

INDIA'S MILITARY POLICY CHALLENGES IN THE 21ST CENTURY

The first macro problem that must be resolved, if India is to rise as a great power, is achieving higher rates of economic growth. The reason for that is simple. A competent military costs money and modern defense capabilities, which are sophisticated and effective, are priced in numbers that boggle the imagination. For a country like India, which has to deal not simply with questions of defense but also questions of development simultaneously, high economic growth becomes the only solution especially in those situations when India cannot choose between the objectives of defense and development. When one begins to think of the revolution in military affairs — the kind of capabilities today that characterize the military forces of the great powers — it is simply impossible for India to acquire such capabilities without sustaining economic growth of at least 7 to 9 per cent per annum consistently.

China is a good example. A country that has experienced close to double-digit growth for more than twenty years since 1978, still finds it hard to develop the kinds of sophisticated military capabilities it seeks to acquire across the board.

Therefore, one must be prepared for the fact that even if the Indian economy were to grow between 7 and 9 per cent consistently for the next twenty years, the best India would be able to do in the area of cutting edge defense technology is to acquire niche capabilities. But those niche capabilities may be enough for the specific strategic circumstances that it faces. The second macro problem that India needs to engage and satisfy is the development of an appropriate national vision and appropriate institutions designed to manage the acquisition of great power capabilities.

What substantive goals, defined in terms of national interest, does India really seek to service? The answer to this question cannot be defined in terms of platitudes like a "just world order." That is a useful phrase for a political campaign. It is a terrible criterion for defense planning and force structuring. The other aspect of this question of defining India's goals and creating the appropriate institutions pertains to the issue of whether India will be able to achieve the right balance between state control and societal autonomy. It is very important to realize that successful states in the modern era have been those that have maintained this balance in the most creative way possible.

The third macro challenge that I would highlight for your consideration is whether India is capable of exploiting the existing structure of the international system to its advantage. In this context, I think India should get rid of the notion of a multipolar world order as a practical outcome in the relevant future. Pursuing chimerical goals like multipolarity does not make for good policy. The international system, for all practical purposes, is going to remain a unipolar system for at least the next half century. By all indicators, if you define power in terms of comprehensive national strength, it is unlikely that the United States will face serious peer competitors for at least another fifty years.

Consequently, the challenge for India becomes, can it develop a viable strategic partnership with the United States that serves both mutual interests and India's own unilateral interests? Can India develop a relationship with the United States that helps it enhance and magnify its own power?

This is not to suggest that the United States is the only power in the international system. Clearly not — there are many others. This is also not to suggest that India's goals ought to consist solely of developing a relationship with the United States, or that India somehow is constrained solely to develop a relationship with the United States and no other. Not true. India has the flexibility to maneuver within the interstices of the international system. But at the end of the day, there is one eight hundred pound gorilla that has to be engaged. And that is the United States. That gorilla is not going to go away. That gorilla has already put its nose for the first time in modern history, into the physical environment of the subcontinent. And it is in India's national interest, and important for its capacity to generate and magnify its power, to develop a productive and a collaborative relationship with the United States that enhances the interests of the two countries.

First, India has to deal with the challenge of neutering internal security threats without undermining its capacity for effective external defense. This is harder to do than is sometimes imagined. It is unfortunate that the principal security threat that India is going to have to deal with on a day-to-day basis is the threat to internal security. There is no running away from this problem. Historically, India dealt with this challenge by essentially throwing manpower at the threat instead of technology. And the reason it did this was simply because it enjoyed a surfeit of manpower and a deficit of technology.

There were two consequences to this strategy. One was that its approach to preserving internal defense was probably not as effective as it could be, because technology could provide that valuable supplement which was not available to India. The second consequence was that preserving internal security became extremely expensive and has now come at the cost of being able to acquire the new technologies required to raise a modern military force. It is a myth that India's manpower is cheap. Maintaining the size and kind of forces that India does, if maintained over the secular period, will undercut its ability to acquire the kind of RMA capabilities that wins modern wars. And this is going to require India to make very painful choices — painful choices about reducing its manpower strength and changing the inter-service budgetary balances, choices that it cannot make today because of the gravity, importance, and burdens of its internal security commitments.

The next micro issue is the need to preserve effective external defense, now in a nuclear shadowed environment. This brings us face to face with the vexed question of whether

India has the capacity to successfully prosecute a limited war. Most commentary so far has focused on the issue of limited war as an example of Indian recklessness. People have chastised the Defense Minister, Mr. George Fernandes, for arguing that limited war in fact represents a solution to India's external security problems. My take on the issue is somewhat different. I believe that limited war should be viewed not as a product of the proclivities of the state, but rather as a predicament resulting from a specific set of structural circumstances.

The transparent presence of nuclear weapons in the subcontinent for the first time makes unlimited wars untenable as a matter of state policy.

This is not simply India's choice — it actually represents a dilemma of the nuclear age. And it is a challenge that faces India both with respect to Pakistan and with respect to China. In both cases, unlimited war is not feasible. There is also no guarantee that war is obsolete. And therefore the challenge of limited war confronts India squarely, both with respect to its northern and its western borders.

What does limited war mean for Indian defense policy? It means that India is now confronted with the task of being required to hit hard and effectively enough to punish an adversary, but not hit so hard or so effectively as to cause inadvertent escalation. This in turn leads to questions like "how do you avoid escalation?" Most commentaries have focused on this aspect of the problem. But there is another aspect to the problem, which has largely escaped attention. Because it is going to demand of India a new style of war fighting that New Delhi traditionally has been uncomfortable with and which historically it has been relatively incapable of. It is a style of war fighting that puts a premium on achieving very speedy decision on the battlefield and then terminating offensive action either before the international community intervenes or before the conflict degenerates into unavoidable attrition. Getting the Indian military to successfully prosecute a fast paced war that generates quick decisions is something that we have not seen in fifty years of India's independence. It is also the kind of war that traditionally the United States was not very good at. We preferred wars that allowed us plenty of time to mobilize, plenty of time to deploy, and then plenty of time to be able to grind down the adversary at our convenience. If India is to be able to prosecute the opposite kind of war, as the United States is now proficient at — fast, decisive, and yet limited — it is going to require an investment in new technologies and new operating skills apart from new doctrines and new concepts of operation.

Third, if India is to become a great power of the sort that it seeks to become, it also has to become a net provider of regional security, both in the sub-continental and in the extra sub-continental arenas. This is easier said than done; yet at one level it is the quintessential part of the definition of a great power. After all, what is the meaning of having great power capabilities if at the end of the day you cannot extend net security to others? And yet any Indian attempt to provide the kind of regional security that I am talking of, even in the sub-continental arena, is fraught with hazards because it risks deepening intra-regional rivalries and it risks deepening the suspicions India's weaker neighbours have of its capabilities and its intentions. Finally, will India develop the organizational structures that are required to maintain and operate these capabilities if it seeks to provide the kind of regional security that is to be expected of a great power?

The fourth micro problem pertains to whether India can acquire an effective nuclear deterrent without breaking the bank. My view is that nuclear weapons are important for India's security in some limited sense, but it is also essential to remember that they are actually relatively obsolescent technologies. Nuclear weapons are now over fifty years old and they are generally unusable as instruments of international politics.

SECURITY THREATS ANALYSIS ON ASEAN

The emergence of India as South Asia's military power had raised other countries concern especially Southeast Asian countries on the impact on security. In reality, India's emergence as a military power would in fact present a security threat, either directly or indirect on Southeast Asian countries because of its geographical location with South Asia. This emergence has a similar scenario when the Southeast Asian Nations (SAN) were worried when China emerged as a military power. The geographical location aspect is a measurement for Southeast Asia countries' concern which is located near to East Asia and is compel to share the South China Sea (SCS). China's action in claiming the right on a particular region in SCS using military approach has become a standard for researches to predict India's superpower actions. SAN had witnessed China utilizing the gunboat diplomacy in SCS which several times had trigger military tension with SAN the armed forces in SCS. The close geography location of Southeast Asian Nation (SAN) and China, besides the fact that they share the South China Sea (SCS) has become a platform for researches to assess the impact of India's emergence. India's power over the Indian Ocean and its close sea position with Southeast Asia region has become subject to SAN's concern.

"As China is on the verge of developing its maritime capability, it is looking at its southern shores more cautiously. It is also vital for China to fight any challenges that come from the south given its conflicting territorial claims. It is also important for China to be able in position to control the sea lanes during times of crises or escalation of tension... If China needs to be recognized as a superpower its ability to control the southern sea is vital (K.S Balakrishnan,1999:50)".

The emergence of China as a superpower and SAN's concern are almost similar to the anxiety on the emergence of India. The close geography location with the region has become a factor that triggers SAN's concern. At the same time, India's authority in the Indian Ocean which is an ocean that connects Southeast Asia with the West is almost a similar scenario as China's control on SCS. The Southeast Asian region is situated amidst the two of the world's very important ocean; Indian Ocean to the west and South China Sea to the east which is dominated by two superpowers of the world that is India and China. SAN's concern on India is not only about geographical aspect but also involved other factors such as politics, military and regional threats.

In analyzing the impact of India's emergence towards SAN, it is necessary to examine the early history and relations of India with SAN. At an early stage especially during the establishment of ASEAN, India had its own different opinion with SAN. SAN's objective to set up ASEAN is to create a non-aligned zone of freedom and peace. In other words, ASEAN tries to avoid the domination of any superpower over the Southeast Asian region (Zin Mahmud,2005:11 14). From India's point of view, ASEAN is established as another political pact and defense similar to the establishment of SEATO (Southeast Asian Treaty Organization) supported by the United States. India had been uncomfortable ever since the US facilitated Pakistan, particularly when it sent airplane carrier tanker, USS Enterprise, to the Indian Ocean during the Indo-Pakistan war in the year 1971 (K.S Balakrishnan, 2000:51). It had influenced India to strengthen its relationship with the Soviet Union. Nevertheless India had not objected or opposed the establishment of ASEAN. Although India is concerned with the expansion of superpowers, especially the US in the Asia Pacific, yet India is not against the presence of Soviet Union in this region. It had raised conflict of interest between India and ASEAN, whereby during the Cold War ASEAN had been more comfortable with the presence the United States than the Soviet Union (K.S Balakrishnan, 2002:32).

The early relationship of India-ASEAN was also influenced by ASEAN criticizing India's action during Pakistan's internal crisis in 1971. According to ASEAN, India should not have interfered in the conflict between West Pakistan and East Pakistan (Bangladesh). India's military presence supporting West Pakistan was seen as meddling in the internal affairs of a country's sovereign. This incident had soured India-ASEAN's relationship. ASEAN had tried to improved the relationship with India by inviting India as an ASEAN's dialogue partner in the1970s, however it was aborted when India resort to recognized the Vietnam's puppet government in Cambodia in 1979. It is contrary to ASEAN's stance that opposed Vietnam's invasion and occupation over Cambodia. This state of affairs had caused the ASEAN-India relationship to deteriorate. The Communist regime Vietcong control on Vietnam backed by Soviet Union in 1975 indicated US's defeat and withdrawal. It had indirectly opened a room for India to strengthen the relationship with Vietnam's communist regime.

In fact Vietnam-China's strained relationship since the Sino-Vietnamese war in 1979 was a great opportunity for India to strengthen its relationship with China's enemy (R.S Sassheen, 1987:111). India also viewed US's withdrawal from Vietnam a an opportunity for China to conquer Southeast Asia (Pushpindar Singh,1987:60). India's high concerned of China's development in Southeast Asia for India was involved in the Sino-India war in 1962 (Asian Defense and Diplomacy, May 2005:10 11). To avoid SAN misunderstanding India's relationship with Vietnam and Russia, India through Indira Gandhi adopted a wise approach to support the decision during the ASEAN Conference in Bali 1976, for the purpose of creating regional peace and stability.

Military modernization and development of India had also influence SAN 's perception on India. Rajiv Ghandi's decision to develop the navy force to strengthen the control of Indian Ocean had aroused SAN's concern. India's choices lead by Rajiv Ghandi, in several South Asian ethnic conflicts particularly involving ethnic Indian in Sri Lanka, Maldives and Fiji had also raised SAN's concern (Zin Mahmud,2005:11 14).

This is because ethnic Indians is a large ethnic community in several SAN countries. Hence, ASEAN is worried of any conflict with Indian ethnic in SAN that will open an opportunity to India to interfere in internal affairs.

In strengthen its control over Indian Ocean, India has rapidly developed its maritime defense strategy by combining capacity and military force directed to the national defense of land, air and sea including land border, archipelago, maritime asset and important trade route. Indian also intends to develop its navy that can operate beyond geo–strategic area, covering the entire Indian Ocean and Southeast Asia. USS Enterprise's presence in the Indian Ocean during the Indo-Pakistan war in 971 to aid Pakistan had vested a large awareness on India to emerge as a maritime power in its interest in the Indian Ocean.

"U-S Pakistani ties annyoyed India relation with Washington in many ways. The 1971 Indo-Pakistani War for the first time witnessed the threat of their alliace with the US. US dispatched its aircraft carrier USS Entreprise during the war. Though India was able to liberate Bangladesh, it for the first time learned the importance of protecting Indian Ocean. It was at this time India realised that it must be a maritime power in the region and to ensure that no countries are able to dictate terms in the Indian Ocean"(K.S Balakrishnan, 2000:51-52).

The interest to defend Indian Territory had started since 1960, following the development competition of big powers in the Asia Pacific and South Asia that could threatened India's security. Although since 1960 India had not extensively developed its maritime defense strategy, the military development had still enable India to protect its strategic territories.

India perceives its control on Indian Ocean as important considering it is a route linking Europe and East Asia (K.M Panikkar,1995:93). India's aims to develop several military harbors in some islands neighboring Southeast Asian countries, also raised concerned. India's military settlement proposal in Nicobar and Andaman islands of Benggal Bay had received Indonesia's protest due its extremely close location to Indonesian territory.

Although India is prioritizing developments in South Asia, the expanding influence of China in Asia Pacific is alarming India. This is because China have started strengthening ties with Myanmar and Bangladesh, two countries sharing borders with India (Haris Zalkapli,2005:24 25). Additionally, China's decision to develop Tibet and Xinjiang rapidly stimulated India's interest, as both of these areas sharing borders with the western part of India. China-Pakistan and China-Myanmar relationship equally had elevated India's concern on China (Philips HJ Davies,2001:55). Similarly, close diplomatic ties and India-Vietnam's military cooperation also had provoked China's attention. This is because military training between India, Korea Selatan and Vietnam and witnessing India sending five warships and Kilo submarines in October and November of 2002 has enabled India to experience training South China Sea. In term of nuclear threats, SAN is increasingly worried about nuclear crisis between India and China. This is because the geography of Southeast Asia is located in the heart of both superpower nations.

On the 16th of May 2001, India's Prime Minister on an official visit to Malaysia had delivered a speech on India's decision to maintain the defense doctrine that uses nuclear weapons as device of deterrence and respect ASEAN's stand for regional peace. (Asian Defense and Diplomacy, December 2002:27). Although in 2001 India had announced its up-to-date ability in successfully developing a sub based deterrent that is capable to strike in seconds, the nuclear doctrine practiced by India is not a first strike policy (Asian Defense and Diplomacy, December 2002:27). India's nuclear development success can directly be deterrence towards China (Dipankar Banerjee, 1999:12 14). Even though this is a miraculous achievement and pride to India, for Southeast Asia it is a disturbing development. This is because ballistic missile blast from Indian Ocean will need to pass over Southeast Asia and South China Sea to reach to China. On the other hand, land ballistic missile would pass areas that are neighboring Southeast Asia to reach the target in China. ASEAN's airspace would also be use if India decides to explode its airborne nuclear deterrent towards China (Philips HJ Davies,2001:55).

Security is the main objective of India in conducting its nuclear weapons development program. India views its nuclear weapon development program as efforts to prevent confrontations from Pakistan and China. Therefore, India has positioned its military at all borders with both countries and located their nuclear weapons that are always ready to face threats (Suhaimi Mokhtar,Mac 2002:62). Indian is also very careful with Pakistan because the conflict among these two nations may trigger war that has happen in 1971 (Asian Defence Journal,1997:78). India's firmness in safeguarding the security through the position of military forces at its border was perform tactically and began in December 2001. President Vladimir Putin speculated that, "they (India) do not want war, but they will go to war when the circumstances forced them to do so" (Suhaimi Mokhtar,August 2002:49). In easier words, "nuclear weapons can prevent nuclear weapons" and India can always be ready to face nuclear threat from the foreign countries (Kenneth Waltz,1979:188-189). This theory is an idea that can convince one country to guarantee the safety of the country under threats (Asian Defence Journal,1997:72). The ownership of nuclear weapons will cause the aggressor to cancel its intention when they find out that the stated country has nuclear weapons (Howard H. Letner,1997:210). To this date, India's security is said to be guaranteed base on the theory of deterrence.

Although the India-China early relation was majorly influenced by border conflicts that resulted in military development, yet it does not mean the cold relationship will continue. This is because, both countries are always attempting to repair their relationship and tackle the misunderstanding. Since year 1962, both countries have carried out 15 settlement negotiations to resolve the crisis of their 2,500 miles border (Asian Defense and Diplomacy, May 2005:12). Although negotiations constantly failed, it demonstrated both country seriousness and readiness to find solution through diplomacy. India-China's relationship improved after Indian Prime Minister, Atal Behari Vajpayee's official visit to China in 2003. It was a visit focusing towards restoration of the relationship and overcoming unsolved problems. This visit can be concluded that both countries were not attempting to threaten one another. Vajpayee explained that:-

"The simple truth is that there is no objective reason for discord between us, and neither of us is a threat to the other.this

simple profound principles should form the badrock of the future India-China partnership"(Asian Defence And Diplomacy, August *2003:9)*

India-China's relationship restoration was reinforced through military cooperation and training between both countries. Being both maritime superpower nations that controls Indian Ocean and South China Sea the ties can be built through training and military cooperation. Hence, in November 2004 witness the first time ever India and China conducted a joint military training (Asian Defense and Diplomacy, December 2003-Januari 2004). It is the extended collaboration of both countries at ministry level, after the head of state effort in 2003. This tie has brought new radiance in the relation between both countries and could lessen Southeast Asia's concern of a clash between the two superpowers.

Although Southeast Asia had long worried about the current development of India's political and military, it does not mean that Southeast Asia has doubted India. This is because Southeast Asian Nation (SAN) had already adopted a constructive engagement approach with India, especially to strengthen diplomatic ties and economic cooperation of India-SAN (Mustafa Climb,2001:43 44). ASEAN had invited India to become a dialogue partner to ASEAN and performed close economic cooperation for India is a strong country in terms of economic development (K.S Balakrishnan,2001:5-6). The Indian government had given positive reaction on ASEAN efforts whereby India had helped the security cooperation through ASEAN and ARF. In fact India collaborated in the Confident Building Measure of ASEAN by engaging in a friendly visit and carrying out joint military training. These efforts had increase understanding between countries and enhanced each others trust. India had attempted to convince the trust of SAN by proving that India is not a power that will threaten SAN's security where India invited those nations to visit and survey its military harbor in Andaman and Nicobar islands. In fact to strengthen the present relationship, India participated in SAN's informal security and military activities, such as taking part in the Langkawi International Maritime and Air Exibition (LIMA) in Langkawi.

INDIA'S REEMERGENCE AS A STRATEGIC RIVAL TO CHINA

The challenges that China's geo-strategists had foreseen in 1950s or even earlier from a potentially strong India finally began to take shape in 2000s. India has emerged as the most formidable competitor (after the US) to China in the Asian theater over the last decade. It's posing as a serious competitor to China in military, diplomatic, economic and even in soft power domains.

In military terms, post-1998 India has been enjoying, what this author calls *strategic capital*, in the sense that, unlike the rise of China, India's military rise is not only not feared but it is felt to be desirable by the countries in the Asia-Pacific like Japan, Australia, South Korea, and ASEAN as a group. Most importantly even the US sees India's military rise in its own interests. Interestingly, a rising India is making full use of this capital by emerging as a formidable military power over the last decade, apart from unveiling even more ambitious military plans for the future.

Chinese security analysts are anxiously observing the growing presence of the Indian military in the Pacific. Indian army representatives have attended the Pacific Armies Management Seminar (PAMS) meetings for some years. India hosted PAMS in 2004, while it was Fiji's turn to hold it in September 2006. Similarly, India has been participating in the Asia-Pacific Chiefs of Defense Conference ever since 1998. The scale of India's participation in the Pacific has raised a major question in China: "Are we all ready to accept India as a against China, the first time it has taken such a step with offensive tactical missiles.

Besides the army, India has also given focused strategic attention to its naval modernization, which has become, along with the US's naval presence, the most serious challenge to

China, not only in the Indian Ocean but also in the western Pacific. When it set up the Far Eastern Naval Command (FENC) at Port Blair in the Andaman and Nicobar islands in 2005, India further accentuated what President Hu Jintao has called China's "Malacca Dilemma". The command also acts as a base for the Indian navy to carry out maritime operations in the South China Sea and the Western Pacific, which are the two sensitive maritime domains for Beijing.

Taking lessons from its military defeat in 1962, mainly due to its failure to deploy air force, the Indian defense planners have shifted their focus to boosting India's air power in both the eastern and western sectors. Expressing his anxieties over India's growing air presence in the Himalayas, Andrei Chang, the Hong Kong editor in chief of the Canadian journal Kanwa Defense Weekly, pointed out, "Along the India-China border, air power has been shifting in favor of India. First of all, India has quite a number of airports in Assam and the disputed territory of Arunachal Pradesh, making troop maneuvers easier." Also once India started procuring 126 aircraft, both the Eurofighter Typhoon and the French Dassault Rafale, in a defense deal worth more than US$20 billion, India began to enjoy a great advantage over the Tibetan skies, thereby seriously threatening the Chinese nuclear deterrent against it.

In 2008 for the first time the Indian Air force stationed its most advanced fighter jets, the Su-MKI30, at four Indian Air Force bases in north eastern India—Tezpur, Avantipur (Baghhdogra) , Chhabua and Hashimara. Kunming, Chengdu and Chongqing. In 2008 India reactivated the 2.1-km airstrip at Daulat Beg Oldi (DBO) in northeastern Ladakh.. The highly strategic ALG is located close to the Chinese controlled portion of Kashmir, also referred to as *Aksai Chin*. It is just eight kilometres from the Karakorum Highway that links Pakistan with China.

Diplomatically India has emerged as the main rival to China after Japan in East Asia. Despite China's diplomatic offensive, India became a member of East Asia Summit (EAS) in 2005 mainly due to hard lobbying by Japan and South Korea.

The Chinese scholars interpreted India's entry into EAS as one more step forward to realize the East Asian Community (EAC) modeled on the EU, a concept initiated by Japan. China sees the EAC in terms of a Japan-ASEAN axis and a Japanese attempt to restore its prominent political and military role in the region.

China blames India's democracy for its poor economic performance compared to what China has achieved under its own economic model (the "Beijing Consensus" i.e. economic growth under tight political control). However, a rising democratic India in concert with major Asia-Pacific democracies such as Japan, South Korea, and Australia and the United States is creating what China calls the "axis of democracies" or an Asian NATO against China. Beijing perceives the formation of this bloc as a move to contain its influence in East Asia and the 10-nation ASEAN.

In a major diplomatic setback to China, on 19 November, 2011, due to strong support from India and Japan, the US participated for the first time in the sixth East Asia Summit held in Bali, Indonesia. Honolulu in October 2010 as the "Indo-Pacific" theater, a newly emerged and integrated theatre joining the Indian and the Pacific oceans. On 19th Dec 2011, India, Japan and the US, the three maritime democracies, held their first-ever trilateral dialogue in Washington, which was widely reported by the Chinese media as yet another component of containment strategy. The next trilateral meeting is scheduled to be held in Tokyo, Japan in 2012.

In the economic domain India, despite all of its economic growth over the last two decades, has still not emerged as an economic challenger to China. China's huge economic edge over India has enabled China to outbid India in various energy deals. Its membership of APEC has enabled it to have a much greater share of global trade than India. However, China's economic lead over India is not going to survive for long. One school of economists already see India as the most serious economic competitor to China in the medium to long term time horizon given India's institutional and demographic advantages over China. India has already emerged as a serious rival of China in attracting FDI, which is a very sensitive economic issue for China.

With the completion of Golden Quadrilateral Highway project in 2007, India has taken the first all important step in addressing the core obstacle in attracting FDI, which was poor physical connectivity.

The results of better connectivity became instantly obvious when India attracted an FDI amount worth US$34.6 billion compared to US$78.2 billion by China in 2009. These figures stood at 3.6% and 38.4% respectively in 2000. Morgan Stanley predicted that India's GDP growth rate would overtake China's in 2013; the World Bank projected it might happen a year earlier in 2012. But the IMF's World Economic Outlook says it's already happened: China grew by 10.3% last year; India grew by 10.4%.

Yong Dali says, "as India's manufacture sectors develop and China's service sectors become more competitive, it is possible that these two countries' trade competition in Southeast Asia will become more serious". China for a long time reaped handsome dividends on the availability of its low cost labor force. However, China has begun to loose on providing cheap labor due to the rising income levels of its manpower employed in the manufacturing sector. The main challenge China faces here is posed by India.

A 2007 Goldman Sachs report forecasts that China will get old before it gets rich. China is the fastest aging country among the developing economies. In fact, the report predicts that China will be an "aged society" in 2027. In India, on the other hand, in 2020 the average age in India will be only 29 years, compared with 37 in China and the United States, 45 in Western Europe, and 48 in Japan. Moreover, 70 percent of Indians will be of working age in 2025, up from 61 percent now. Also by 2025 the proportion of children younger than 15 will fall to 23 percent of India's total population, from 34 percent today, while the share of people older than 65 will remain around just 5 percent.

Soft Power

The other domain where India has emerged as a serious rival to China is the soft power domain. India's concurrently growing soft power has further intensified the competition between these two pre-modern the United States. India, just like China, is not only a nation-state, it's also a civilization-state which is a very important element of soft power, as Nye says. India is the only country that can share the Chinese claim to great power status based on its 5000 year-old civilization. However, China is in no mood whatsoever to share this privilege – especially with India, a country that it militarily defeated in 1962. But more importantly, the rise of a civilization-state like India challenges China's historically constructed exclusivist political notion of the *Middle Kingdom*. As John Lee argues, "The Chinese see the idea of Asia as having a Chinese core (i.e. *Middle Kingdom*) with a number of cultures and polities in the periphery while itself is at the centre. Those cultures and polities are either tributary to the Middle Kingdom or considered 'barbarians.' Thus a rising civilization-state such as India uniquely threatens the core political idea of another civilization-state, China." The rise of India has created a rare phenomenon in international politics where a civilization-state with more than one billion diverse people is growing economically at good pace under a democratically elected government. Joseph Nye argues that India has considerable soft power advantage over China in being a democratic country. The fact that India can grow at more than 7% over the last two decades under a democratic polity is an ideological threat to the authoritarian China. In fact, one can argue that a "New Delhi Consensus," meaning economic development under a democratic rule, is a far better model for the Third World than the "Beijing Consensus" based on economic development under tight political control. John Lee opines, "The traditional Chinese response to Western expectations that it pursue political reform is to point out that contradiction to this reasoning".

Also, the communist regime in China used to sell the argument to its own people that democracy is causally related to India's previous economic stagnation, and thereby China has derived legitimacy for its authoritarian rule. However, democratic India's economic success over the 2000s has put the CCP in quite an uncomfortable position. The Chinese citizenry, at least among the intellectual class, has begun to develop an extremely positive outlook towards Indian democracy. As Jinxin Huang argues: One anonymous Chinese scholar believes that it is India's decentralized democracy that has managed to hold together a poor, populous, and linguistically and religiously diverse country. According to her/him, 'democracy has created a shared commitment for all those who live in India regardless of religious and ethnic backgrounds.' In short, for the first time ever, the Chinese are finding that India's democracy is an advantage.

China's Response Strategy

In the 1950s and early 1960s, when Beijing realized that India was reducing its diplomatic and strategic space by emerging as its main Asian peer competitor, it taught New Delhi a lesson and emerged as *primus inter pares* in the developing world. It established what John W. Garver has called *entente cordiale* with Pakistan by giving it diplomatic, political and military support. It openly sided with Pakistan in the 1965 war. However, the real diplomatic master stroke on the part of Beijing that de-hyphenated it with India and put it in the big league with the two super powers, occurred when China accepted the US offer of an alliance to corner early 1970s. Now it is perfectly logical to ask how Chinese leaders are going to respond to a resurgent India that is being re-hyphenated with China. This author opines that China has developed a four-pronged strategy to "manage" the rise of India. Importantly, all the four components of this strategy are in place simultaneously. These components are:

- A carrot and stick policy to sabotage growing Indo-US ties
- To intensify military encirclement of India
- To deepen *entente cordiale* with Pakistan
- To keep India out of regional and global institutions .

Beijing's carrots to India include rhetorically affirming India's great power ambitions (e.g. India's *zhong he guoli* or "comprehensive national power"), China's declaration that it wants India to play a bigger role in global politics, and cultivating India-China "friendship." More importantly the Chinese carrot also included heightened diplomatic engagement with India over the 2000s. For example, high profile leaders visited India, including Li Peng in January 2001, Premier Zhu Rongji in January 2002, Premier Wen Jiabao in April 2005, President Hu Jintao in November 2006, and Premier Wen Jiabao again in December 2010. The timing of such visits creates an interesting pattern. Each of these visits has followed a high profile visit from the US to India. For example, Li Peng and Zhu Rongji's visits followed President Bill Clinton's March 2000 visit; Wen Jiabao's first visit followed Secretary of State Condoleezza Rice's March 2005 visit; Hu Jintao's visit followed President George W. Bush' visit in March 2006; and Wen's second visit followed President Barack Obama's orbit. I strongly believe that this pattern will continue in the foreseeable future as well.

Another component of the Chinese carrot to India is deepening trade ties with India. With more than US$61 billion as of 2011, China has emerged as India's single largest trading partner. During Wen's visit to India in December 2010 he proposed to raise bilateral trade to US$100 billion by 2015. As Ziad Haider, a research fellow at the Stimson Centre in Washington D. C. argues, "Stronger economic ties will create stronger constituents for peace in both countries and raise the threshold for conflict. In what scenarios would India deem siding with the USA against China worth jeopardizing its commercial links with China?"

The pragmatic Chinese have complemented the carrot by using the stick of periodically reminding India that Sino-US relations are exclusive, both have deep economic engagement, and their views on global security issues converge. Besides, both are permanent members of UNSC, and this can harm Indian interests, especially on the issue of nuclear proliferation. China also likes to remind India that both the US and China have strong relations with India's Achilles' heel, Pakistan. The second component of this strategy is China's intensified military encirclement of India. For example, China completed Golmund-Lhasa railway in 2006, thereby dramatically reducing the troop deployment time on Indian borders. It completed its fifth airfield in Tibet in October 2010.

Over the last decade Beijing has deployed state-of-the-art medium and intermediate range missiles with nuclear warheads in Tibet that have a very short flight time (meaning no warning time). It has been constructing seaports around India in Bangladesh, Sri Lanka, and Pakistan under the "string of pearls" strategy. The latest "pearl" in this string included a base on the Seychelles, completed in December 2011.

It's going to station three aircraft carriers, one each in the South China Sea, Western Pacific, and Indian Ocean by Zhang Li explicitly argues, Pakistan is a hedge against uncertainties in Indo-China relations given the Tibet factor and now increasingly the US factor. A similar view is proffered by Ye Hailing when he argues that "the influence of the US on Indian foreign policy and the temptation of becoming a member of a so-called 'Democracy Community' cannot be ignored by India. It is not very wise for China to expect Indians to take China's engagement with Pakistan kindly."

China has widened the Karakorum highway, making it suitable for transportation of military vehicles and building the Diamer-Bhasha dam in PoK. In the construction of the Gwadar port, China provided much of the technical assistance and 80 percent of the funds. Giving a further boost to their strategic ties during the visit of the Chinese Premier to Islamabad in 2005, the two governments signed the "*Treaty of Friendship, Cooperation and Good-neighborly Relations between the People's Republic of China and the Islamic Republic of Pakistan.*" By this treaty, argues Gurmeet Kanwal, China has guaranteed the territorial integrity of Pakistan. In April 2008 China promised Pakistan it would provide financial support for purchasing a Chinese 250 JF-17 Thunder jet fighter fleet and F-22 frigates. In a strategic tit-for-tat for the Indo-United States civilian nuclear deal signed in 2006 that came into effect in 2008, Chinese companies in June 2010 signed a contract in Shanghai in relation to two 650-megawatt Chashma-3 and Chashma-4 reactors, in addition to a 2004 deal under which China supplied Chashma-1 and Chashma-2 to Pakistan .

As a fourth and final component of its strategy, China has been playing a villainous role to keep India out of important global and regional institutions despite its rhetoric of acknowledging India's "great power"

This Chinese stance is diametrically opposite to what India did in the 1950s when the UNSC seat was being offered to India on a platter and India refused the privilege guided by its *moralpolitik*. Also, China left no stone unturned to keep India out of the EAS in 2005. Though China invited India to the Shanghai Cooperation Organization as an observer in 2006, it did so only along with Pakistan. It tried to obstruct the Nuclear Suppliers Group waiver to India in 2008. Similarly, India had secured full support from the US, Japan, and Vietnam among others to get entry into APEC, but it's inclusion was halted by Chinese reluctance at the 2007 summit to lift the moratorium on new members.

INDIA'S LIKELY PATH: SOFT BALANCING AND LIMITED HARD BALANCING

For the foreseeable future, India will likely pursue soft balancing, limited hard balancing and diplomatic engagement with China. The limited hard balancing involves asymmetrical capability acquisition and the building of additional strength on the border and naval assets in the Indian Ocean. India is currently augmenting its nuclear capabilities and placing them on different platforms to create a triad, while also strengthening its conventional capabilities. Some of these weapons, especially the aircraft-based nuclear systems and Prithvi short-range ballistic missiles, are meant for deterring Pakistan, though they also contribute to a triangular deterrent relationship among China, India, and Pakistan. These capabilities could form a powerful asymmetrical deterrent and defense capability, though they wouldn't constitute a force equal to China's in an all-out conflict. However, a full spectrum of nuclear deterrent deployment is delayed by the slow pace at which India develops and deploys its indigenous missile capabilities.

On the diplomatic front, possibilities exist for further strengthening the soft balancing coalition with the United States, Japan, and ASEAN countries, despite a short-term hiatus in the development of the coalition caused by U.S. policies under Trump. India and Japan have initiated an Asia-Africa economic growth corridor to compete with the Belt and Road Initiative, but progress has been limited thus far. These mechanisms offer a convenient stopgap between active military balancing and doing nothing in the face of China's expansionist policies. In addition, diplomatic engagement through institutional forums and regular summit meetings are likely to be the preferred option for both. China in particular seems to use these venues to reduce the intensity of Indian opposition and to mitigate the possibility of India forming anti-China coalitions.

Why is it difficult for India to engage in full-fledged hard balancing, whether it be internal balancing through military capability or external balancing via formal military alignment with other major powers? The first obstacle is the capability discrepancy. In 2017, China spent some $150.5 billion on defense, while India spent around $52.5 billion. Second, even though trade relations favor China, they are important for India's economic progress as well. Third, it's hard to find reliable alliance partners, and the formation of hard-balancing alliances could push China to step up border clashes, encourage Pakistani support for the insurgency in Kashmir, and increase China's activities in the Indian Ocean. Finally, a strategy of soft balancing gives India some diplomatic freedom to hedge and bargain with potential allies such as the United States and Japan as well as with China itself. Soft balancing may be the least objectionable way to avoid intense security competition with China and an arms race that will disproportionately hurt India. However, the ball is in Beijing's court in terms of whether or not India goes for intense hard balancing in the years to come.

Policymakers in Washington should not expect a radical realignment by India involving a hard-balancing coalition with the United States, given that India prides its strategic autonomy so much. Indian elites also have ambitions to become "the next China," or at least a leading power in the 21st century, and a close military relationship with Washington would not fulfill that objective unless the United States is willing to accommodate India more than it has done so far. Moreover, India's strategic and economic relationships with Russia and China make hard and fast alignment with Washington a difficult proposition.

What policy planners in both New Delhi and Washington should work toward instead is pursuing as much cooperation and coordination as possible. They should seek to promote soft balancing and institutional mechanisms to restrain China's expansionism in the Indo-Pacific. This will require more strategic subtlety and an effective counter to the Belt and Road Initiative. To counter China effectively, the United States, India, and Japan need to use economic and diplomatic instruments more than they are doing now, because military power cannot substitute what the smaller states in the region are yearning for: economic and infrastructure development without too many preconditions.

4

China's Growing Military Presence Abroad Brings New Challenges

Increasing contributions to UN peacekeeping and the rising presence of Chinese security forces abroad are pushing Beijing to engage with questions of international law it has not previously had to consider.

China's involvement in UN peacekeeping contributions has been on the rise for some time. China is also stepping up its own military and security operations abroad to protect its commercial and strategic interests, particularly in Africa. In doing so, China is exposing itself to a more complex set of issues – including international legal issues – with which it is only just starting to grapple.

China's contribution to UN peacekeeping over the last 10 years has expanded dramatically. In September 2016, it pledged $1 billion to help fund UN peace, security and development activities, while in 2018 it supplied 10.3 per cent of the UN peacekeeping budget, up from 3.93 per cent in 2012. China is also the largest contributor of peacekeeping forces among the five permanent members of the Security Council. As well as its regular troop contributions, it has also established a stand-by rapid deployment force(opens in new window) of 8,000 peacekeeping troops.

For China, increased involvement in UN peacekeeping offers what it likes to refer to as a 'win-win' situation. China's contribution is very valuable at a time when peacekeeping is in need of resources, given the cutbacks from the other four permanent members of the Security Council in both financial and personnel contributions, waning US support for the UN and pressures on the UN budget.

At the same time, the increased role in UN peacekeeping helps to cement China's image as a 'responsible stakeholder' in the international order. China's contributions to peacekeeping missions also help to promote stability in countries in which China has significant strategic and commercial interests, such as Senegal, South Sudan and Mali.

China's increased involvement in UN peacekeeping has coincided with the adoption of a more pragmatic position in relation to its traditionally staunch adherence to the principles of state sovereignty and non-intervention.

China was initially sceptical of the UN's Responsibility to Protect(opens in new window) (R2P) doctrine, endorsed by member states in 2005, which seeks to protect populations from gross human rights violations, and which can include recourse to use of force by the international community, if authorized by the Security Council under Chapter VII of the UN Charter. Over time, though, Beijing has softened its stance to intervention and has gradually acknowledged the ability to respond to humanitarian catastrophes in certain circumstances, for example voting in favour of the Intervention Brigade in the Democratic Republic of the Congo in 2013.

The softening of China's stance on non-intervention is also evident in the significant rise not only in the involvement of Chinese troops in UN peacekeeping, but also in the deployment of Chinese military and security forces in a number of African states in order to protect China's investment and infrastructure projects located there.

In 2017, China established its first foreign naval base in Djibouti, and in 2018 it held military drills in several African countries. The significant increase in China's military presence in Africa since 2015 gives rise to a number of more complex issues for both China and the local communities involved. According to a recent report, China's growing military and security presence in Africa is leading to concern in some local constituencies. The fact that China's state-centric perception of security and development downplays the importance of human rights is likely to compound these tensions on the ground.

NEW INTERNATIONAL LAW IMPLICATIONS

The growing presence of Chinese peacekeeping, police and security forces abroad also carries implications for China in a number of different areas of international law with which it has only recently started to grapple. These include the law on the use of force and, given that many Chinese infrastructure projects are situated in fragile states, the law of armed conflict.

The mushrooming presence of Chinese companies and investments abroad also carries implications for the Chinese state, and for the companies concerned, under international human rights law (particularly the UN Guiding Principles on Business and Human Rights(opens in new window)). The international law on state responsibility could also be relevant if security companies owned or employed by the Chinese government, where their actions are attributable to China, become complicit in breaches of international law by other governments (such as human rights abuses).

Compared to other areas of international law, such as international economic law and the law of the sea, China has not invested much to date in education in these areas, which may leave it exposed as it increases its global footprint. It was clear from a recent Chatham House roundtable at Columbia Law School in New York that China is now seeking to rapidly upskill in these areas.

China's global economic and security ambitions appear to be tilting China towards a more interventionist approach, which is extending beyond UN peacekeeping contributions towards security and military missions of its own. Time will tell how China will respond to the challenge of burnishing its image as a good global citizen while maintaining an approach to peacekeeping, security and development which is closely informed by its own economic and security interests.

CHANGE OF POWER STATUS AND THE SPEED OF CHINA'S RISE

Entering the 21st century, there are more and more predictions about when China will become a superpower. Some guess that China will be as strong as the United States in the coming decade, some bet that in 20 years and some predict its rise in year 2040. In spite of those disagreements among scholars, the forecasts were all based on the speed at which China's total power has been growing in recent years, without any consideration of the influences of the other powers' growth.

As we are aware that China's power status is related to that of the other states, when forecasting China's future power status, we should not only take account of the speed of China's power growth but also the growth of the other states' power. To foresee the future change of China's power status, we should clarify the conditions for ascent and descent of international power status.

Conditions for Ascent and Descent of Power Status

As a state's power status is determined by quantitative comparisons of powers among states, the change in power status of a state depends on the difference in power growth rates between two states in a given period of time.

Based on the afore-mentioned formula of a state's power status, the expression for the change of a state's power status should be $Sc = A(1 + Ra)/B(1 + Rb)$ “ A/B, (here Sc refers to the result of a change in power status of two states A and B; where A and B indicate the original power for State A and State B respectively; while Ra and Rb indicate the actual growth rates of the two states, respectively). The expression shows that the change of a state's power status depends entirely upon the power growth rates (*Ra* and *Rb*) of the two states over a certain period of time. That is, the state with a faster power growth rate will rise, and the other will fall, and the statuses remain unchanged if the growth rates of the two state powers are the same. Over a fixed time period, the difference in power growth rates for the two states may result in three possibilities for change of a side's power status: rising, falling or unchanged. The three scenarios may result from 13 different situations, in which there are five for ascent, five for descent and three for no change.

It will be a political issue if a state is able to rise to a superpower in a few decades, but only an historical issue if a state rises to a hegemon over hundreds of years. As the atrophy of a state's power is a significant factor for the rapid rise of other states' power statuses, it creates an important scenario for a shift of power between two states. Therefore, power atrophy is an important political issue deserving more attention than power growth. A state's power increases in most years, decreases occasionally and very rarely has zero growth. Thus, the probability of the 10 scenarios of power-status change varies. Often both states enjoy positive power growth simultaneously; it is less common for one state to have a positive power growth while the other has a negative one; it is rare for both states to have negative power growth and is even less common that one state incurs zero power growth. When two states simultaneously have positive or negative power growth, it takes a longer time for their power gap to change and their power statuses to shift, and the probability of power-status shift is small. If one of the two states incurs zero power growth, their power gap will change relatively rapidly and there will be a higher probability for their power status to shift. However, the fastest change in the two states' power gap or their power statuses will occur when the two states have opposite power growths, i.e. one state's power increases and the other's decreases ($Ra > 0 > Rb$ or $Ra < 0 < Rb$). Because national power grows in most years and opposite power growths of two states tend to shift power statuses easily, the factors leading to power atrophy are more significant than the factors enhancing national power in terms of changing the power gap and power status between states.

Political turbulence can cause a state's comprehensive power to diminish severely and rapidly, and it alters a state's power status at a faster rate than does economic development. Being defeated in a war, state disintegration, civil war, social turmoil and political movements all work effectively in shifting power status. The shift of power status between China and the Soviet Union after the Cold War serves as a typical example. In 1991, prior to collapse, the Soviet Union was the only competing superpower in the world rivalling the United States, and its power status drastically differed from that of China. However, as the succeeding state of the former Soviet Union after its collapse, Russia's comprehensive power endured a drastic fall and as a result its geographical area was reduced by about 24%, its population reduced by 48%, its economy decreased by 11%, and the size of its military was cut by 33.7%. At that time Russian comprehensive power was still greater than China's, however, its power status fell into the same class that China belonged to.

The power gap between them was only in degree and no longer in character. Thereafter, Russia's economy declined for years, its military capability was severely weakened, and its political power was diminished internationally. Even though it is hard for us to figure out in which specific year the power-status shift occurred, we are quite certain that China's comprehensive power surpassed that of Russia during the 1990s. Up to 1999, sustaining only military superiority over China, Russia fell far behind China in aspects of political power and economic power. In 1999, Russia's GDP accounted for only one-fourth or one-third of China's GDP of $1 trillion.

Economic crisis can cause a nation's power to decrease rapidly and it works as a faster agent than economic development in changing the power gap or power status between two states. The East Asian Financial Crisis during 1997–98 widened the power gap between China and the Southeast Asian countries and meanwhile reduced the disparity of economic power between China and Japan. The East Asian Financial Crisis decreased China's annual economic growth rate to 7% from 9% prior to the crisis while it caused negative and zero economic growth, respectively, for Indonesia and Japan. Indonesian GDP fell to $50 billion in 1998 from $190.3 billion in 1995 (in 1998 its currency exchange rate fell to US$1:IDR7500 from $1:IDR2321 in 1996) and it recovered to $208.3 billion in 2003, with only a 9.5% increase from its GDP in 1995. In that period, Japan's GDP reduced from $5083.1 billion in 1995 to $4326.4 billion in 2003, a total reduction of 15%. During the same period, China's GDP (by currency exchange rate) doubled from $704.1 billion in 1995 to $1409.9 billion in 2003. Therefore, in the eight years from 1995 to 2003, the economic gap between Indonesia and China had been widened from 3.7 times to 6.8 times, while the economic gap between China and Japan narrowed from 7.2 to 3.0 times. In terms of PPP, China's economy even surpassed Japan's, causing a shift in their economic power rankings.

Political Factors Determining the Fluctuation of China's Power Status

According to the principle that opposite power growths among states tend to change power status between states easily, we come to realize that in 10 years (by 2015) whether China can sustain the existing power status will be determined mainly by the likelihood of political crisis that may cause China's power status to descend. Since its foundation in 1949, China's power status has undergone a spell of four rising and three falling periods. During 1950–58 China's power status had been rising. During that period, the Korean War tremendously raised both China's military power status and her domestic and international capabilities of political mobilization. Between 1952 and 1958, China's GDP increased by as much as 1.9 times. During 1959–63 China's comprehensive power atrophied severely. The Anti-Rightwing Movement led the Chinese government to adopt the policies of 'Great Leap' and 'People's Commune', which resulted in an overall economic crisis.

It was not until 1964 that China's economy recovered to the same level of 1960. In 1959, Sino–Soviet relations began to deteriorate and China was facing joint pressures from both the United States and the Soviet Union. During 1964 and 1965, China's national power enjoyed a brief rising period but fell again during 1966–76.

In May 1966, the Cultural Revolution occurred and the country was immersed in turbulence and chaos when the government's ability to maintain order was severely hampered, economic activities stagnated, and the military weakened. However, in the same period of time, many Asian states such as Japan, South Korea and Singapore had industrialized their countries and their power status was rising rapidly in relation to China's.

From 1978 to 1988 was a period when China restored its social order, increased its domestic mobilization capability and normalized relations with the United States and the Soviet Union.

Consequently, China had again enhanced its international political capability, and its economy sustained an average annual growth as high as 10.2%. The political events of 1989–93 slowed China's economic growth, and dramatically reduced its domestic and international political mobilization capabilities.

Thus, China's power status fell as her political power diminished in such a drastic manner. From 1993 to 2004 was the third period when China's power status ascended.

During this interval, China gradually emerged from the international isolation which had started in 1989 and its capabilities of domestic and international mobilization once again increased. During 1993–2004, China's economy sustained an annual growth of 9.2% and the 1997 East Asian Financial Crisis accelerated the ascendance of China's economic power status. Ever since the founding of the People's Republic of China, each of the three major descents of China's power status was traced back to a political crisis rather than wars or economic difficulties. Therefore, we can believe that as long as there is no future political crisis, China will be able to avoid a fall in its power status.

Based on the principle that national power usually sustains growth in the majority of years, the author argues that the major external elements affecting the speed of rise of China's power status will be: (1) US military commitments and an increase or decrease of its international mobilization capabilities, and (2) the pace of political integration of the European Union (EU). According to the current growth of the comprehensive strengths of major powers, the author assumes that no other single nation, except the United States, could have larger comprehensive power than China in the next 10 years.

Although each individual European state has smaller comprehensive power than China, the EU as a unified power will have a superior status to China's. If the political integration of the EU results in an international player with national character in the next 10 years, our references for judging China's future power status should include both the United States and the EU.

Some people suppose that China's future power status would fundamentally depend upon China's economic growth. They obviously have neglected the political and military powers of the United States and the EU.

China possesses a huge supply of low-paid labour, therefore in the next 10 years China's economic growth will be faster than that of the United States and the EU. It is also quite possible for China to narrow its economic gap with the United States and the EU. Nevertheless, there is uncertainty with regard to the development of the military and political powers of China, the United States and the EU in next 10 years.

In 10 years from now, China may narrow its military gap with the EU but the change of its military gap with the United States will depend on its military containment against Taiwanese secessionists. A favourable security environment will constrain the EU from large military expenditure.

Therefore, in the next 10 years, China's military strength will grow faster than that of the EU and will reduce the military gap between the two. Nevertheless, the change of military disparity between China and the Unites States will be determined by the rates of military investment of the two sides. As a result of the pro-independence group introducing a timetable for Taiwan to achieve legitimate independence by 2008, the Chinese government will inevitably enhance its military capability to contain Taiwanese secessionists.

If the Chinese government was to launch a military attack against Taiwan's independence, it would be possible for China to narrow its military gap with the United States. If the United States continues to wage wars against smaller states while China has no need to attack Taiwanese secessionists militarily, the US military budget will increase faster than that of China's, thus the military power gap between China and the United States would be enlarged.

In the coming decade, China will probably reduce the disparity of its political power with that of the United States, but in the meantime her advantageous political power with relevance to the EU may diminish. In the 1990s, global democratization and marketization increased the US international mobilization capability to a historical peak.

With little resistance from the UN Security Council, the United States obtained UN authorizations on waging the Gulf War in 1991, the Somali War in 1996, the war in Kosovo in 1999 as well as the war in Afghanistan in 2001.

Many countries provided military and economic support to the United States during these wars. However, the United States current unilateral policy caused its international political mobilizing capability to fall sharply from 2003.

Without any UN authorization, the United States waged war in Iraq under the excuse of alleged Iraqi possession of weapons of mass destruction. The US action encountered strenuous objections from many traditional European allies, headed by France and Germany.

As no weapons of mass destruction have been discovered in Iraq, US international influence has been seriously weakened.

In the next 10 years, hegemonic position will drive the United States to continue its unilateralist foreign policy. Meanwhile, China will maintain its multilateral diplomacy to harmonize relationships with her neighbours, the EU and the developing countries of other regions.

Their opposite foreign policies will reduce the political power disparity between China and the United States. Presently, China has greater political power than the EU because China is a single state while the EU is a regional organization with inconsistent foreign policies adopted by its member states. In 1999, the EU introduced the Euro which entered circulation in 2002 and finally established a single currency system on the EU market.

In the year 2004, the political leaders of EU member states signed the European Constitution laying a legislative foundation for the EU to become a single state entity. If the EU constitution is approved by its member states, it will establish its own three-in-one entity of administrative institutions including a council, a committee and a foreign ministry.

Future political integration of the EU will enhance its character as a large national state, which may help it to narrow its political power disparity with China.

Based on the above analysis, if we assume that both the United States and the EU act as single states, the comprehensive national power gap between either China and the United States or the EU and China will probably be narrowed by the year 2015. China's comprehensive power status may rank third in the world.

In 10 years and beyond, it may be possible for China to reduce its economic power disparity with the United States and the EU even though its economic power may still be smaller than theirs. China will narrow its military power gap with the EU but its overall military strength will still be weaker than that of the United States or the EU. In terms of political power, China will narrow the gap but still cannot catch up with the United States. China may maintain her political power superiority over the EU but the disparity between the two may be reduced by further political integration of the EU if all its member states ratify the EU Constitution before 2015.

We have discussed why China enjoys the leading power status among the major powers with the exception of the United States. Based on the principle that a nation's power status ascends in accordance with a faster growth rate, we may presume that China will strengthen its power superiority over Japan, Russia and India within the next 10 years. If the EU becomes a single state entity by 2015, Britain, France and Germany will no longer be regarded as individual international players. Thus, we only assess here the power status between China and three other states: Japan, Russia and India.

With regards to economic power, low-cost labour and a rapidly expanding domestic market will ensure China a faster economic growth than Japan and Russia in the next 10 years. According to World Bank data based on PPP calculations, Japan, Russia and China have GDP per capita in 2001 of $26,940, $8230 and $4580, respectively. This indicates that China's labour wage level was less than 18% of Japan's and 56% of Russia's. Low-cost labour guarantees foreign investors long-term high profits in China. At the end of 2005, China adopted a floating exchange rate according to World Trade Organization regulations and the Renmenbi (RMB) will appreciate continuously over the next 10 years.

The increase in RMB exchange rate will make China's economic growth appear even faster. Although it enjoys the same advantage of low-cost labour as China, India is far behind China in aspects of opening-up to foreign investment as well as other economic reforms. Therefore, the Indian economy will continue to grow at a slower pace than that of China.

In terms of military power, it is anticipated over the next decade none of the three states, namely Japan, Russia and India, will be involved in military conflict with the United States.

Therefore, the military spending of these states will increase slower than China's. Even though India and Russia are both faced with the threat of separatism in Kashmir and Chechnya, respectively, they do not face direct military protection of these separatists by the United States.

As a result, the threat to Russia and India, from the separatists in these two regions, will not be comparable to that caused by the Taiwanese secessionists. Japan is under US military protection, hence its military investment will not increase as fast as that of China.

The Japanese government has decided to reduce its 2005–09 military expenditures to $233 billion, i.e. 3.7% less than its average annual military spending in the previous five years.

As a result of the danger of Taiwanese independence, China is faced with potential military clashes with the United States in the Taiwan Straight. China's military spending in the next 10 years will increase much faster than that of Japan, Russia and India. This will in turn reduce the military disparity between China and Russia and at the same time make its military superior to Japan and India.

In terms of political power, China's endeavours in East Asian regionalization will effectively enhance its ability for political mobilization over the next 10 years. China will have the opportunity to further improve its relations with the EU and that will strengthen China's influence on global affairs. India, Russia and Japan, however, will have few chances to further enhance political influence in their own regions. Although India has already been a leading nation in South Asia, the South Asian regionalization has much less momentum than the East Asian. The Eastern expansion of the EU is constraining Russian political influence in East Europe and the former Soviet Republics. To sustain its special relationship with the United States, Japan has adopted a policy undermining the establishment of the East Asian Community. This policy is similar to that adopted by Great Britain with regard to the EU.

Japan's policy against East Asian regionalization may ultimately weaken its political influence in East Asia. In terms of global affairs, both India and Japan may have the opportunity to become permanent members of the UN Security Council but they will have little chance of obtaining the power of veto. What they actually obtain may only be a position of permanent/non-permanent membership without substantially increased power. Russian political impact on global affairs will further diminish as it is still trapped in a regressive inertia following the collapse of the Soviet Union.

MODERNIZING CHINA'S MILITARY: PROGRESS, PROBLEMS AND PROSPECTS

In early February 1991, China's High Command was stunned to realize just how far behind modern militaries the People's Liberation Army had fallen. The opening days of the Gulf War convinced PLA analysts that they were witnessing a revolution in military affairs (RMA). American stealth bombers penetrated Iraqi airspace undetected to strike their targets in Baghdad and elsewhere with impunity, while the allied naval armada sat comfortably offshore in the Persian Gulf, well outside the range of Iraqi defenses, launching wave after wave of air strikes and cruise missile attacks. The surgical bombing substantially degraded Iraqi air defenses, while electromagnetic warfare attacks blinded command and control networks. Allied information warfare experts spread viruses into Iraqi computers, scrambling software programs and causing confusion.

With its intelligence eyes and ears incapacitated and its air defenses knocked out, Iraq had no effective defenses against carrier-based air strikes or the saturation bombing of the elite Republican Guards by B-52 and B-1 bombers (which flew round-the-clock missions). Once the allied ground invasion began, Iraqi tanks (ironically, many of them of Chinese origin) became easy fodder for the far more advanced allied tanks, which could target them with laser rangefinders and used night vision equipment to illuminate the desert battlefield. In the infantry offensive that followed, allied units (which were linked to each other by means of global positioning systems, or GPS) quickly decimated Iraqi ground forces. Finally, when Saddam Hussein was forced to play his trump card—Scud missiles potentially armed with biological and chemical weapons—American antimissile defenses were able to intercept many of them in flight after calculating trajectory and targeting coordinates and relaying them to Patriot missile battery commanders via satellite within minutes of the Scud launches.

The Gulf War, with its awesome display of firepower, stealth, electronics, computers, and satellites, revealed that warfare had made a quantum leap into a new era. It was a profound shock to the PLA, but it was not the first time that the Chinese brass had been forced to acknowledge their military shortcomings. Twelve years earlier, during China's punitive attack on Vietnam, the PLA found it difficult to carry out a modest cross-border incursion to subdue a few small cities and suffered enormous casualties against smaller, albeit experienced, opposition. The Chinese army had proven incapable of carrying out a coordinated ground assault from three directions. Command and communications were disjointed, and Chinese forces fell victim to their own "friendly fire." Nor did the PLA bring any air power to bear on their adversaries. As a result, battle-hardened Vietnamese troops were the ones who "taught lessons" to the PLA.

The weaponry that the allied forces threw at Iraq, which was generations ahead of what China had encountered on the Vietnam border in 1979, forced China's generals to the harsh realizations that a new, high-technology era of warfare had dawned and that the Chinese military was unprepared to deal with it. The shock of the Gulf War was all the more traumatic because, since the Vietnam fiasco, China's military had begun a fairly comprehensive modernization and reform program. Deng Xiaoping, who chaired the Central Military Commission, Marshall Ye Jianying, and General Yang Shangkun all harshly criticized the PLA's bloated size, disorganization, political factionalism, lax discipline, and combat ineffectiveness. Deng, Ye, Yang, and others accordingly set in motion a series of initiatives intended to truly "modernize" the military (although military modernization came distinctly last in the "Four

Modernizations"). Throughout the 1980s, the PLA was restructured to prepare, first, for "people's war under modern conditions," and then for "limited war." The changes reconfigured ground forces, consolidated military regions, began combined arms and joint service exercises, undertook a new recruitment drive along with the demobilization of redundant and incompetent personnel, and pursued new weapons procurement programs. The PLA had been implementing reforms for more than a decade when the Gulf War starkly demonstrated that it was still operating in terms of a bygone era of warfare.

CHINA: MILITARY MODERNISATION AND STRATEGY

Military modernisation cannot be seen in isolation from economic modernisation, and both go hand-in-hand. This aspect needs to seep in the decision-making process. The emerging international environment today forms a strategic triangle of which the two obvious participants are the US and China; empirically speaking, India should be the third power forming this triangle. What we need to look into is where China is heading especially in light of the fact that as a nation, China has been far ahead of India since the past decades. It was in 1996 that the Chinese government passed a law that reunification was the sacred duty of the PLA. We need to question whether that duty ends with Taiwan, or does it go any further? Arunachal Pradesh is well-entrenched in the Chinese thinking and strategy and India should not be complacent about that. In this regard, India also needs to increasingly focus upon logistics infrastructure in the border areas. This has been visible in the official Defence White Papers which have spelt out the strategy of active border wars. In today's date, the Indian Air Force will prevail over the PLA Air Force given that even though PLAAF stands way ahead, however, in terms of professional capability of its personnel, the IAF holds the edge.

A facet that stands opposed to vociferous Chinese claims of a 'peaceful rise' is the robust military modernisation that the

PLA has undertaken since the past decades. The entire debate centering on China's 'peaceful rise' is meant for public consumption. Beijing has chosen to undertake swift and robust modernisation of the PLA by planning to make up for its poor hardware capabilities while at the same time enhancing abilities to wage asymmetric warfare in the space, cyber-space and information warfare domains. The post-1991 Gulf War period witnessed the Chinese leadership take note of the rapidly changing nature of modern warfare. As a response, the leadership of the PLA set upon a path of reform aimed at building a more professional force in a corporate and institutional sense, and a more capable force in the operational sense. The Chinese White Paper on national defence issued in 2004, stated that the objective of the PLA was to win local wars under the conditions of informationisation. The 2010 Annual Pentagon Report on the *Military and Security Developments Involving the People's Republic of China* underlines this Chinese emphasis on the concept of informationisation which would enable integrated joint operations that require integration of the entire PLA with common information systems.

The primary obstacles acknowledged by the Chinese military leadership in realisation of integrated joint operations at the moment include:

- Inadequate training
- Shortage of qualified staff of PLA personnel
- Equipment
- Tactics of the other services.

In an effort to rectify this existential paucity, the PLA reportedly is undergoing robust training for integrated joint operations on future battlefields. In line with the strategic requirements of high mobility operations and three-dimensional assault, the PLA has been moving from regional defence to trans-regional mobility. The units are becoming small, modular and multi-functional in organisation through appropriate downsizing and structural reform. While accelerating the development of aviation, light mechanised and information counter-measure forces, it is giving priority to the development of tactical missiles, surface-to-air missiles and special operations forces, so as to increase its capabilities for land-air integrated operations, long-distance manoeuvres, rapid assault and special operations.

The PLA has chosen to justify pre-emptive military action at the operational and tactical level under the guise of a 'defensive posture' at the strategic level. The Chinese doctrinal concept of "active defence" *(jiji fangyu)* thus, could be interpreted as a tactic of employing the weak against the strong. Although stated to be defensive in purpose, the doctrine seeks to take the initiative and stay on the offensive from a conflict's earliest stages in order to bring hostilities to a swift and more importantly, a favorable conclusion. The concept is in concurrence with the doctrine that puts a premium on surprise, pre-emption, indirect/asymmetrical confrontation and concentrated strikes on the most critical platforms and capabilities of the adversary, particularly its C4I2SR systems, and on high-value psychological targets. The effort is to overwhelm and undermine the adversary's will to resist during the early stages of conflict.

Thus, the focus on anti-access, area-denial strategies, procuring platforms with the capability and intention to deter, prevent or complicate the intervention of the US (and/or others) in a Taiwan-like scenario. From an Indian stand point, the scenario is applicable to a Tibet-like situation. China's force structure for long-distance air and naval operations is consistent with a limited regional force projection capability. The production of conventional missiles and upgrading the quality and survivability of China's nuclear arsenal from silo-based to road-mobile and from liquid-fuelled to solid-fuelled, accentuates PLA's aim to render its strategic nuclear forces as more survivable and hence provide a far more credible deterrent.

Realising the shortcomings in inter-service cooperation and actual experience in joint exercises and combat operations, the Chinese leadership appears to be stressing more upon asymmetric strategies to leverage China's advantages while exploiting the perceived vulnerabilities of potential opponents, for e.g., the counter-space and cyber warfare programmes. As computer technology increasingly integrates itself into modern military organisations, including the PLA, military planners shall assign it the twin role of being both a target and a weapon. Cyber forces are most likely to be integrated into an overall battle strategy as part of a combined arms campaign.

China's negotiating strategy is to resolve the dispute when the Chinese are in a much stronger position in terms of comprehensive national strength so that they could bargain from a position of strength—an instance is Beijing's strengthening of its military capabilities and infrastructure development in Tibet. PLA's larger aim is that of radically boosting rapid military deployment in the border areas with India. Would enhance China's military capability and enable Chinese coercive diplomacy especially with regards to the border dispute with India.

The PLA realised that modernising its military had become inevitable in wake of Gulf War I—which eventually became the catalyst for its military modernisation campaign. China's thrust areas of modernisation have been the strategic forces, navy and air force with heavy defence budget allocations with every passing year. China's intent as it formulates its strategy is one in which it envisions a multi-polar world and a uni-polar Asia. India needs to take serious note of its lagging logistics mechanism and infrastructure in the border areas which have been neglected. Significantly, the armed forces have to be made a part of the policy formulation, especially while formulation of India's China policy.

The PLA is greatly driven by strategy. There needs to be a wider understanding that Chinese military strategy is not a defensive one but an offensive one. It is a strategy that is tailored in a sense to go well beyond the enemy lines of communications. The concept of 'informationisation' that the PLA is greatly emphasizing upon can be related to RMA-based warfare. However, the levels of information warfare platforms in the Chengdu and Lanzhou MR are very low. The campaign strategy of the PLA can be attributed to the lessons learnt from Gulf War I. As the higher ranks of the PLA advocate the military strategy of active defence, there is an understanding that is emerging that the PLA is less likely to enter a conflict unless and until it is absolutely confident of victory.

Although, a lot of speculation has been raised regarding the rising Chinese defence budget, it is still too low in order to achieve full-spectrum dominance like the US military. China is focusing a lot on the levels of training including both tactical and technical training, with multiple platforms for training. Another area of focus are the modernisation levels vis-à-vis equipment which will further reflect upon their usage in future battlefield environments as China readies to confront Taiwan, Vietnam, Japan, South China Sea region or South Asia.

From an Indian stand point, it is important to note as to how this equipment would be used in terms of future warfare. Another important facet is how China is coping up with all these technological advances despite the US embargoes.

CHINA'S NATIONAL MILITARY STRATEGY

The national military strategy that will now be discussed finds its roots in the late 1970s and early 1980s, when Deng Xiaoping reassessed the international security environment and made the decision to make economic modernization the central task for the coming decades. Deng's decisions not only sent the Chinese nation down a new and different path, but sent the PLA down a new road as well. It stands to reason that a modernizing, outward-looking China seeking a leading role in the mainstream of the international order would require a new type of defence establishment and a new military strategic direction than that of a previously autarkic China seeking to lead the "Third World." What follows then is a description of what Chinese strategic planners might term the general thrust of the national military strategy "during the new historical period" and into "the cross-century period." It is current to the extent that the latest policy decisions coming out of the 15th Party Congress and 9th National People's Congress are incorporated as adjustments. But we should bear in mind that the general direction of China's NMS has been evolving for more than a decade. Consequently, there is both continuity and change to report.

National Military Objectives

China's national military strategy seeks to achieve three sets of national military objectives: *Protect the Party and Safeguard Stability*, *Defend Sovereignty and Defeat Aggression*, and *Modernize the Military and Build the Nation.*

These three objectives not only define what it is the PLA must achieve as a military force, but highlights the unique role it plays in the political economy of the PRC. Significantly, these three national military objectives are derived from and are mutually supportive of China's three national security objectives. The formulation of these three national military objectives are strictly those of the author's and not authoritative PRC formulations. However, they should be familiar to students of the PLA because China's top military leaders often allude to them or aspects of them in public statements.

For example, in the April 1998 issue of *International Strategic Studies*, Deputy Chief of the General Staff Lieutenant General Xiong Guangkai states that the "basic objectives" of China's armed forces are to "consolidate national defence, resist aggression, defend the nation's sovereignty over its territorial land, sea, airspace as well as its maritime interests, and safeguard national unity and security."

In May 1998 Chief of the General Staff Department (GSD) General Fu Quanyou provided this iteration: "the PLA's mission is to strengthen the national defence, fend off aggression, safeguard territorial sovereignty and the rights and interests of territorial waters, and maintain national integrity and safety." As yet another example, in 1996 Defence Minister Chi Haotian offered that the "basic objectives" of China's national defence are to "solidify the defensive capacity, resist foreign invasion, and safeguard the unification and security of the country."

Although the three national military objectives that this chapter posits are seemingly self-explanatory, it is worthwhile to briefly discuss each because through them we achieve a greater appreciation of just what it is the PLA is attempting to achieve, the challenges it faces, and a flavor for the organizational culture of this massive defence establishment.

Protect the Party and Safeguard Stability. The first and foremost mission entrusted to the PLA, and a national military objective, is to be the guardian of the CCP. The past two decades of professionalization and modernization have not altered the fundamental fact that the institutional loyalty of China's armed forces and the personal commitment of it top leaders is to the maintenance of the regime and the primacy of the CCP. The PLA remains the party's army.

China's "national command authorities" are the leaders of the Central Military Commission (CMC), which is a party organization under the Central Committee. It is worth remembering that it has only been 71 years since the "Red Army" was founded. The revolutionary heritage of that army and its roots as a communist insurgent force that saved the fledgling CCP from annihilation in the 1920s and 1930s is not too distant a memory for some of the current PLA leaders. Minister of Defence and CMC Vice Chairman General Chi Haotian (66 years old) joined the PLA as a young man in the early 1940s during the "twin struggles" against the Nationalists and the Japanese and he spent a good part of his later career as a senior political commissar. The constant self-propagandizing within the PLA to remind the troops that the party is the focus of their loyalty has not abated as the Chinese armed forces have attempted to become a more proficient military force. Indeed, the first among the "Five General Requirements" issued by Jiang Zemin for all PLA soldiers is to be "politically qualified."

It is often argued that today the party and ideology mean less and less in China. For the general populace and even some civil cadre that may be truer than not. However, the party and ideology still count for quite a lot in the PLA. The "new nationalism" that has been ascribed to the PLA is not necessarily at the expense of the Party and it may just be that in today's China the PLA is the only institution over which the CCP "centre" in Beijing still has near total control from one end of the nation to the other. The constant public affirmations of the PLA's top leaders of the primacy of the Party is no more empty rhetoric than the statements of the top U.S. military leadership affirming the primacy of the Constitution and the principle of civilian control over the military.

In August 1997, PLA Academy of Military Sciences Commandant General Xu Huizi encapsulated many of the above thoughts in an article in *China Military Science.*

After entering the new historical period, Deng Xiaoping repeatedly stressed that our military situation is that of the party commanding the gun, instead of the gun commanding the party; the military must follow the party's instructions, and must not at any time wave its own flag.... Comrade Jiang Zemin referred to the principle of the party commanding the gun as our military 'soul.'

For these reasons, the PLA must be prepared to defend the CCP with military force against domestic challenges as well as external threats. Over the past few years much of the internal security mission of the PLA has passed to the People's Armed Police (PAP). However, the PAP is ultimately under the control of the CMC and the "regular" PLA has not been absolved from its requirement to provide for the defence of the party. One of the many reasons the PLA was called upon to converge on Beijing in the Spring of 1989 was because the PAP was incapable of handling a situation that was viewed by the CCP leadership to be burgeoning into a direct threat to the rule of the regime and the CCP. The PLA also pursues the related military objective of safeguarding internal stability. Some domestic challenges and threats may be aimed at the state, not the party per se. Examples would be acts of violence by separatist factions in non-Han China such as in Tibet or Xinjiang. Still other threats to stability with which the PLA must deal are natural disasters and manmade disasters. In these situations the PLA is often called upon to provide disaster relief, internal humanitarian assistance, as well as fight back the forces of nature such as floods or large-scale fires.

At the risk of being guilty of unsubstantiated generalization, I would offer that the top leadership of the PLA remains a very conservative group, which is virulently opposed to any domestic circumstance that could lead to instability (*luan*). The up-and-coming generation of leaders (colonel and above) are probably no less so. The chaos of the Cultural Revolution touched many of this latter generation personally and tragically and they fully understand the cost China paid in terms of development and modernization. And if in their hearts some dismiss as irrelevant Communist ideology, they may still see the CCP as the only political force in China that can successfully keep the nation together and lead it into the future.

Defend Sovereignty and Defeat Aggression. This national military objective brings us to the classical warfighting mission of the Chinese armed forces. Militaries exist to fight and so does the PLA. It is worth pointing out that the PLA considers itself a defensive force. Its leaders often declare that China since 1949 has never fought a war of aggression and has gone to war only when other nations have attacked China first or threatened its territory. Officially, Chinese will argue that their intervention in Korea (1950), the war against India (1962), the Sino-Soviet clashes of the late 1960s, and the incursion against Vietnam (1979) were all conflicts foisted upon China in defence of its sovereignty. Hence, they would couch their warfighting objective in terms of defence against aggression and the preservation of the nation's sovereignty. Moreover, the PLA rejects the notion of fighting as part of a formal alliance, proudly claiming that no Chinese combat troops are stationed on foreign soil, nor does Beijing desire to do so.

However, as mentioned earlier, China's definition of "sovereignty" is much broader than just the sanctity of its borders. The PLA defence of China's sovereignty also includes being capable and prepared to employ force to achieve national unification and assert Beijing's maritime rights. Chi Haotian has commented directly on these points in the past. In a May

1996 interview he was reported to comment that China's national defence policy "is aimed at protecting China's territorial land, waters, and air space as well as China's maritime rights and interests against foreign aggression. It is also aimed at safeguarding China's unity.... In the last decade, Beijing's use of the PLA to assert its claims to resources in the South China Sea has raised a great deal of concern within the region and beyond. As far as China's unification goes, only the issue of Taiwan remains unresolved. Although Beijing claims it prefers to settle this issue in a peaceful manner, China's leaders will not renounce the use of force. This puts a tremendous amount of pressure on the PLA for obvious reasons. As we review China's analysis of its security environment later in this chapter, it will become clear just how much the PLA must accomplish as a professional military force.

Modernize the Military and Build the Nation. The modernization of the military deserves its own place among the PLA's national military objectives. The top civilian and uniformed leadership of the PRC consider China's overall modernization and the modernization of the military (often referred to as "army building") to be mutually dependent and supporting national objectives. "Strengthening national defence and army building," declared Jiang Zemin at the 15th Party Congress, "is the basic guarantee for national security and the modernization drive."

The Chinese believe that without a modernizing and capable military the nation will not be able to enjoy the security from external threats it requires to continue to concentrate on economic reform. Without a capable military China cannot secure the internal stability it requires to modernize in the civil sector. Without a capable and modernizing military China cannot hope to secure any of its national security objectives in the realms of sovereignty or unification. Finally, without a modern PLA whose capabilities ultimately comport with China's (anticipated) economic, technological, and political strength, the PRC will not be able to take its seat at the table of world leaders in Beijing's much hoped for multipolar international order. While both civil and military leaders subscribe to these views, the tension in the system revolves around the fact that military modernization is not proceeding at the same pace as economic modernization. Moreover, by long-standing political fiat going back to the beginning of the Dengist period, the decision *not* to invest state treasure in military modernization at the expense of economic reform still stands. Jiang Zemin reaffirmed this tenet at the 9th NPC in March 1998. Speaking to a full session of the PLA's delegation to the NPC, Jiang lectured that:

> It is also very important to correctly handle the relationship between economic development and the building of national defence. Building a modernized army and national defence is a guarantee for the country's safety and modernization drive. This is something the whole party and the whole nation always care very much about. The level of China's productive forces is still not high, and our economy is not that strong. Therefore, we must concentrate our energies on economic development. *Without a highly developed economy, it is also impossible to promote the modernization of national defence and the army. We must always insist on taking economic development as the central task while paying adequate attention to modernizing national defence...*

Outwardly, at least, the top PLA leadership supports this basic line and does not question its validity. A serious challenge to the party leadership on this account should not be anticipated. Yet, as the men who are responsible for modernizing the military in a world (as we will later see) which they view as basically hostile, they do evince concern about how far behind economic development military modernization can lag. For example, General Xu Huizi has cautioned that "we must also understand that national wealth does not equate to military strength; there are many examples both past and present, in China and overseas, where a nation has been wealthy while its military was weak. We must try to keep our military quality development level at a level compatible with national defence security; keeping it at a level appropriate to China's international status as a great nation is a choice on which we must insist." Defence Minister Chi Haotian made a more direct commentary on this point in 1996 in a lengthy article in *Qiushi*. "The building of national defence," stated Chi, "cannot exceed the limitation of tolerance of economic construction, *nor can it be laid aside until the economy has totally prospered.*"

As a result of this contradiction, the leadership of the PLA is going to have to be very focused in how it approaches the modernization of the military. The decisions they make (and are making) in this regard will to a large extent drive some of the major national military strategic concepts in their overall NMS.

The corollary to "modernizing the military" is "building the nation." Not only is the PLA's modernization expected not to be a drain on the state's coffers, but military modernization is also expected to enhance the economic, scientific and technological level of the state. The military, says Chi Haotian, is expected to do so by leading and participating in "key state projects," by bringing science and technology to the rural areas of China, by transferring superior military technologies to the civilian sector, by providing the nation with a pool of PLA veterans who are technically advanced relative to their civilian counterparts (the PLA as a "big school"), and providing infrastructure to the hinterlands.

These, then, are the broad national military objectives the PLA seeks to achieve. To achieve these goals China's military planners need to articulate strategic concepts, or courses of action. Before they can do that, however, they must think through the environment in which they must operate, now and in the future. They must employ a "filter" that highlights both challenges and opportunities.

THE MILITARY BALANCE BETWEEN CHINA AND OTHER COUNTRIES

There is no method of describing or analyzing the balance of military power that will be suitably applicable in all cases.

The balance will differ depending on the two countries being weighed against each other, while considerations of the ways in which these countries utilize military force leaves one comparing apples and oranges. Including into the mix comprehensive assessments of war-making capabilities (dynamic balance) makes the issue even more complex. Measuring the balance of military power between China and Vietnam or between China and the Philippines is far different from measuring the balance between China and Taiwan. Furthermore, US involvement on behalf of one side could change these bilateral balances considerably, and much could depend on how the Japan-US and US-South Korea alliances would function in light of such involvement.

However, Chinese military capability with regard to Taiwan, the US, Japan, and other countries does not seem to have been enhanced to the degree suggested in the mid-1990s by those observers who view China as a threat. Were China to resort to the use of nuclear weapons, of course, there would clearly be an overwhelming asymmetry in the military balance between China and Taiwan or between China and Japan, but this is not a factor that has only just arisen in the 1990s. In the area of nuclear weapons, though, there is also a tremendous imbalance between the US and China which has not changed for the past several decades.

There have admittedly been some changes in the balance between Taiwan and China. The purchase of Su-27 fighters from the Soviet Union without doubt improved China's air capabilities, but the F-16 and Mirage 2000 fighters introduced by Taiwan are far greater in number and importance. That China has begun extensive deployment of short- and medium-range ballistic missiles is noteworthy, but in cases where the option of employing weapons of mass destruction has been ruled out, the use of ballistic missiles would be of questionable significance and accomplish little.

With regard to capabilities that have not changed, there have been no demonstrable improvements made in China's amphibious assault capabilities. This means that, unless it could achieve overwhelming air superiority, China would find it extremely difficult to execute an amphibious assault across the Taiwan Strait; this fact has not changed. Any operation designed to land forces on Taiwan would require months of advance preparation, and with such build-ups almost immediately discernible in the modern age, the Taiwanese side would have plenty of time to prepare. This analysis has thus far only looked at the military balance between China and Taiwan. Were the US to offer its assistance to Taiwan, the inconsequential degree to which the military balance has changed would become even more apparent. US involvement has made, and will continue for some time into the future to make, an amphibious assault on Taiwan by China a practical impossibility. China could still launch a ballistic missile offensive against Taiwan, but the counterstrike capability of the US - in cruise missiles and other weapons - greatly exceeds that of Taiwan.

Given the considerable possibility that the US would indeed stand on the side of Taiwan in a crisis, the military balance in the area of the Taiwan Strait is in no way clearly advantageous for China, i.e., China would have a low probability of achieving its objectives.

MISSIONS AND STRATEGIC TASKS OF CHINA'S ARMED FORCES

China's national strategic goal is to complete the building of a moderately prosperous society in all respects by 2021 when the CPC celebrates its centenary; and the building of a modern socialist country that is prosperous, strong, democratic, culturally advanced and harmonious by 2049 when the People's Republic of China (PRC) marks its centenary. It is a Chinese Dream of achieving the great rejuvenation of the Chinese nation. The Chinese Dream is to make the country strong. China's armed forces take their dream of making the military strong as part of the Chinese Dream. Without a strong military, a country can be neither safe nor strong. In the new historical period, aiming at the CPC's goal of building a strong military in the new situation, China's armed forces will unswervingly adhere to the principle of the CPC's absolute leadership, uphold combat effectiveness as the sole and fundamental standard, carry on their glorious traditions, and work to build themselves into a people's military that follows the CPC's commands, can fight and win, and boasts a fine style of work.

In the new circumstances, the national security issues facing China encompass far more subjects, extend over a greater range, and cover a longer time span than at any time in the country's history. Internally and externally, the factors at play are more complex than ever before. Therefore, it is necessary to uphold a holistic view of national security, balance internal and external security, homeland and citizen security, traditional and non-traditional security, subsistence and development security, and China's own security and the common security of the world.

To realize China's national strategic goal and implement the holistic view of national security, new requirements have been raised for innovative development of China's military strategy and the accomplishment of military missions and tasks. In response to the new requirement of safeguarding national security and development interests, China's armed forces will work harder to create a favorable strategic posture with more emphasis on the employment of military forces and means, and provide a solid security guarantee for the country's peaceful development. In response to the new requirement arising from the changing security situation, the armed forces will constantly innovate strategic guidance and operational thoughts so as to ensure the capabilities of fighting and winning. In response to the new requirement arising from the worldwide RMA, the armed forces will pay close attention to the challenges in new security domains, and work hard to seize the strategic initiative in military competition. In response to the new requirement coming from the country's growing strategic interests, the armed forces will actively participate in both regional and international security cooperation and effectively secure China's overseas interests. And in response to the new requirement arising from

China's all-round and deepening reform, the armed forces will continue to follow the path of civil-military integration (CMI), actively participate in the country's economic and social construction, and firmly maintain social stability, so as to remain a staunch force for upholding the CPC's ruling position and a reliable force for developing socialism with Chinese characteristics.

China's armed forces will effectively perform their missions in the new historical period, resolutely uphold the leadership of the CPC and the socialist system with Chinese characteristics, safeguard China's sovereignty, security and development interests, safeguard the important period of strategic opportunities for China's development, maintain regional and world peace, and strive to provide a strong guarantee for completing the building of a moderately prosperous society in all respects and achieving the great rejuvenation of the Chinese nation. China's armed forces mainly shoulder the following strategic tasks:

- To deal with a wide range of emergencies and military threats, and effectively safeguard the sovereignty and security of China's territorial land, air and sea;
- To resolutely safeguard the unification of the motherland;
- To safeguard China's security and interests in new domains;
- To safeguard the security of China's overseas interests;
- To maintain strategic deterrence and carry out nuclear counterattack;
- To participate in regional and international security cooperation and maintain regional and world peace;
- To strengthen efforts in operations against infiltration, separatism and terrorism so as to maintain China's political security and social stability; and
- To perform such tasks as emergency rescue and disaster relief, rights and interests protection, guard duties, and support for national economic and social development.

Strategic Guideline of Active Defense

The strategic concept of active defense is the essence of the CPC's military strategic thought. From the long-term practice of revolutionary wars, the people's armed forces have developed a complete set of strategic concepts of active defense, which boils down to: adherence to the unity of strategic defense and operational and tactical offense; adherence to the principles of defense, self-defense and post-emptive strike; and adherence to the stance that "We will not attack unless we are attacked, but we will surely counterattack if attacked."

Shortly after the founding of the PRC in 1949, the Central Military Commission (CMC) established the military strategic guideline of active defense, and later, in line with the developments and changes in the national security situation, had made a number of major revisions of it. In 1993 the military strategic guideline of the new era was formulated, which took winning local wars in conditions of modern technology, particularly high technology, as the basic point in making preparation for military struggle (PMS). In 2004, the guideline was further substantiated, and the basic point for PMS was modified to winning local wars under conditions of informationization.

China's socialist nature, fundamental national interests and the objective requirement of taking the path of peaceful development all demand that China unswervingly adhere to and enrich the strategic concept of active defense. Guided by national security and development strategies, and required by the situation and their tasks in the new historical period, China's armed forces will continue to implement the military strategic guideline of active defense and enhance military strategic guidance as the times so require. They will further broaden strategic vision, update strategic thinking and make strategic guidance more forward-looking. A holistic approach will be taken to balance war preparation and war prevention, rights protection and stability maintenance, deterrence and warfighting, and operations in wartime and employment of military forces in peacetime. They will lay stress on farsighted planning and management to create a favorable posture, comprehensively manage crises, and resolutely deter and win wars.

To implement the military strategic guideline of active defense in the new situation, China's armed forces will adjust the basic point for PMS. In line with the evolving form of war and national security situation, the basic point for PMS will be placed on winning informationized local wars, highlighting maritime military struggle and maritime PMS. The armed forces will work to effectively control major crises, properly handle possible chain reactions, and firmly safeguard the country's territorial sovereignty, integrity and security.

To implement the military strategic guideline of active defense in the new situation, China's armed forces will innovate basic operational doctrines. In response to security threats from different directions and in line with their current capabilities, the armed forces will adhere to the principles of flexibility, mobility and self-dependence so that "you fight your way and I fight my way." Integrated combat forces will be employed to prevail in system-vs-system operations featuring information dominance, precision strikes and joint operations.

To implement the military strategic guideline of active defense in the new situation, China's armed forces will optimize the military strategic layout. In view of China's geostrategic environment, the security threats it faces and the strategic tasks they shoulder, the armed forces will make overall planning for strategic deployment and military disposition, in order to clearly divide areas of responsibility for their troops, and enable them to support each other and act as an organic whole. Threats from such new security domains as outer space and cyber space will be dealt with to maintain the common security of the world community. China's armed forces will strengthen international security cooperation in areas crucially related to China's overseas interests, to ensure the security of such interests.

To implement the military strategic guideline of active defense in the new situation, China's armed forces will uphold the following principles:

- To be subordinate to and in the service of the national strategic goal, implement the holistic view of national security, strengthen PMS, prevent crises, deter and win wars;
- To foster a strategic posture favorable to China's peaceful development, adhere to the national defense policy that is defensive in nature, persevere in close coordination of political, military, economic and diplomatic work, and positively cope with comprehensive security threats the country possibly encounters;
- To strike a balance between rights protection and stability maintenance, and make overall planning for both, safeguard national territorial sovereignty and maritime rights and interests, and maintain security and stability along China's periphery;
- To endeavor to seize the strategic initiative in military struggle, proactively plan for military struggle in all directions and domains, and grasp the opportunities to accelerate military building, reform and development;
- To employ strategies and tactics featuring flexibility and mobility, give full play to the overall effectiveness of joint operations, concentrate superior forces, and make integrated use of all operational means and methods;
- To make serious preparations to cope with the most complex and difficult scenarios, uphold bottom-line thinking, and do a solid job in all aspects so as to ensure proper responses to such scenarios with ease at any time and in any circumstances;
- To bring into full play the unique political advantages of the people's armed forces, uphold the CPC's absolute leadership over the military, accentuate the cultivation of fighting spirit, enforce strict discipline, improve the professionalism and strength of the troops, build closer relations between the government and the military as well as between the people and the military, and boost the morale of officers and men;

- To give full play to the overall power of the concept of people's war, persist in employing it as an ace weapon to triumph over the enemy, enrich the contents, ways and means of the concept of people's war, and press forward with the shift of the focus of war mobilization from human resources to science and technology; and
- To actively expand military and security cooperation, deepen military relations with major powers, neighboring countries and other developing countries, and promote the establishment of a regional framework for security and cooperation.

NEW FAULTLINES FOR FUTURE

Apart from these perennial problems as also these broad trends, the new transformation of China during these last two decades has since resulted in creating a series of more immediate challenges which have the potential for creating crises in case these are not attended to and resolved in time. These new faultlines may not appear to be very explosive at first glance yet, given the nature of China's evolution during these last 50 years, China does not seem fully prepared to deal with such contingencies and it will have to devise more sophisticated strategies and channels of expression to redress rather than suppress these issues. Therefore, depending exclusively on the framework of the law and order problem and on its instruments of state suppression its conventional approach to internal threats will only further aggravate the situation. Thus it is China's difficulties in containing the spread and implosion from these new issues while also working on long-term solutions that makes China's internal defence so threatening in its potential. Some of the more specific threats to China's internal defence come from the following activities and processes:

Uneven Regional Development-A recently published book, The Political Economy of Uneven Employment-A case of China, written jointly by Hu Angang of the Chinese Academy of Science and Wang Shaoguang, a professor at the Yale University, notes that the inter-provincial economic gap in China has been growing at a rather rapid pace. According to these authors, in 1978, only 15 provinces, municipalities or autonomous regions belonged to either the high (i.e. per capita GDP higher than 150 per cent of the national average) or low (i.e. per capita GAP lower than 75 per cent of national average) income groups, compared with 22 in 1994. In 1994 no province or autonomous region in western China had a per capita GDP higher than the national; while in east China the per capita GDP in all provinces with the exception of Hebei ranked higher than the national average. China's inter-provincial GDP gap is significant even by international averages. In 1994, Shanghai's per capita GAP was 14 times higher than that of Guizhou, far greater than the income gap between the poorest and richest provinces in most other countries. The figure for France was 2.15 in 1988, 1.43 for the United States in 1983, 4.0 for Indonesia in 1983 and 3.26 for India in 1980. Similarly, in terms of its rural-urban divide, while the average urban household income in China stands at above $3,000 per year the average rural household income stands less than $950 per year. According to one 1997 report by the World Bank, China's income inequality ranked among the worst in the world. Reasons for this lie in rapid loosening of controls and preferential treatment for faster development. But this has also seen provinces and other sub-state actors becoming increasingly financially autonomous of Beijing and these growing income gaps can have grave political consequences in the long run. Already, regional conflicts have become frequent, threatening national unification and political stability that has since come to be Beijing's prime concern.

Regional Imbalance: East versus West-The most basic grievance which then finds a variety of expressions has been China's continued regional imbalance which has further complicated ground realities of China's minorities' continued unrest since centuries. Especially, China's Western Region has been particularly neglected even during China's economic boom of the last twenty years. Western China accounts for 56 per cent of the country's land mass and 23 per cent of its population. According to China Almanac, for 1997, the income for farmers in the west averaged at $168 while it averaged at $362 for those in the east. West China, which is the home for China's mineral and hydrocarbon resources, houses their nuclear facilities and nuclear test-site also houses over 80 per cent of China's minorities. But it remains land-locked and shares borders with countries that remain unstable both internally as also in their ties with Beijing. As a result, indices of its development actually show a negative growth during the 1990s. Its per capita income for example, has fallen from being 56 per cent to that of east China in 1983 to becoming just 40 per cent by 1999. And with 23 per cent of China's population, therefore, this region now accounts for only 13 per cent of China's consumer spending. This situation has been created by the fact that Deng Xiaoping had chosen to go for a "get rich fast" policy which has resulted in confining China's economic boom to coastal cities. Similarly, of $300 billion FDI actually invested in China, its Western Region has received only 3 per cent of it while the bulk of this has been concentrated in China's coastal provinces.

Floating Population: Migration-Traditionally, Mao had perceived of a policy where all Chinese were tied down to their communes and mobility was not really a great strength of Chinese society. From there, China today has changed into a highly mobile society which has been partly forced by the inherent requirements of a rapidly growing industrial economy.

But the Chinese institutions and polity have still to learn to deal with this new reality. Demographic estimates, for example, indicate China's urbanisation rate will reach 50 per cent by 2030, when China's total population is expected to stabilise at 1.6 billion. Factoring in such a calculation, approximately 15 to 16 million itinerant farm workers will annually head to the cities in the next 30 years. China's urbanisation rate now stands as low as 30 per cent, compared with the world average of 40 per cent. According to a sample survey by China's Development Research Centre, in Beijing's Haidian, Chaoyang and Fengtai districts, 110 primary schools were found teaching 20,000 children from the migrant families. Forced by the grave unemployment situation from the readjustment of the industrial structures of State-owned

Enterprises, many big cities have been trying hard to control the inflow of farmers, mostly through economic and administrative means. As a result, 5 million people leave Sichuan province alone every year to seek opportunities in these coastal cities. This floating population has been particularly responsible for integrating China's deprived sections and exposing them to the rapid development and riches of the other parts of their country thus enlightening them of their deprived status.

SOE Reforms and Unemployment-Rapid reforms of China's State Owned Enterprises (SOEs) and the resultant laying off of workers and unemployment has been another major subject of debates during more recent years. This has especially come to notice due to regular reports of riots and demonstrations that, at first look, appear completely alien to China's communist ethos. Across the country, these recently laid off demoralised and impoverished workers have been reported to be attacking their Communist Party managers and looting their own factories. With China's rapid development during these last three decades and its increasing integration with the global market including its expected entry into the World Trade Organisation, China has been trying to restructure its economic institutions, industries and infrastructure to make it commensurate to global expectations. Pollution, for example, has lately come to be one major issue that has affected the close down of various industries. This reflects the changing profile of economic priorities. According to figures provided by China's State Economic and Trade Commission, by the first half of the year 2000, China had closed down 36,000 badly maintained and illegal coal mines which is expected to reduce this year's production by 302 million tons as also dislocate large numbers of its beneficiaries. Similarly, by June this year, China has closed down 5,600 oil refineries for their faulty and environment damaging practices. These SOEs have also been the main culprit for China's unemployment trends. China officially admits that as on June 2000, they still had 11.2 million laid-off workers from its SOEs as unemployed. Of these 5 million had been laid off from SOEs during 1999 alone. Though many of these have also been rehabilitated yet, these new trends are beginning to create their own pressure points for China's domestic peace.

Drug Trafficking and its By-products-Apart from the flaws in China's developmental strategies and initiatives leading to imbalances and side-effects, some of these trends have also actually encouraged criminal activities as means of making fast money.

Thanks to the external linkages of these activities, they have also become difficult to control and begun to threaten China's domestic peace. The external linkages of China's internal unrest have since brought in difficulties of expanding drug-trafficking, spread of small arms, money laundering and AIDs epidemic which had all evolved as by-products of China's internal unrest. To quote from the speech by China's Vice Minister for Public Security, Zhao Yongji, delivered at the national conference in Shenzhen in January 2000, "If effective measures are not adopted, the illegal activity poses a threat to social stability.

Last year, 2,011 cases of smuggling involving drugs, guns and other goods valued at 680 million yuan ($82 million) were uncovered by border police, ninety-one military weapons were seized along China's southwestern borders and more than 1,600 kilograms heroin seized and 2,027 arrested during 1999.27 According to China National Narcotics Control Commission, the number of 'registered' drug addicts in China itself stands at 682,000 for 1999.28 AIDS, which does not appear a national security problem at first glance has also since developed a threatening profile by its sheer rapid spread in certain sensitive regions like Yunnan and Xinjiang.

This happens to be another problem closely linked to drug-trafficking. In China, AIDS has been spreading especially around its border with Myanmar and from there moving to its major cities obtaining for China the notoriety of being the fourth largest in Asia and the 17th largest HIV carrier in the world. In Asia only Thailand, India, Myanmar have been counted as ahead of it. At a function organised to kick off China's AIDS Alert campaign during December 1999, Vice Minister for Health,

Yin, Dakui, confirmed that by September 1999, China had accounted for 15,088 HIV positive cases of which Yunnan province alone accounted for nearly 60 per cent of this figure.

According to outside experts, however, these HIV carriers in China have been shooting up from 10,000 in 1993, 30,000 in 1994, 100,000 in 1995, 300,000 in 1998 and 500,000 in 1999.29 Other Chinese experts put the figure as likely to hit upto 1 million by year 2000.30 This prediction is based on the argument that, like all other countries, there will be time of rapid increase in the numbers of HIV carriers following a preliminary period of slow spread and that China seems now in this second phase already.

Overreaction to Corruption and Crime-Though China has since allowed ten political parties to exist and express their opinions, China continues to be very sensitive to any expression of dissidence, of any kind. Especially, following their experience of student demonstrations at the Tiananmen Square during May-June 1989, Chinese leadership has become increasingly skeptical of any gatherings or associations.

Their hard-handed treatment of the religious group, Falun Gong, has been one such example in more recent years. Going by the fact that Chinese history's bloodiest rebellions, the Boxer Rebellion and the Taiping Rebellion, had both begun with a charismatic religious figure preaching on non-political issues, explains China's over-reaction to Falun Gong during recent times.

Falun Gong, which was founded by one Li Hongzhi in 1992 has gathered millions of followers over these years and to indicate their commitment to this sect, over 1,500 are believed to have died by refusing medical help which seems to be at the core of their preaching.

Starting from their get together sessions from the historic day of China's 50th anniversary celebrations on October 1, 2000 at Tiananmen Square, Chinese authorities have acted tough and sent thousands of their followers to labour camps for "education and reform through labour." In fact, Ammesty

International has already documented 190 executions of Falun Gong followers during January 1997 to March 1999, with thousands of others having been detained.

Similarly, corruption is another issue that has gradually come to be a hyper issue for the political elite. Recently, in August 2000, China heavily publicised the death sentence handed down to a former vice-chairman of the National People's Congress, Cheng Keijie for accepting bribes worth $4.9 million. Similarly, China's mayor and party secretary, Chen Xitong, had also been sentenced to death for accepting bribes during 1997. While all these things may not portend any immediate national crisis yet, in the longer-run these must be seen as symptoms of a deeper malaise in China's management of its Internal Defence.

5

India's Military Strategic Roadmap

In recent years, India has developed multiple strategies to deal with China's rise and threatening postures on both its land border and in the Indian Ocean. They include limited balancing based on asymmetrical arms buildups and informal coalitions with like-minded states and regular diplomatic engagement with Beijing both bilaterally and through multilateral forums. But the most significant non-traditional soft balancing efforts have been in building limited strategic partnerships with the United States and Japan as well as participation in ASEAN Forums, along with other regional groupings such as the Shanghai Cooperation Organization (SCO). The strategy is also based on institutional denial by not agreeing to China's membership in the South Asian Association for Regional Cooperation and, most prominently, refusing to join the Belt and Road Initiative (BRI). There have been some efforts at creating counter economic cooperation initiatives with regional states as alternatives to BRI. The Africa Growth Corridor with Japan was planned in 2017 as a limited alternative to BRI, although it is yet to take full shape.

None of these strategic options has diminished the palpable differences in Beijing's behavior toward India. As discussed in my just released volume, The China-India Rivalry in the Globalization Era by Georgetown University Press, the relations between the two Asian giants have remained a "managed rivalry" with ups and downs in terms of 'hostile' or 'friendly' interactions. Economic globalization has helped to reduce the intensity of the rivalry, but not to eliminate the issues that the two states compete over. Since May 2018, a limited détente is visible as China is facing considerable economic pressures from the Trump administration. The Modi-Xi summit in Wuhan in May 2018 and the several meetings between the two leaders at forums such as SCO and BRICS have helped to smoothen rough feathers since the July-August 2017 standoff in the Doklam plateau in the trijunction between Bhutan, China and India. The Trump administration's trade policies have generated worries in both China and India as the United States has imposed tariffs on both countries, even though New Delhi has been trying to develop improved economic and strategic relationships with Washington. China, however, offers the most significant challenge to India's core interests as Beijing's larger goals in the Indo-Pacific clash with India's. Thus far, India's response has been limited to China's expansionist policies. Why are India's strategic options so constrained and why has soft balancing become such an important strategic tool for India?

The first is economic. China has emerged as India's lead trading partner and during 2017, China traded some $84 billion worth of goods and services with India involving a trade surplus of $52 billion for Beijing. Despite, all protestations from India, this huge trade gap is unlikely to change anytime soon, as Indian manufacturing and consumer industries are heavily dependent on Chinese products for cost and other reasons. India's alternative strategy of developing products domestically through the "Make India" program has not advanced far in the face of the Chinese economic onslaught.

The second is the nonavailability of reliable partners to joining a balancing coalition who are not hampered by China's wedge strategy. China's approach toward India has always involved an effort to make sure India doesn't form active balancing coalitions with parties, including the United States, Japan and Australia—the so-called Quadrilateral grouping. This is a form of wedge strategy, and China practices such a strategy in different regions by weaning potential partners in Southeast Asia and elsewhere through economic carrots and sticks.

Third is the U.S. strategy under President Donald Trump. Trump is not exhibiting a deep strategic vision vis-a-vis India as his predecessors George W. Bush and Barack Obama did. Trump wants America to withdraw from many of its commitments, including those involving India, without realizing how hard it was to build a rapprochement between the two 'estranged democracies.' For the past seventy years, almost all U.S. alliance partnerships have been jointly built around their economic and military relationships. Trump is placing economic tariffs on allies and adversaries alike, hoping to bifurcate the two. India is also included in that list of targeted countries. In addition, Trump's immigration policies, in particular reducing the H-1 and student visas, are hurting potential Indian applicants more than those from most other countries. These policies are doing little to befriend India, and hence Modi has now decided to pursue a more appeasing strategy toward China. Under Trump, the United States is not a credible partner in the eyes of most allies, including India.

The lack of reliable partners is a challenge partially because India is unable to fulfill the requirements they expect of New Delhi. The United States is an unreliable partner for India despite its frequent statements of good intent. The lifting of sanctions on India in the nuclear nonproliferation area through the 2005 U.S.-India Nuclear Accord was a major symbolic act that allowed India to bypass many a stricture of the non-proliferation regime. India was expected to buy several U.S. reactors, but the nuclear resurgence in India did not happen due to the country's inability to come up with a strong antiliability bill. In the meantime, the Fukushima accident in Japan generated much nuclear pessimism which has dampened the civilian industry's growth worldwide.

Finally, India has a strong instinct for strategic autonomy, a hangover from its nonaligned days. Any time when pressures mount from multiple great powers, India has found the return to strategic autonomy an appealing option. Today, India is once again showing that it may pursue autonomy more than any other strategy because of the threats coming in different manifestations from China and the United States.

Vacillating U.S. Policies

The United States has in the meantime been distracted by a number of other considerations. One of them is its interactions with China. The Trump administration, despite threats of trade sanctions, has not led an effective balancing coalition against Beijing, and the two areas this has manifested is in it's inability to prevent the Chinese island reclamations and naval buildup in the South China Sea, along with the Chinese navy's increasing forays in to the Indian Ocean.

The Obama pivot to Asia strategy did nothing to dampen Chinese expansionism into the Indo-Pacific. Its deterrent effect was nil. Instead, by helping generate a fear of future containment, it probably encouraged Beijing to accelerate its naval expansion. So, China perceived a short-term window of opportunity to maximize its strategic presence in South China Sea and the Indian Ocean before the United States brought in additional forces and military deployments.

More importantly, America's withdrawal from the crucial Trans Pacific Partnership (TPP) has signaled to China that soft balancing through this particular economic instrument will not happen. The Trump administration's lack of interest in regional institutions also hampers soft balancing efforts. Washington is developing heavy weapons. including aircraft carriers. for deployment in the Pacific, but Beijing is not planning a major arms race based on an equivalent strategy. The incremental pace with which China militarizes the region is not creating an imminent crisis, and the United States has not been able to muster domestic or international support to confront China in a preventive manner. The occasional joint military exercises such as Malabar and the freedom of navigation naval visits in the South China Sea are not producing the outcome of restraint—let alone containment.

China is using economic globalization and interdependence for its military and naval expansion in such a manner that no parties feel that the threat is strong enough to justify the costs of balancing China in an effective or urgent fashion. For effective balancing coalitions to emerge, the security threat has to be seriously felt by affected states.

India, like other potential allies of Japan and the United States, is thus restrained from adopting any strategy that goes beyond limited hard balancing and somewhat vigorous soft balancing toward China. The limited hard balancing depends on unequal arms purchasing and deployment, but the soft balancing relies on regional and international institutions as well as lower level strategic partnerships to constrain China's threatening behavior. The intended message appears to be that these soft balancing instruments could be upgraded to hard balancing if the threats become overwhelming. It's possible that allies in Southeast Asia, particularly ASEAN countries such as Vietnam and Indonesia, are also not keen on actively balancing China, although there is some interest in soft balancing among Vietnam, Indonesia, Malaysia and Singapore—and this is giving India more opportunities in this is regard.

So, what strategic options does that leave India with? A continuation of current low-key balancing is not a bad strategy, as hedging will allow India a certain kind of maneuverability in the short and medium term. However, India needs an alternative to the BRI, and this is where New Delhi may have a chance to build or rebuild its links with neighboring countries and beyond. The Asia-Africa Growth Corridor initiated by Japan and India in May 2017 has yet to take off. This was supposed to be an answer to China's BRI by focusing on quality infrastructure, digital connectivity, and improvements in health and agriculture as well as human skills development in countries in Africa and Asia. There is also a plan supported by Japan to develop infrastructure in India's Northeast, connecting the region to Southeast Asia and China. The latter may also allow linking with select BRI components if China is willing to collaborate in a selective fashion. Not allowing all neighbors to fall into a dependent relationship with China is in India's interest, though New Delhi still needs to keep the United States, Japan, ASEAN and Australia as potential allies in case Chinese nationalism and expansionism turn sour.

Strategic autonomy or a form of nonalignment may be another option, but this will not necessarily bring security to India in the current atmosphere, as China is unlikely to respect India's autonomy. Instead, it may expect reverence and allegiance to its expansionist schemes. In order for China to meet its strategic goals, it needs to weaken India as a challenger in the Asia Pacific region or otherwise mellow India's possible objections.

China's tactical signals of friendship are unlikely to last. Today or tomorrow, China will likely turn against India, unless it is willing to bandwagon or remain neutral in China's expansionist policies. This is because China's goals under Xi Jinping are ambitious: it seeks to replace America as the next hegemonic power, which India will have a tough time reckoning with. As China pursues this, it will have to expand its naval footprint in the Indian Ocean as its economic investments under the BRI projects increase, which will leave India will leave feeling threatened.

Does India have a Strategic Vision?

The absence of a proper strategic vision in Washington today limits India's strategic options. The question is: does India also lack a strategic vision? Are the Indian elite and society at large aware of the challenges India faces in the ongoing strategic competitions in the region? What can India do to avoid being subjugated once again by powerful actors, if not directly this time? Will the East India Company syndrome repeat itself? The Chinese BRI has many elements of East India Company syndrome, such as opening trading posts and then converting them to naval bases—a process that would leave the oceans under Chinese control. Chinese policies are turning smaller parties into overly dependent clients, and they will have to make substantial territorial and economic concessions to China, as happened to Sri Lanka in the leasing of the Hambantota port for ninety-nine years to China in December 2017. This is a bit akin to the British acquisition of Hong Kong and Macau from a weak Chinese empire in the 1800s. China has also brought in large number of its workers to the construction projects and encouraged its citizens buy the houses and real estate it has developed on these island states. It is increasingly involving itself in the domestic politics of the client states, tactics that East India Companies adopted as well.

Grand strategy may not offer all the answers, but strategies that leave a nation ready to face different contingencies is necessary to survive and prosper in a highly competitive international environment. Linking domestic performance and international performance is critical as well. This is where India lags. Despite an impressive economic growth rate, now above 7 percent, it faces all the challenges of a weak state, such as being unable to provide basic public goods, be it in infrastructure, water provisions, education, electricity or health services. Urban planning and development are archaic, while India's hygienic standards look medieval at best. India's political and bureaucratic class is yet to imbibe the need for becoming strong developmental agents to transform their country on an urgent basis. Many of them seem more interested in the acquisition of private wealth at the cost of the state and its agencies. Even if they are supporters of development, their slow pace in approving and implementing developmental schemes is in effect hurting India's larger goal of emerging as a global power that can withstand challenges coming from China and others. This also affects India's possible emergence as a lead power to emulate and follow. Indian electoral politics are generating many of the tendencies of a fragile democracy, with communal forces increasingly shaping the agenda. An intolerant political dispensation will hurt India's soft power substantially and its claim for a global leadership role. There has to be something others can imitate or value in the governance and politico-economic structures of a global power. Effective grand strategy must thus begin at home.

The strategic challenges the twenty-first century brings into India are multifarious. New Delhi needs much more nimbleness in diplomacy and to develop different instruments for balancing and engagement. Soft balancing using international and regional institutions, limited alignments and economic instruments such as denial are crucial components—even when the country develops strong defensive and deterrent capabilities for hard balancing purposes. Diplomatic engagement is equally important, but summit level meetings and agreements need to be followed through and the decisions made must be carried out in a timely manner. Tactical moves by the leaders ought to be translated into coherent grand strategic policies. Avoiding an intense rivalry with China is necessary for India to grow economically, although its rise may be hampered by increasing international, regional and domestic pressures.

INDIA UNBOUND

Progress on the resolution of either of these conflicts, especially the one over Kashmir, would liberate India's political and diplomatic energies so that the country could play a larger role in the world. It would also finally release India's armed forces from the constraining mission of territorial defense, allowing them to get more involved in peace and stability operations around the Indian Ocean. Even with all the tensions on the subcontinent, the armies of India, Pakistan, and Bangladesh have been among the biggest contributors to UN peacekeeping operations. The normalization of Indo-Pakistani relations would further free up some of the best armed forces in the world for the promotion of the collective good in the greater Middle East, Africa, and Asia.

Even as the Kashmir and China questions have remained unsettled, India's profile in its extended neighborhood has grown considerably since the early 1990s.

India's outward economic orientation has allowed it to reestablish trade and investment linkages with much of its near abroad. New Delhi is negotiating a slew of free- and preferential-trade agreements with individual countries as well as multilateral bodies including the Association of Southeast Asian Nations (ASEAN), the Gulf Cooperation Council (GCC), and the Southern African Development Community.

Just as China has become the motor of economic growth in East Asia, a rising India could become the engine of economic integration in the Indian Ocean region.

After decades of being marginalized from regional institutions in different parts of Asia, India is also now a preferred political partner for ASEAN, the East Asian Summit, the GCC, the Shanghai Cooperation Organization, and the African Union. Moreover, it has emerged as a major aid donor; having been an aid recipient for so long, India is now actively leveraging its own external assistance to promote trade as well as political objectives.

For example, India has given $650 million in aid to Afghanistan since the fall of the Taliban. Meanwhile, the search for oil has encouraged Indian energy companies to tail their Western and Chinese counterparts throughout the world, from Central Asia and Siberia and to western Africa and Venezuela.

On the security side, India has been actively engaged in defense diplomacy. Thanks to the strength of its armed forces, India is well positioned to assist in stabilizing the Indian Ocean region. It helps that there has been a convergence of U.S. and Indian political interests: countering terrorism, pacifying Islamic radicalism, promoting democracy, and ensuring the security of sea-lanes, to name a few. The Indian navy in particular has been at the cutting edge of India's engagement with the region — as was evident from its ability to deploy quickly to areas hit by the tsunami at the end of 2004. The Indian navy today is also ready to participate in multinational military operations.

Axes And Allies

The end of the Cold War freed India to pursue engagement with all the great powers — but especially the United States. At the start of the 1990s, finding that its relations with the

United States, China, Japan, and Europe were all underdeveloped, India moved quickly to repair the situation. Discarding old socialist shibboleths, it began to search for markets for its products and capital to fuel its long-constrained domestic growth. Economic partnerships were easy to construct, and increasing trade flows provided a new basis for stability in India's relations with other major powers. India's emergence as an outsourcing destination and its new prowess in information technology also give it a niche in the world economy — along with the confidence that it can benefit from economic globalization.

Barely 15 years after the collapse of the Soviet Union, India's omnidirectional engagement with the great powers has paid off handsomely. Never before has India had such expansive relations with all the major powers at the same time — a result not only of India's increasing weight in the global economy and its growing power potential, but also of New Delhi's savvy and persistent diplomacy.

The evolution of Sino-Indian ties since the 1990s has been especially important and intriguing. Many see violent conflict between the two rising Asian powers as inevitable. But thanks to New Delhi's policy of actively engaging China since the late 1980s, the tensions that characterized relations between them from the late 1950s through the 1970s have become receding memories. Bilateral trade has boomed, growing from less than $200 million in the early 1990s to nearly $20 billion in 2005. In fact, China is set to overtake the European Union and the United States as India's largest trading partner within a few years. The 3,500-kilometer Sino-Indian border, over which the two countries fought a war in 1962, is now tranquil. And during Wen's visit to India in April 2005, India and China announced a "strategic partnership" — even though just seven years earlier New Delhi had cited concerns over China as a reason for performing nuclear tests, prompting a vicious reaction from Beijing.

India has also cooperated with China in order to neutralize it in conflicts with Pakistan and other smaller neighbours. In the past, China tended to be a free rider on regional security issues, proclaiming noninterference in the internal affairs of other nations while opportunistically befriending regimes in pursuit of its long-term strategic interests. This allowed India's subcontinental neighbours to play the China card against New Delhi when they wanted to resist India's attempts to nudge them toward conflict resolution. But now, Beijing has increasingly avoided taking sides in India's disputes, even as its economic and security profile in the region has grown.

China is not the only Asian power that India is aiming to engage and befriend. Japan has also emerged as an important partner for India, especially since Japanese Prime Minister Junichiro Koizumi has transformed Japanese politics in the last few years. During a visit to New Delhi just a couple of weeks after Wen's in April 2005, Koizumi announced Japan's own "strategic partnership" with India. (This came despite Japan's harsh reaction to India's nuclear test in 1998, which prompted Japanese sanctions and an effort by Tokyo to censure India in the United Nations and other multilateral forums.) Amid growing fears of a rising China and the incipient U.S.-Indian alliance, Japan has elevated India to a key player in its long-term plans for Asian security.

Recognizing the need to diversify its Asian economic portfolio, Tokyo has also, for political reasons, begun to direct some of its foreign investment to India (which has overtaken China as the largest recipient of Japanese development assistance). Since the start of the Bush administration, Japan has also shown increasing interest in expanding military cooperation with India, especially in the maritime domain. India, too, has recognized that it shares with Japan an interest in energy security and in maintaining a stable balance of power in Asia. Japan actively supported India's participation in the inaugural East Asian Summit, in December 2005, despite China's reluctance to include New Delhi. Neither India nor Japan wants to base their political relationship exclusively on a potential threat from China, but both know that deepening their own security cooperation will open up new strategic options and that greater coordination between Asian democracies could limit China's impact.

India's relations with Europe have been limited by the fact that New Delhi is fairly unimpressed with Europe's role in global politics. It senses that Europe and India have traded places in terms of their attitudes toward the United States: while Europe seethes with resentment of U.S. policies, India is giving up on habitually being the first, and most trenchant, critic of Washington. As pessimism overtakes Europe, growing Indian optimism allows New Delhi to support unpopular U.S. policies.

Indians consistently give both the United States and the Bush administration very favorable marks; according to a recent Pew Global Attitudes poll, for example, the percentage of Indians with a positive view of the United States rose from 54 percent in 2002 to 71 percent in 2005. And whereas a declining Europe has tended to be skeptical of India's rise, the Bush administration has been fully sympathetic to India's great-power aspirations.

Still, India does have growing economic and political ties with some European powers. Although many smaller European countries have been critical of the U.S.-Indian nuclear deal, the continent's two nuclear powers, France and the United Kingdom, have been supportive. Paris, in particular, bet long ago (well before Washington did, in fact) that a rising India would provide a good market for high-tech goods; with this in mind, it shielded New Delhi from the ire of the G-8 (the group of eight highly industrialized nations) after India tested nuclear weapons in May 1998.

In the last several years, the United Kingdom has also started to seize economic opportunities in India and has been generally accommodating of New Delhi's regional and global aspirations.

In the wake of the Soviet Union's collapse, India also worked to maintain a relationship with Russia. The two states resolved residual issues relating to their old semi-barter rupee-ruble trading arrangements, recast their 1971 peace and friendship treaty, and maintained military cooperation. When President Vladimir Putin succeeded Boris Yeltsin, in 2000, India's waiting game paid off. A newly assertive Moscow was determined to revive and expand its strategic cooperation with India. New Delhi's only problems with Moscow today are the weakening bilateral trade relationship and the risk of Russia's doing too much to strengthen China's military capabilities.

Charm Offensive

At the end of the Cold War, the prospect of India's building a new political relationship with the United States seemed remote. Washington had long favored Pakistan and China in the region, India had in turn aligned itself with the Soviet Union, and a number of global issues seemed to pit the two countries against each other. Yet after the Cold War, India set about wooing the United States. For most of the Clinton administration, this sweet-talking fell on deaf ears, in part because Clinton officials were so focused on the Kashmir dispute and nonproliferation. Clinton, driven by the unshakable assumption that Kashmir was one of the world's most dangerous "nuclear flashpoints" and so needed to be defused, emphasized "preventive diplomacy" and was determined to "cap, roll back, and eventually eliminate" India's nuclear capabilities. Of course, Clinton's approach ran headlong into India's core national security concerns — territorial integrity and preserving its nuclear option. Pressed by Washington to circumscribe its strategic capabilities, New Delhi reacted by testing nuclear weapons.

But even as it faced U.S. sanctions, New Delhi also began to proclaim that India was a natural ally of the United States. Although the Clinton administration was not interested in an alliance, the nuclear tests forced the United States to engage India seriously for the first time in five decades. That engagement did not resolve the nuclear differences, but it did bring Clinton to India in March 200o — the first American presidential visit to India in 22 years. Clinton's personal charm, his genuine empathy for India, and his unexpected support of

India in the 1999 war with Pakistan succeeded in improving the atmospherics of the relations and in putting New Delhi on Washington's radar screen in a new way.

It took Bush, however, to transform the strategic context of U.S.-Indian relations. Convinced that India's influence will stretch far beyond its immediate neighborhood, Bush has reconceived the framework of U.S. engagement with New Delhi. He has removed many of the sanctions, opened the door for high-tech cooperation, lent political support to India's own war on terrorism, ended the historical U.S. tilt toward Pakistan on Kashmir, and repositioned the United States in the Sino-Indian equation by drawing closer to New Delhi.

India has responded to these sweeping changes by backing the Bush administration on missile defense, the International Criminal Court, and finding alternative approaches to confronting global warming. It lent active support to Operation Enduring Freedom in Afghanistan by protecting U.S. assets in transit through the Strait of Malacca in 2002, agreed to work with the United States on multinational military operations outside of the UN framework, and, in 2005 and 2006, voted twice with Washington against Iran — an erstwhile Indian ally — at the International Atomic Energy Agency.

India also came close to sending a division of troops to Iraq in the summer of 2003 before pulling back at the last moment. Every one of these actions marked a big departure in Indian foreign policy. And although disappointed by India's decision to stay out of Iraq, the Bush administration recognized that India was in the midst of a historic transformation of its foreign policy — and kept faith that India's own strategic interests would continue to lead it toward deeper political cooperation with Washington.

New Delhi's persistence in reaching out to Washington since 1991 has been driven by the belief that only by fundamentally changing its relationship with the world's sole superpower could it achieve its larger strategic objectives: improving its global position and gaining leverage in its relations with other great powers.

But India's ability to engage everyone at the same time might soon come to an end. As U.S.-Chinese tensions grow and Washington looks for ways to manage China's influence, questions about India's attitude toward the new power politics will arise: Can India choose to remain "nonaligned" between the United States and China, or does India's current grand strategy show a clear bias toward the United States?

The nuclear pact unveiled by Bush and Singh in July 2005 — and consolidated when Bush went to New Delhi in March 2006 — was an effort by Washington to influence the ultimate answer to that question. Bush offered to modify U.S. nonproliferation laws (subject to approval by Congress, of course) and revise the global nuclear order to facilitate full cooperation with India on civilian nuclear energy. New Delhi, in return, has promised to separate its civilian and military nuclear programs, place its civilian nuclear plants under international safeguards, and abide by a range of nonproliferation obligations. India's interest in such a deal has been apparent for a long time. Having failed to test weapons before the Nuclear Nonproliferation Treaty was drafted, in 1968, India was trapped in an uncomfortable position vis-à-vis the nuclear order: it was not willing to give up the nuclear option, but it could not be formally accommodated by the nonproliferation regime as a nuclear weapons state.

India's motives for wanting a change in the nuclear regime are thus obvious. But for the Bush administration, the deal is less about nuclear issues than it is about creating the basis for a true alliance between the United States and India — about encouraging India to work in the United States' favor as the global balance of power shifts. Ironically, it was the lack of a history of mutual trust and cooperation — stemming in part from past nuclear disputes — that convinced the Bush administration that a nuclear deal was necessary.

An Impossible Ally?

Many critics argue that the Bush administration's hopes for an alliance are misplaced. They insist that the traditionally nonaligned India will never be a true ally of the United States. But such critics misunderstand India's nonalignment, as well as the nature of its realpolitik over the past 60 years. Contrary to a belief that is especially pervasive in India itself, New Delhi has not had difficulty entering into alliances when its interests so demanded. Its relationship with the Soviet Union, built around a 1971 peace and friendship treaty, had many features of an alliance (notwithstanding India's claim that such ties were consistent with nonalignment); the compact was in many ways a classic response to the alignment of Washington, Beijing, and Islamabad. India has also had treaty-based security relationships with two of its smaller neighbours, Bhutan and Nepal, that date back to 1949-50 — protectorate arrangements that were a reaction to China's entry into Tibet.

In fact, there is no contradiction between India's alleged preference for "moralpolitik" (in opposition to pure power politics, or Machtpolitik) and the Bush administration's expectation of an alliance with India. New Delhi is increasingly replacing the idea of "autonomy," so dear to Indian traditionalists, with the notion of India's becoming a "responsible power." (Autonomy is thought appropriate for weak states trying to protect themselves from great-power competition but not for a rising force such as India.) As India starts to recognize that its political choices have global consequences, it will become less averse to choosing sides on specific issues. Alliance formation and balancing are tools in the kits of all great powers — and so they are likely to be in India's as well.

That India is capable of forming alliances does not, however, mean that it will necessarily form a long-term one with the United States. Whether it does will depend on the extent of the countries' shared interests and their political capacity to act on them together. The Bush administration expects that such shared interests — for example, in balancing China and countering radical Islam in the Middle East — will provide the basis for long-term strategic cooperation. This outcome is broadly credible, but it is by no means inevitable, especially given the United States' seeming inability to build partnerships based on equality. When it comes to facing a rising China, India's tendency to engage in regional balancing with Beijing has not come to an end with the proclamation of a strategic partnership between the two nations.

Indeed, preventing China from gaining excessive influence in India's immediate neighborhood and competing with Beijing in Southeast Asia are still among the more enduring elements of India's foreign policy. Despite Western concerns about the military regime in Myanmar, New Delhi has vigorously worked to prevent Yangon from falling completely under Beijing's influence, and India's military ties with the Southeast Asian nations are expanding rapidly. In 2005, when Pakistan pushed for giving China observer status in the South Asian Association for Regional Cooperation, India acted quickly to bring Japan, South Korea, and the United States in as well. Given India's deep-seated reluctance to play second fiddle to China in Asia and the Indian Ocean region — and the relative comfort of working with a distant superpower — there is a structural reason for New Delhi to favor greater security cooperation with Washington.

In the Middle East, too, India has a common interest with the United States in preventing the rise of radical Islam, which poses an existential threat to India. Given its large Muslim population — at nearly 150 million, the third largest in the world — and the ongoing tensions stemming from the subcontinent's partition, India has in the past acted on its own to avert the spread of radical Islam. When Washington aligned with conservative Islamic forces in the Middle East during the Cold War, India's preference was for secular nationalist forces in the region. When the United States acted ambivalently toward the Taliban in the mid-1990s, India worked with Russia, Iran, and the Central Asian states to counter the Taliban by supporting the Northern Alliance. Now, although some in India are concerned that alignment with the United States might make India a prime target for Islamist extremists, there is no way India can compromise with radical Islam, which threatens its very unity.

But shared interests do not automatically produce alliances. The inequality of power between the two countries, the absence of a habit of political cooperation between them, and the remaining bureaucratic resistance to deeper engagement in both capitals will continue to limit the pace and the scope of strategic cooperation between India and the United States. Still, there is no denying that India will have more in common with the United States than with the other great powers for the foreseeable future.

While New Delhi has acknowledged that U.S. support is necessary for India's rise to be successful, Washington has recognized India's potentially critical role in managing emerging challenges to global order and security. As a major beneficiary of accelerating globalization, India could play a crucial role in ensuring that other developing countries manage their transitions as successfully as it has, that is, by taking advantage of opportunities while working to reduce the pain of disruption. Given the pace of its expansion and the scale of its economy, India will also become an important force in ensuring that the unfolding global redistribution of economic power occurs in an orderly fashion. Meanwhile, India could become a key player in the effort to modernize the politics of the Middle East. If nothing else, India's success in ensuring the rights and the integration of its own Muslim minority and in reaching peace with Pakistan would have a powerful demonstration effect.

To secure a long-term partnership with India, Washington must build on the argument of "Indian exceptionalism" that it has advanced in defense of the recent nuclear pact, devising a range of India-specific policies to deepen cooperation. India is unlikely, however, to become a mere subsidiary partner of the United States, ready to sign on to every U.S. adventure and misadventure around the world. It will never become another U.S. ally in the mold of the United Kingdom or Japan. But nor will it be an Asian France, seeking tactical independence within the framework of a formal alliance.

Given the magnitude of the global security challenges today, the United States needs more than meek allies. It should instead be looking to win capable and compatible partners. A rising India may be difficult at times, but it will act broadly to defend and promote the many interests it shares with Washington. Assisting India's rise, then, is in the United States' own long-term interest.

INDIA'S MILITARY POWER AND DEMOCRACY

India has a penchant for blacklisting foreign arms producers without considering negative effects it has on India's military preparedness. This is the reason why recent reports of irregularities in the procurement of seven Barak anti-missile defence systems and 200 missiles from Israel Aircraft Industries Ltd (IAI) have caused serious concern to the Indian Armed Forces. They fear that the Government may get forced to blacklist IAI as per the provisions of defence procurement procedure. Should that happen, India's defence modernisation plan would suffer irretrievable damage.

Having seen the adverse effects of banning Bofors, HDW and Denel, they dread a similar fate for a large number of ambitious plans under implementation. IAI is deeply involved in most of the major modernisation plans of the three services. In addition to the upgradation of fighter aircraft (Jaguar, MIG-21, MIG-29 and Mirage-2000), transport aircraft (AN-32) and all helicopters of MI series, it is supplying three Airborne Early Warning and Control System (AWACS) systems to India. It is also the prime supplier of unmanned aerial vehicles to the three services. Most importantly, IAI is involved in a number of developmental projects. India simply cannot afford to cut off all dealings with it. The saga of banning Bofors, HDW and Denel cannot be repeated.

Bofors

After carrying out trials of various guns on offer, India opted for Bofors 155 mm FH-77B towed artillery system. A contract for 410 systems was signed with the Swedish firm in 1986 for Rs. 1437.72 crore. The contract included transfer of technology for subsequent manufacture of guns in India. India had planned to produce 1,840 pieces within the country to equip 92 artillery regiments. However, with the exposure of kickbacks, the Government banned Bofors for all future dealings. It had the following effect:-

- Although India had paid for transfer of technology, it failed to utilise it. India lost an opportunity to create a base for further development of artillery weapon systems. As a result, indigenous competence to manufacture and maintain guns remained stunted.
- As spares could not be procured from Bofors, middlemen thrived making huge profits. In the absence of adequate spares, the Army had to cannibalise parts from some guns to keep other guns functional. Essential maintenance also suffered.
- Without help from Bofors, India is struggling to carry out overhauling of guns in the stipulated time frame. It is feared that delay in overhaul will adversely affect extension of useful life of the gun systems. Indigenous capacity installed with a Base Repair Workshop is far too less and it will take unacceptably long to overhaul the complete inventory.
- The Navy was already using Bofors guns on some ships and they faced difficulties in ensuring regular supply of spares.
- Indian inventory of 84 mm Carl Gustav Rocket Launchers suffered as Carl Gustav subsequently became a subsidiary of Bofors and thus, came under the ban.

Denel

Discussions were in final stages with Denel of South Africa for 155 mm howitzers (both towed and self-propelled) when it emerged that Denel had employed unacceptable means to grab contract for the supply of NTW-20 Anti-Material Rifle. It was alleged that Denel had engaged middlemen to offer bribes to obtain sensitive information about the internal proceedings of the Commercial Negotiation Committee. The Government decided to blacklist Denel in 2005 and cancel all orders placed on it. The development was highly unfortunate. Bhim project was almost concluded with Denel's T-6 155mm turret from the G-6 being mounted on Arjun hull.

An initial order had also been placed on a public sector undertaking. With the blacklisting of Denel, Indian Army's Field Artillery Rationalisation Plan suffered a crippling blow. The total requirement envisaged by 2025 is 3600 artillery guns of 155mm/52 calibre. The current inventory is of 410 Bofors guns only. Therefore, India desperately wants to procure 400 additional gun systems (220 wheeled and 180 tracked) on priority to meet inescapable minimum requirement.

Field trials in respect of wheeled systems were carried out in 2003 to ascertain compliance of Services Qualitative Requirements. Three competitors participated-Denel, Soltam Atmos 2000 and FH77 of SWS Defence. All the three systems failed to meet specified standards. Retrials of duly improved versions were held in 2004. With the blacklisting of Denel, the choice got limited to Soltam and FH77. As per the press reports, FH77 emerged far superior to Soltam and was the choice of the Army. However, due to politically sensitive reasons, the Government incorrectly termed the case as a single vendor situation and decided to float fresh tender enquiries with reformulated Qualitative Requirements. Tender for wheeled guns was floated in March 2007 and the second tender for tracked guns followed soon thereafter. It is learnt that 12 producers of guns have been invited.

Nearly 20 years have passed since the induction of Bofor guns; no new gun system has been procured. Due to ban on Bofors and Denel, India has shut doors on two major producers of guns and thereby limited its choice. Continued shortage of suitable 155mm/52 calibre gun systems implies major gaps in India's defence preparedness. Additionally, India's quest for indigenous production of 155 mm ammunition also suffered a major blow. Work on a new ordnance factory in Nalanda to manufacture 155mm ammunition for Bofors guns has got stalled, as Denel was to provide technical know-how. Hundreds of crores of rupees have also gone down the drain.

HDW

The case of HDW makes instructive reading. A contract was signed with the German firm in December 1981. India was to get two HDW 209 class fully built submarines and sub-assemblies and components for assembling two other submarines in India.

HDW was also to provide required training to Indian personnel. HDW delivered two submarines in 1987 and two more were assembled in India in due course. As allegations of bribery and kickbacks became public, the Government decided to blacklist the company.

It was also decided not to build any more submarines of the same class. Marlog, a company jointly owned by HDW and Ferrostal, took over the responsibility to fulfil all contractual obligations.

There are just a handful of competent submarine manufacturers in the world. By blacklisting HDW, India antagonized one of the leading producers and thereby deprived itself of the benefits of latest technological advancements.

HDW is the world leader with the most advanced air-independent propulsion system. Continued collaboration would have given a boost to indigenous submarine building competence. Additionally, India would have acquired wherewithal as regards maintenance, overhaul and repair support.

As India had not received the complete drawings and NATO identification numbers for all spare parts of the submarines, it faced immense problems in procuring them from other sources. Middlemen made huge profits. The Navy wanted to increase the offensive punch of the submarines by mounting Exocet missiles on it. As HDW could not be engaged, others laid unacceptably harsh conditions. Indian plans for the upgradation of the submarine entailed an increase in their length and that could be done only by HDW. To sum up, by blacklisting HDW India deprived itself of maintenance support, upgradation opportunities and development of indigenous skills.

POTENTIAL DRIVERS OF MILITARY CHANGE IN INDIA

In the past 20-30 years, several developments have challenged the traditional paradigm of Indian defence organization. It is not always clear which of these developments is more important or what are the best responses, or even how relevant these are for a country like India. Moreover, there are disagreements about how these developments fit into the debate over increased jointness and integration.

The most obvious driver for military change is the modernization of India's conventional forces and the development of new force structures and doctrines. This combines several sub- factors like the nuclearization of the military balance with Pakistan, the Revolution in Military Affairs, Chinese military modernization, and the debate over power projection/"out of area" operations for the Indian military.

Traditionally the Indian military was very Pakistan-centric and kept a traditional British defensive doctrine based on holding and strike corps. Since the Sundarji reforms of 1980s, there has been a steady effort to mechanize the Indian army and make it more mobile and capable of executing operations both in a nuclear environment and high- tech/network warfare (the Cold Start just being the most infamous example).

The military was searching for "strategic space" to be able to utilize its superior conventional capabilities to give options for policymakers. In its search for military options for policymakers, the military was influenced by the experiences of successful limited war in Kargil in 1999. The military also perceived that because of the lack of options between "do nothing" and "all-out warfare" in the 2001-02 Crisis with Pakistan, policymakers felt compelled to engage in their own clumsy halfway option of coercive diplomacy.

Beyond dealing with a nuclear Pakistan, the armed services have also been tasked to come up with plans and capabilities for dealing with a larger and more powerful China.

This presents them with a challenge that goes beyond the modernization of capabilities and also includes raising new military formations, acquiring new capabilities and technology, developing new doctrine, and developing an infrastructure in contested border regions, while at the same time avoiding any actions that strain the delicate relationship with China.

The raising of more specialized mountain units, deployment of deep strike assets (like Brahmos cruise missiles and Su-30 aircraft), and the development of security infrastructure has been by most accounts slow and inadequate.

On the other hand, during the past 20 years, while the military was pushing for conventional modernization, a large part of the Indian Army's actual duties have been "sub-conventional" or, as is often termed in India, an "aid to civil authorities." This has involved long counter-insurgency campaigns in the Northeast, Punjab, Jammu and Kashmir, support to paramilitary forces fighting the ongoing Naxel insurgency, cross-border terrorism, and constabulary duties along many disputed borders (India has about 8,500 miles of disputed borders). A large part of an entire generation of officers in the Army has spent most of their active duty careers dealing with internal insurgencies rather than conventional operations against Pakistan. There is more to the debate over what power projection capabilities India needs than just the issue of military modernization. The issues include the familiar missions the Indian military has engaged in, such as the evacuation of Indian civilians from conflicts (Gulf Wars, Lebanon in 2006, Libya in 2011, etc.), Indian participation in the UN, and other international peacekeeping missions, and regional constabulary and soft-security needs (dealing with smuggling, piracy, humanitarian assistance and disaster response (HADR), etc.). More ambitious arguments were made about the ability to project hard power, including sea control in the Indian Ocean Region, amphibious operations, and assistance to friends in adjacent regions.

The question of power projection is also linked to another driver for military change in India: the increasing interaction and exposure to international militaries and international military norms. Since the early 1990s, when India opened up its economy and moved away from non-alignment, the Indian military has vastly increased mil-to-mil ties with nations in Southeast and East Asia, the United States, Western Europe and others through bi- and multilateral exercises, military exchanges, cooperation on non-traditional security issues, and particular peacekeeping operations.

More than ever before, the Indian military and defence establishment see how various trends and ideas are shaping other militaries and defence establishments and there is a desire to learn "best practices" and to be able to have greater cooperation or even interoperability with them by becoming more like them. For example, the Ministry of Defence (MoD) created new organizational structures to manage military diplomacy.

MODERNISING THE INDIAN INFANTRY

Why has it taken the Army so long to conceive an upgrade package for the oldest, most potent and intensely employed fighting arm, the Infantry, even after the so-called revolution in military affairs?

The foot soldier, the original and most versatile weapon system that is always taken for granted, has emerged from the dubious shock and awe strategy of recent campaigns as its ultimate arbiter. India has paid dearly for the neglect of its infantry in terms of cost, casualties and over-stretch of battle. But the Infantry has never let us down. Kargil was its finest hour. Gen VP Malik, the Army Chief of the time, wryly noted: "We will fight with what we have."

So when for the first time an international conference of Army and defence industry was launched last week to put the forgotten soldier centre-stage, some misgivings were natural. While Army Chief Gen JJ Singh outlined his vision for the soldier system of the future, the conspicuous and total absence of Government - MoD - robbed the conference of any sanctity. In sharp contrast, for a MoD-sponsored defence finance seminar earlier in the month, Government officials and ministers were stepping over each other at Vigyan Bhavan.

Free India's Army came into being in 1947 and within weeks, the Infantry soldiers landed in Srinagar to save J&K from being gobbled up by Pakistani tribal raiders. Since then, the Infantry has not ceased fighting proxy wars there and later, elsewhere too. A former Army Chief, Gen SR Choudhury, who was not from the Infantry, described the Infantry as the Army and vice versa. Field Marshal Montgomery said: An army is considered only as good as its Infantry.

The experience of four wars, several border skirmishes, two out-of-area missions, the ceaseless campaign to counter cross-border terrorism in Kashmir, numerous other insurgencies in the North-East, internal stability operations elsewhere in the country and UN peace keeping operations make the Indian Infantry the most battle-hardened and combat rich force in the world.

The simple and uncomplaining infantryman has given so much to so many for so little. The modernisation of the infantry was first attempted - halfheartedly - in the mid-1980s by the Perspective Planning branch of the Army Headquarters. The bias for mechanised warfare, zealously pursued by Gen Sundarji, was so pronounced that the Infantry modernisation plan was skipped altogether. Guns, tanks, APCs were the weapons in demand. The Infantry was ignored. Had a modest upgrade package been undertaken at that time, infantry would have been more combat contemporary and effective.

Instead, till recently, some soldiers were still using World War II equipment and clothing. Shameful as it was, soldiers had to buy rucksacks and other accoutrements from the market. DRDO is still to come out with a light bulletproof vest. The Army failed to accurately visualize the nature of combat it would fight in the future. Pakistan-sponsored insurgency in Punjab did not alert the nation and the Army to the proxy war brewing in J&K. We defaulted on both counts - anticipating low intensity conflict and cross border terrorism and preparing the Infantry for it.

Despite the sustained counter-insurgency and counter-terrorism campaign in J&K and the North-East since the 1990s, the Army was sluggish in investing in the infantry. The first Gulf War reintroduced the fiction that wars could be won from the air.

The air campaigns in Bosnia and Kosovo temporarily turned fiction into reality. But 9/11 broke the myth of supremacy of air power. Operation Enduring Freedom in Afghanistan lasted 76 days; 65 of these were air operations.

The 11-day land offensive secured a temporary and incomplete victory against the Taliban. Operation Iraqi Freedom on the other hand, fought for 20 days was bereft of any preparatory air campaign though a secret air war preceded it. Unhappily for the US/NATO-led coalition forces, despite their pyrrhic military victories, low intensity wars in Afghanistan and Iraq are continuing in full blaze.

The recent 34-day war in Lebanon and the ongoing campaign in Gaza demonstrate the limits of Israel's military power. Used to decisive victories in less than 10 days, Israeli Defence Forces (IDF) were badgered by Hassan Nasrallah's jihadi militia. Reliance on air power, tanks and guns in Lebanon as substitute for ground troops - infantry - was motivated by casualty aversion. We too have to be sensitive to casualties.

The wars in Lebanon, Iraq and Afghanistan spurred by the growing cult of Osama bin Laden and Hassan Nasrallah require a redefinition of the concept of power and military success. Success would necessarily be an inclusive military victory encompassing post-conflict stability and reconstruction.

For this we need Infantry. The Indian Army should not get overly seduced by high-sounding warfare like 'netcentric' that the West is being diverted into. This is not to suggest we ignore the strides in high-tech warfare. But as a former US NATO Commander noted recently: "This netcentric stuff is great but our men in Baghdad are being blown up with their Humvees by IEDs." He suggested that we address the battle we are fighting before switching to the one we will fight in the future.

India's supreme operational challenge is and will be the maintenance of internal security. Just last month, Prime Minister Manmohan Singh stated this ground reality. The Infantry is at the heart of counterinsurgency and counter-terrorism operations and may well get sucked into anti-Naxal operations as well. Keeping the Army operationally ready for both conventional and unconventional missions is imperative but the emphasis has to be on the business of the day: CI and CT.

The Indian Infantry is belatedly embarking on a modernisation programme to enhance its combat skills through increased lethality, communications, surveillance, mobility and suvivability. These force multipliers will enable the soldier to fight all-weather, 24x7 and on any terrain in the right battle-configuration albeit with the accent on LIC.

The GSQR for the Future-Infantry-Soldier-As a System (F-INSAS) must empower not encumber the soldier. DRDO must compete with domestic and international industry. DRDO has one more chance to make amends for its omissions and commissions. F-INSAS must strike the right balance between the surge of technology and sensibility of the soldier keeping the battle of the future in mind. Defence Minister AK Antony should accord F-INSAS the highest strategic priority.

ARTILLERY MODERNIZATION

In my reckoning Artillery modernization has not made any headway because of two reasons. The first is that-blinded by the labels of 'support' and 'supported', the Army has not yet grasped the full import of the modern artillery on tomorrow's battlefield. The second can best be described by just one word: jinxed.

However like the Infantry, modernization of the artillery has also been a matter of concern in the last decade or so. In these years much has apparently been done but unfortunately without any headway. Actually the process began in the early eighties. But other than 400 Bofors guns procured in the mid eighties we have nothing else to show.

The exercise to procure new towed and mounted self propelled tracked and wheeled 155 mm 52 calibre guns are on. We are also planning to induct a specified number of light weight 155 mm guns for certain areas and missions. It is important at this juncture to focus on ensuring that the process of evaluation and induction moves without any hiccups and delays.

As we induct these guns the space of the contact battle at the tactical level will increase to a 30 km envelop thus enhancing our ability to destroy, maneuver, and defeat. Similarly we need to pay more attention to the requirements of the Artillery at the operational and strategic level. In this context even though we have been inducting the Prithvi, the BrahMos and the Agni series, the process has been based on the developmental projects of the DRDO and not on the basis of a well thought through conceptual framework.

The subject of rocket and missile artillery thus merits deeper examination. We require more systems that can provide coverage between the 30 to 100 Km ranges. Besides, the liquid propellant based Prithvi imposes certain operational limitations. Admittedly the Smerch rocket system has filled this gap to some extent but much more needs to be done. Firing platforms like the guns and rocket and missile launchers are just one of the four pillars upon which comprehensive artillery capability is structured.

The other pillars are communications to include artillery command and control systems, surveillance systems and the ammunition systems. In the Kargil war our communications and surveillance systems were not adequate. Thus the guns could be exploited to only 30 percent of their potential.

In principle surveillance and target acquisition capabilities must exceed our delivery systems ranges by at least 30 percent. The ideal would be 50 percent. We have been working on this for a while but more needs to be done.

We should be able to establish a comprehensive surveillance and target acquisition grid by using a mix of ground and air/ space based sensors to include satellites, aircraft, drones, helicopters and tethered balloons. On the ground besides, electro optical devices and thermal cameras we will also require a sufficient number of weapon locating radars some of which should be employable in the mountains. The surveillance grid must allow for transmission and exchange of data to all shooters and decision makers in real time. The problems of surveillance in the mountains merit special attention.

Advancements in ammunition technology have led to a dramatic enhancement in the lethality and destructiveness of the artillery. With improved conventional munitions (ICM) the kill capacity of the ordinary shell has gone up in multiples. Smart and intelligent munitions now permit pinpoint accuracy enabling the artillery to engage and destroy fortifications and tanks from long ranges. We must induct such sophisticated ammunition speedily. However while doing so the challenge lies in getting the mix right since sensor/seeker based munitions are relatively very expensive.

FACTORS AND PROCESS OF INDIA'S MILITARY DEVELOPMENT

The emergence of India as a new military power in South Asia has prompted researchers to study and describe factors and political development in South Asia. According to Chris Smith (1994) the political upheaval, conflict and war during India's early history are the many elements that have influenced Indian policies formation after achieving independence in 1947. Factors such as history, leadership, security, national interest, internal and external conflicts and the situation in the international system have given significant impact to develop the reinforcement of the defense system to strengthen the safety and security level. The emergence of India as a new power in the region South Asia is related to the military modernization development in China during the end of 1980. Additionally, these two superpowers were involved in war related to border dispute in 1962. This conflict has left a significant impact to India in addressing and developing their military capabilities. The situation deteriorated when China attempted to expand power in Southeast Asia which has propelled India to toughen their maritime defense force in an effort to prevent the influence of China's military development in Southeast Asia and South Asia. Michael Leifer (1996:17) also stated that China's action to claim the island in South China Sea in February 1992 encouraged India to increase security surveillance in Indian Ocean waters.

Scalapino (1975:122) explained that the development of expansion and power among Soviet Union and United States has also motivated India's awareness on security threats. This factor is proven important because superpower involvement in South Asia and Southeast Asia had influenced India to increase the defense system. Expansion and competition of the superpowers in the South Asia involve aspects such as strategic alliances, military aid, containment policy, service support, technology and so forth . Even the support and assistance of the superpowers on countries in the South Asian region is considered as factor to the increase in military technology and development. India's military modernization in late 1980s was seen by Shekhar Gupta (1975:62) as an obvious desire for India to emerge as a new military power in the region of South Asia and Asia in general. This is because if it is studied, India has allocated large amount of expenditure in the development of military during the late 1980, in fact India was one of the largest arms importer in the world between year 1985-1989.

Since 1947 under Nehru's administration, India practiced a 'non alignment' policy and socialism. He adopted a 'do not intervene' and non-aligned policy although there were differences in ideology aspects and emphasize on peace, besides dealing conflict resolution through diplomacy. This is because he himself was a socialist and an idealist. India's defense policy under Nehru can be divided into 2 stages namely among year 1947-1949 and 1950-1962. Because India was granted independence in 1947, Nehru implemented policies that have more tendencies to economic development and did not focus on military development. This is because India was facing an economic recession and social problems during the early phase of his administration. Nehru's policies directly forced budget and national budget to be more focused on economic development. This is the reason why the process of military development and military modernization was delayed during Nehru's era. Although these policies were objected by the other Indian leaders, the concentration was towards economic development.

In 1962, India-China's war directly effected and become the starting point in the change of India's defense policy. In 1962 also India's Prime Minister Nehru died and his death has opened a space for new policies implementation particularly in the development of military. The war between India and China in 1962 was favorable to China due to its strong military compare to India.

This event has triggered India to develop its military power to ensure their defense and security. For this reason the allocation of expenditure on defense has recorded a high increase. Concentration and modernization of India's military entails all three force of defense namely land, navy and air. Additionally emphasis also was focused on the development military technology and research. India has proven its effort and has yielded success whereby in May 18 1974 India has successfully produced its first's nuclear bomb that was tested in Pokran. Realizing their defeat during the China-India war in 1962, India started the move to strengthen its defense and military modernization. With that, India cooperated with the Soviet to receive weaponry supply for the purpose of military developments. India-Soviet's cooperation is visibly successful in modernizing Indian military power until the end 1980, whereby India has owned weapons equipment imported from Soviet such as cannon 155mm, T-72's tank, MIG-21, Mirage's aircraft 2000, and long-range bomber. In terms of allocation, India's defense expenditure recorded an increase, for example at the end of the year 1985, an increase from 2% to 4.2% to 1989 was seen from the GDP. India's allocation and expenditure has been recorded as the world largest importers of arms with cost nearly worth US$ 10 billion.

The superpower development and competition among United State and Soviet Union in South Asian region had aroused security threat and political instability. This is because Soviet Union's communist power evolved in Afghanistan in 1980's, while America's assistance and support has been given to Pakistani for the purpose to prevent Soviet's energy development base on 'containment policy' strategy (V. Longer,1988:56). This development has directly given security threats to India with the superpowers and United States assistance to Pakistan. Developments such as arms race, China-Pakistan relationship, United State-Pakistan and separatist rebellion in Kashmir and Punjab have raised Indian leader awareness to re-examine policies such as the neutral policy and independent region from the grip of superpower and national defense policy (Amit Gupta,1995:448). This current development has prompted India which was under the government of Prime Minister Indira Ghandi to study and make changes on national defense policies. Thus, India has made military development, implemented 'South Asian Doctrine', rejects intervention of foreign power on South Asia's countries internal problem and neutral policy. Therefore, Indira Ghandi infers if any South Asian country accepts the entry of a foreign power, it will be assumed as a threat to regional security especially South Asia. However, all changes that were made by Indira Ghandi have been deferred when she was assassinated by the Sikh militants in 1984 (Amit Gupta,1995:448).

While India was under the administration of Prime Minister Rajiv Gandhi, major changes were made when he realized that the policies implemented previously were ineffective. Internal crisis such as the conflicts in Kashmir and Punjab and threats from outside has prompted to implement more effective new policies particularly in the development of military. This situation had caused India to undergo a more drastic move to develop its nuclear weapons. This is because through the development of nuclear it can create deterrence or prevent enemy's confrontation beside modernizing the military power (V. Longer,1988:305). To create regional peace Rajiv Ghandi implemented policies enhancing relationship with regional countries and superpowers especially Pakistan, China, Soviet Union and US. By early 1990s the international structure has undergone a big change with the collapse of the power of Soviet Union. Soviet Union's down fall gave an effect on India because Soviet Union was a very close ally and had good ties with India (Shekhar Gupta,1995:3). Thus, India realized it should develop its military capabilities more rapidly to ensure national security. This situation motivated India to develop military aspects particularly in the development of nuclear-weapons that can become a prevention of enemy's threats.

India has implemented its nuclear development program to protect national interest, security and create balance of power through quantity and quality of strategic arms possession. These strategic weapons refer to nuclear weapons or modern weaponry of mass destruction and are able to provide an advantage to a country.

This decision is considered a rational decision because India thinks the world is in state of anarchy and in moving towards military modernization. India is developing a powerful military not only in the field of modern defense but also in the aspect nuclear, biology, and chemical (NBC) weapons.

This is because India thinks ownership of nuclear weapons can ensure India's survival, security and progress. When China carried out their nuclear-weapons test in Lop Nor on the 16th of October 1964, this made India realize the importance of nuclear-weapons as device to prevent confrontation in the field of military politics (East Asian Strategic Review,2002:109).

Concern towards China's nuclear-weapon threat occurred because of two reasons namely, unresolved border problem and China channeling nuclear program aid to Islamabad. Since China's nuclear weapon test was executed, New Delhi has been actively practicing nuclear choices (Avery Goldstein,2000:251).

Furthermore India has tried to develop a medium (IRBM) and long distance (ICBM) missile (Bary Buzan,2002:9). Soviet Union has given help in terms of expertise and 2 nuclear reactors to India in 1992. India also received help from Israel for the purpose of countering Islamic bomb.

Edward Mead Earle (1973: 418-420) has underlined 6 key features to emerge as a maritime power are history, physical location, size of region, national population character and institutions of the country to be a maritime power. The maritime interest is base on the need to provide security coverage to hundreds of archipelago, thousands of kilometres of beach, a wide Exclusive Economic Zone area (EEZ) and geographical position interest and the strategic location of the Indian subcontinent which is located in the middle of Europe and East Asia.

This situation has prompted India to design a maritime defense strategy that incorporates capacity and military force that directly protects the nation from land, air and sea which includes land borders, archipelago province, maritime asset and important trade routes. India also aims to develop a navy that can operate transcending geo–strategic area covering the entire Indian Ocean and South-East Asia. This includes the purchase of Admiral Gorshkov aircraft carrier, three Kvirok and two kilo submarines for the navy. India's territorial maritime defense interest has started since the 1960s following the development competition of big powers in Asia Pacific and South Asia that could threaten India's security (Chris Smith,1994:70. Although since 1960s India has not develop its maritime defense strategy extensively but this development will provide significant capacity to ensure security on its strategic territories.

Besides strategic weapon development, India has also implemented a long term plan of conventional military development called the 20 years plan to modernize the defense forces. They allocated USD 20 billions to purchase artillery, tanks, ammonization, surveillance system and visual night aid. This plan involved the purchase of modern and sophisticated defense equipment such as 310 T 90 tanks, Unmanned Aircraft Vehicles (UAVs), 155mm Howitzers cannons, land missile on air, rocket launcher and other equipment (Jane's Defence

Weekly, January 2001:32.). This military development is not just limited to the army, India has also give attention to its air force development which provides modern and sophisticated air defense equipment. They have purchased equipment and aircraft such as the Advanced Jet Trainers, Dassault Mirage 2000s, SU–30 aircrafts, Tupolev Tu bomber–22M3 (Backfire) and many more (Asian military Review, February–March 2000:74).

Their Air force has also large allocation which amounted to USD$30 billion to purchase aircraft and training, surveyor aircraft, AWACS, missile and repair of air defense equipment. For the navy, the Indian government has allocated as much as USD$20 billion to buy 2 airplane carrier tankers, submarines, missiles and surveyor aircrafts besides having cooperation with foreign country in defense.

This military development process has made India emergence as a new military power when India came forward as a nuclear power. The world was stunned by the threat during the South Asia conflict in 1998 (India and Pakistan) that can bring to the use of nuclear in the clash (Muhd Izhar Abu Samah,2001:46-47). Directly the conflict among these two states has enlightened the world with the emergence of India as a military power and as a developed nation in the field of nuclear technology. According to Zin Mahmud (2002:30-31):

"In terms of strength, India exceeds Pakistani, although both have nuclear weapons. Yet India's nuclear power is greater than Pakistan's. In terms of population and economic strength, Indian is also in a higher position than Pakistan."

GREAT POWER STATUS OF INDIAN MILITARY

Although often overshadowed by the rise of China, India's ascent toward great-power status over the past two decades has been one of the most dramatic developments in the international system. In the late 1980s, India was the world's most populous nation but had an economy barely one-third the size of Italy's and an outdated military dependent largely on

Soviet hand-me-downs. Today, India's economy is the world's fourth largest in terms of purchasing-power parity; it will soon overtake Japan for third place if current trends continue. It has risen to become the world's ninth-largest source of industrial output, slightly ahead of Brazil. India has also become a more modern, sophisticated military power, and with the passage of the Indo-U.S. civil nuclear agreement in 2008, India received a key endorsement as a legitimate member of the "nuclear club."

Becoming a "great power" has not always been an explicit objective of Indian foreign policy, and the pursuit of a stronger global role has been controversial in a state with immense domestic needs. However, India's recent rise—particularly in economic terms—has led an increasing number of officials and members of the public to embrace this idea. Leaders of both of India's leading political parties—the ruling Congress Party and Bharatiya Janata Party (BJP)—have stated openly in recent years that they seek great-power status for their country.

India's cultivation of great-power capabilities and influence—and the policy goals it pursues as it amasses strength—are clearly important to U.S. foreign policy. At the global level, India is a large, democratic, developing country that could either help advance or frustrate core U.S. foreign policy aims. In the near term, a rigid Indian alliance with or against the United States is highly unlikely, but a range of options exists in between. On key strategic and ideational issues, India could tilt toward the United States or engage in what scholars Robert Pape and T.V. Paul describe as "soft balancing": using political levers and flexible coalitions with other emerging powers to resist American leadership. This possibility has led CIA officials to characterize India as the key "swing state" in the twenty-first century international system. At the regional level, India's rising clout and improved Indo-U.S. ties create both opportunities and potential pitfalls for American efforts to help manage the maelstrom in Afghanistan and Pakistan. Economic relations between India and the United States are also growing in importance, both bilaterally and in multilateral forums such as the G-20, where India carries increasing weight.

Navigating Indo-U.S. relations effectively requires understanding the motives and means for India's great-power quest. This article attempts to address three basic questions. First, what does great-power status generally mean to India's governing elites? Second, how is the Indian government pursuing its goal of becoming a legitimate great power? Third, how can the answers to these questions guide U.S. foreign policy toward a stable and constructive relationship with India as the latter becomes a more prominent player on the world stage?

MODERNISATION PREPAREDNESS OF THE INDIAN MILITARY

Despite the army leadership's best efforts, the ongoing Revolution in Military Affairs (RMA) had, till recently, almost completely bypassed the Indian Army. For well over a decade the army's efforts to modernise had been thwarted due to political neglect and lack of adequate budgetary support. The funds made available for modernisation are extremely limited and a large portion of these funds is surrendered year after year. For Financial Year 2006-07, a sum of Rs 3,000 crore was surrendered as unspent. The fact that 155 mm ammunition for the Bofors howitzer had to be imported from South Africa during the Kargil conflict in 1999 tells its own tale of persistent shortages. Had the conflict not been confined to the 150 km frontage of the Kargil sector, T-72 and 130 mm medium gun ammunition too would have run short and it would have been politically embarrassing for the government as well as the army. In the plains the army would have had to fight with obsolete Vijayant tanks and several other vintage equipment that were unsuitable for combat. However, sustained efforts by Army HQ have now borne fruit and the army's modernisation drive is once again well underway.

In the prevailing era of strategic uncertainty, while terrorism has become the primary threat, the external and internal threats and challenges faced by India are such that a large army is still required to be maintained. Also, a high degree of preparation and operational readiness is still necessary as conventional war, though improbable, cannot be categorically ruled out. At the same time, heavy capital investments in modern defence equipment are undoubtedly a drain on a developing economy that is ill-equipped to handle the burgeoning defence expenditure. Several eminent analysts have recommended that qualitative upgradation should be accompanied by quantitative downsizing of personnel strength of the army. However, given its responsibilities for border management and the manpower-intensive low intensity conflict that the army is involved in, this is easier said than done.

Future conventional conflict on the Indian sub-continent will in all probability result from the ongoing low-intensity limited war on the Line of Control (LoC) with Pakistan or the unresolved territorial and boundary dispute with China and will be predominantly a land conflict. The Indian Army seriously lacks a potent firepower punch, especially in the mountain sector. Precision-guided munitions (PGMs) have still to enter service in numbers large enough to make a real difference. The reconnaissance, surveillance and target acquisition (RSTA) assets necessary for the optimum exploitation of even the existing firepower assets are grossly inadequate. Automated command and control and decision support systems have been on the drawing boards for several decades but are yet to mature.

In a future conventional war that will be fought under the nuclear shadow, manoeuvre will be extremely limited. This restriction will lead to much greater emphasis being placed on firepower to achieve the laid down military aim. Hence, it is imperative that artillery modernisation is undertaken with alacrity so as to generate firepower asymmetries on the future battlefield. After a long spell of keeping the powder dry, action on modernisation of the Indian artillery is livening up once again. Since January 2008, the Ministry of Defence (MoD) has issued three global tenders for 155mm guns and howitzers for the mountains, the plains and self-propelled guns for the deserts. Summer and winter trials are expected to be held over the next one year and, red tape permitting, contracts may be awarded as early as in the first half of 2010.

Artillery firepower had paved the way for victory during the Kargil conflict. Despite the lessons learnt in Kargil, modernisation of the artillery had continued to lag behind. The last major acquisition of towed gun-howitzers was that of about 400 pieces of 39-calibre 155mm FH-77B howitzers form Bofors of Sweden in the mid-1980s. This gun had proved its mettle in the Kargil conflict. Just when a contract for 120 tracked and 180 wheeled self-propelled (SP) 155mm guns was about to be concluded after years of protracted trials, South African arms manufacturer Denel, a leading contender for the contract, was alleged to have been involved in a corruption scam in an earlier deal for anti-material rifles (AMRs). The other two howitzers in contention, from Soltam of Israel and BAE (Bofors) of Sweden did not meet the laid down criteria according to the COAS and Army HQ recommended fresh trials, setting the programme back at least three to four years. Another key issue was that the howitzers that had been offered were technology demonstration models and not guns that were in actual service with the home country armies.

The probability of the next conventional war breaking out in the mountains is far higher than that of a war in the plains. With this in view, the artillery recently conceptualised a requirement for a light-weight towed howitzer of 155mm calibre for employment in the mountains. Neither the present Bofors howitzer nor its replacement will be capable of operations in the mountains. A light-weight 45-calibre 155mm howitzer weighing less than 5,000 kg, with a light but adequately powered prime mover, is ideal for the mountains. The gun-train should be capable of negotiating sharp road bends without the need to unhook the gun from the prime mover. The two British 45-calibre 155mm howitzers that competed for the US contract for a similar howitzer some years ago – the UFH (Ultra-lightweight Field Howitzer) and the LTH (Light-weight Towed Howitzer) – could be considered for licensed production with transfer of technology.

In January 2008, the MoD floated a Request for Proposal (RfP) for 140 pieces of ultra-light 39 calibre 155mm towed howitzers for use by the Indian Army's mountain formations and, presumably, by its rapid reaction divisions – as and when these are raised as it will be easy to transport by air. 140 howitzers will be adequate to equip seven medium artillery regiments and will cost approximately Rs 3,000 crore. The RfP has been reportedly issued to UK's BAE Systems (which now owns Bofors), for the M777 howitzer claimed to be the lightest in the world at under 4,220 kg, and to Singapore Technologies for the Pegasus SLWH.

India has floated a global tender for the purchase of 400 155mm towed artillery guns for the Army, to be followed by indigenous manufacture of another 1,100 howitzers, in a project worth a whopping Rs 8,000 crore. The RFP was issued to eight prospective bidders including BAE, General Dynamics, Nexter (France), Rhinemetall (Germany) and Samsung (South Korea). An RfP has also been issued for 180 wheeled self-propelled guns for around Rs 4,700 crore for employment by mechanised forces in the plains and semi-desert sectors.

Since the Bofors 155mm Howitzer was introduced into service, the indigenously designed and manufactured 105 mm Indian Field Gun (IFG) and its (not so) light version, the Light Field Gun (LFG), have joined the 75/24 Indian Mountain Gun, the 100mm Russian field gun and the 122mm Russian howitzer on the obsolescence list. Approximately 180 pieces of 130mm M46 Russian medium guns have been successfully "up-gunned" to 155mm calibre with ordnance supplied by Soltam of Israel. The new barrel length of 45 calibres has enhanced the range of the gun to about 40 km with extended range ammunition.

A contract for the acquisition of two regiments of the 12-tube, 300mm Smerch multi-barrel rocket launcher (MBRL) system with 90 km range was reported to have been signed with Russia's Rosoboronexport in early-2006. This will be a major boost for the long-range firepower capabilities of the army. If this weapon system had been available during the Kargil conflict, Pakistan's brigade HQ and forward airfield at

Skardu and other targets deep inside POK could have been hit with impunity. Extended range (ER) rockets are being introduced for the 122 mm Grad MBRL that has been in service for over three decades. The ER rockets will enhance the weapon system's range from 22 to about 40 km. A Rs 5,000 crore contract has also been signed for the serial production of the Pinaka MBRL weapon system, another DRDO project plagued by time delays and completed with help from Larsen and Toubro and the Tatas.

The modernisation plan of tube artillery alone is likely to cost Rs 13,000 crore. The major acquisitions will be of initial lots of 400 towed howitzers of 155mm calibre, with a barrel length of 52 calibres, costing about Rs 4,000 crore, 140 ultra-light weight 155mm towed howitzers, with a barrel length of 45 calibres, costing Rs 3,000 crore and 180 SP 155mm howitzers costing Rs 5,000 crore. The "Shakti" project for a command and control systems for the artillery, called Artillery Combat Command and Control System (ACCCS), has reached the stage of maturity and is now being fielded up to the regimental level.

The BrahMos supersonic cruise missile (Mach 2.8 to 3.0), with a precision strike capability, very high kill energy and range of 290 km, was inducted into the army in July 2007. It is a versatile missile that can be launched from TATRA mobile launchers and silos on land, aircraft and ships and, perhaps in future, also from submarines. Fifty BrahMos missiles are expected to be produced every year. Efforts are underway to further increase its strike range. BrahMos Aerospace has orders worth Rs 3,500 crore from the army and the navy, which has opted for the anti-ship as well as the land attack cruise missile (LACM) versions. These terrain hugging missiles are virtually immune to counter measures due to their high speed and very low radar cross section and are far superior to sub-sonic cruise missiles like Pakistan's Babur. Chile, Kuwait, Malaysia and South Africa have shown interest in acquiring this missile.

The Indian army is extensively engaged in ongoing internal security (IS) and counter-insurgency operations (CI) and simultaneously needs to prepare itself for a future border conflict that may spill over to a larger conventional war in the plains. In keeping with these twin requirements, Army HQ have apparently decided to upgrade the IS and CI capabilities of infantry battalions as well as enhance their Infantry firepower-mobility-EW (electronic warfare) punch for a possible war in the plains against Pakistan or in the mountains against China. The Army Chief's modernisation vision is to "adapt to high-end technology, improve night-fighting capability... (and) information technology, information warfare and network centric warfare."

Despite its large-scale employment on border management and extensive commitments in Internal Security and Counter Insurgency operations, infantry modernisation had been languishing for several decades when the Ministry of Defence (MoD) finally cleared a visionary plan to modernise the army's infantry battalions by according "in principle" approval in the form of Modification 4B to the war establishment (WE) of a standard infantry battalion in 1998. However, no funds were specially sanctioned for this purpose till the BJP-led NDA government approved the expenditure of Rs 3,500 crore in September 2003. Thereafter, approval had to be sought on file for each new weapon system or piece of equipment on a "case-by-case" basis as has become the norm. It is by now well-known how each such case chronicles the saga of an uphill struggle to get approval first from the MoD, then MoD (Finance) and, finally, the Ministry of Finance (MoF). All this is only possible after the DRDO has first certified that the weapon system or equipment in question cannot be developed and manufactured indigenously and such a certificate is hard to come by.

While 250 Kornet-E anti-tank guided missiles (ATGMs) with thermal imaging sights have substantially increased the anti-tank capability of infantry battalions, most efforts to modernise the equipment held by infantry and Rashtriya Rifles (RR) units are aimed at enhancing their capability for surveillance and target acquisition at night and boosting their firepower for precise retaliation against infiltrating columns and terrorists holed up in built-up areas. About 200 hand-held

BFSRs with practical ranges up to seven to eight km where clear line of sight is available, 2,000 hand-held thermal imaging devices (HHTIs) with ranges up to 2,000 metres for observation at night and stand-alone infra-red, seismic and acoustic sensors with varying capabilities have enabled infantrymen to dominate the Line of Control so completely that infiltration has come down to almost a trickle.

The newly acquired weapons, which complement these surveillance and observation devices, include: 1,500x84 mm rocket launchers, including some disposable ones; 1,000 AMRs (anti-material rifles); 8,000 UBGLs (under-barrel grenade launchers); 4,000 new generation carbines; 300 bullet proof vehicles; and, several hundred accurate sniper rifles. However, the numbers acquired and the ammunition stocks are still inadequate and need to be made up more rapidly. While the INSAS 5.56 mm assault rifles have now been in service for almost 10 years and proved to be effective, the light machine gun (LNG) version is still facing teething problems and the carbine version for close quarter battle has not found favour with the army. New 5.56 mm assault rifles of bull-pup design with an integrated laser range finder and grenade launcher are under development. Efforts are also being made to provide infantry platoons and sections with integrated GPS-based navigation system, secure light-weight walkie-talkie radio sets and better protective gear with a helmet that incorporates a built-in head-up display.

The mechanised infantry is now equipped with the BMP-2 ICV Sarath of which over 1,000 have been built since 1987. A new variant is the 81 mm Carrier Mortar Tracked Vehicle (CMTV) that is based on the chassis of the Sarath ICV and has been indigenously developed to enhance the integral firepower available to mechanised infantry battalions. Other variants include a command post, an ambulance, armoured dozer and engineer and reconnaissance vehicles. Mechanised reconnaissance and support battalions need better surveillance radars, fire-and-forget ATGMs and effective night fighting capability. However, their capabilities can be upgraded on a lower priority compared with infantry battalions that are engaged in border management and IS/CI operations.

The army's infantry battalions also need their own mini or micro UAVs like Elbit's Skylark or Rafael's Skylite, among others, to partly reduce the extent of patrolling necessary in internal security environment and to improve their surveillance capability in conventional conflict. These UAVs should have a range of about 10 to 15 km, should be light-weight (less than 10 kg), hand-launched, carry a single payload, e.g. a daylight video camera or infra-red camera for night operations, and should be inexpensive enough to be dispensable. A mini ground control station should be authorized at battalion HQ for planning and control. Ideally, these should be indigenously designed and developed and locally manufactured.

A new DRDO project, that is reported to be ongoing, aims to equip future soldiers with lightweight force multipliers. Soldiers of the future will have miniaturised communication and GPS systems, small power packs, weapon platforms and smart vests with fibre-optic sensors.

The soldiers will also have better and lighter combat fatigues, boots, belts, ammunition pouches, rucksacks and rations in the form of meals-ready-to-eat. Though somewhat akin to the US Army's Land Warrior programme, the Indian Army programme for modernisation of infantry battalions will result in only incremental changes. However, these would be significant enough to make a difference on the battlefields of the Indian sub-continent. The infantryman's average combat load is approximately 27 kg, including the 3.06 kg 5.56 mm INSAS assault rifle and its "on weapon" ammunition. If this can be reduced by even a few kg, it will enable the soldier to improve his agility in battle and counter-insurgency operations. Ultimately an infantryman has to be prepared to engage in hand-to-hand combat and agility can make a difference between life and death.

For over 350 infantry battalions, plus about 150 Rashtriya Rifles, Assam Rifles and Territorial Army battalions, these major changes will be extremely costly to implement and will spill over at least 10 to 12 years – that is, if the funds can be found. What is certain is that there is no alternative to making the financial commitment that is necessary to enhance the operational capabilities of the army's infantry battalions. Without modernising this cutting edge of its sword, the army will soon begin to resemble the armies of India's lesser neighbours.

The indigenously designed Arjun main battle tank (MBT) has been in the pipeline for over two decades. Though the tank has many good features, it has consistently failed to meet the army's GSQR for an MBT and orders have been placed for only 124 tanks to be manufactured. The lack of progress on the Arjun MBT had slowed down the pace of armour modernisation. India then signed a deal with Russia to acquire 310 T-90S tanks in the year 2000. Subsequently, India began to assemble these tanks at Avadi. It has recently been reported that in addition to these, India has decided to acquire another 347 T-90S tanks and assemble them within the country.

The first Indian assembled T-90S (Bhishma) rolled off the production line on January 8, 2004. While T-90S Russian tanks have provided new teeth to India's strike formations in the plains and corrected the imbalance that had resulted from Pakistan's acquisition of T-80 UD from Ukraine and the Al Khalid tanks jointly designed with China, a large number of T-72 (Ajeya) tanks are still awaiting modernisation. The lack of a suitable fire control system and night fighting capability are major handicaps. As soon as the obsolescent Vijayanta tanks are phased out of service, it will be time to also discard the old T-55s as well as they can no longer be either upgraded or modernised. Armour modernisation is now proceeding apace and can be classified as a success story.

The air defence (AD) of mechanised forces is another area that is crying for attention. The Kvadrat missile system that has been the backbone of AD for strike formations since the early 1970s are now ageing and need urgent replacement. With the DRDO's indigenous Akash medium-range and Trishul short-range missile projects not making major headway, it is time to start looking at import substitutes. In fact, the assets of Army Air Defence corps of the army are grossly inadequate to provide effective protection against enemy aircraft during war. This young corps requires substantial capital infusion to really come into its own.

Another DRDO project that is way behind schedule is the Nag anti-tank missile system. The antiquated Jonga-mounted SS-11 B1 anti-tank guided missile (ATGM) system has been replaced in missile battalions by MILAN shoulder-fired ATGMs. However, a vehicle-mounted missile system like the Nag is definitely necessary for reconnaissance and attrition tasks. The experimental Plan AREN tactical communications system for strike formations needs early replacement. The ability to carry broadband data needs to be enhanced in particular. Even the more recent static communications network called ASCON lacks ISDN capability for the real-time transmission of maps and streaming video.

While some Stentor long-range BFSRs have been in service for over a decade, medium-range radars are still to be acquired. At least about 30 to 40 weapon locating radars (WLRs) are required for effective counter-bombardment, especially in the plains, and only a few have been procured so far. Israeli Searcher-I unmanned aerial vehicles (UAVs) have been introduced into service but these are few in number and it will be a long time before these will really make a difference by providing a real-time surveillance capability so that ground forces can initiate action even as a fresh input is received. Only a small number of Searcher – II UAVs, with an upper ceiling that makes them suitable for the mountains, have been acquired.

An automated command and control and decision support system for use by the General Staff is still a far cry and so are supporting systems like the battlefield surveillance system and air space management system. The urgent requirement of real-time satellite reconnaissance systems has still not been accepted despite the nuclear overhang under which the armed forces now operate. Even though the cameras on India's remote sensing and cartographic satellites now have sharply enhanced resolutions, less than one metre, military-grade photographs of still better resolution are needed to be purchased from the open market. These sources may dry up quickly during war.

A "system of systems" approach must be followed so that scarce RSTA and communications resources can be synergistically configured and optimally exploited. The war in Iraq fought in March-April 2003 was based on the concept of "network-centric warfare" in which surveillance sensors, targeting systems and "shooters" are fused together in a seamless "system of systems" that reduced response time between the acquisition of a target and its destruction to 15 to 20 minutes. While such a system may take over a decade to establish, a beginning must be made right away.

PGMs are increasingly gaining currency as weapons of choice in conflict on land, both to accurately destroy critical hard targets quickly as well as to avoid or at least minimise collateral damage.

During the Gulf War I in 1991, despite all the CNN-generated hype of smart bombs flying unerringly through ventilators, PGMs formed less than 10 percent of the total high explosive dropped over Iraq and were rather inaccurate. The "collateral" destruction of an air raid shelter harbouring women and children has been too well documented to bear recounting.

The coalition forces did not destroy a single Iraqi Scud missile launcher. In Kosovo, PGMs accounted for about 30 per cent of the ordnance dropped and accuracies had improved considerably by 1999.

In the post-September 11, 2001 retribution inflicted on the Taliban militia and its al Qaeda supporters in Afghanistan, the share of PGMs had risen to nearly 60 percent. In Gulf War II in Iraq, the ratio of PGMs went up to nearly 70 per cent. The Indian artillery does not have any PGMs worth the name. Only limited quantities of the Russian Krasnopol PGM have been imported for the Bofors 155 mm howitzer. Among others, the Bofors Bonus PGM is a suitable candidate, subject to successful trials in the deserts and the mountains.

Finally, the approach to army modernisation must be more focused; the priorities must be clearly established and then adhered to. The government must give a firm commitment in terms of funds and the Ministry of Defence must streamline its procedures and processes for speedy procurement of high priority weapons and equipment. It is time to institute a rolling, non-lapsable defence modernisation fund of Rs. 25,000 crores as a viable method of ensuring that defence procurement is not subjected to the vagaries of annual budgets.

The present situation is disturbing and, if allowed to go on indefinitely, will seriously compromise the army's preparedness to fight the next border war that inimical neighbours like Pakistan can be expected to thrust on India.

6

China's Military Rise and the Indian Challenge

The 19th Congress of Chinese Communist Party (CCP), arguably the most significant political event in China, marked the emergence of Chinese President Xi Jinping as an undisputed leader of China who asserted his authority and leadership in the party to the extent that he has become the first CCP leader to have his contribution attached to his name when Congress unanimously approved incorporation of Xi's ideological contribution into the Party Constitution as 'Xi Jinping's Thought on Socialism with Chinese Characteristics for a New Era'.

The content and the tenor of the address reaffirmed emphatically that China will continue to be more assertive in advancing its interest with an integrated 'soft and hard power approach'. As Xi charted for China a roadmap for the future, he did so by contextualising China's global standing at a time when America seems to have become more inward looking and the global balance of power is undergoing a dramatic transition. His address, though largely focussed on domestic gains and achievements, was also a manifesto for China where he attempted to integrate both normative and ideational components, which he summed as 'Chinese Dream', and the hard power to realise the goals he has set out for China. China's military modernisation and reforms are intrinsic to its goals of expanding its political and economic footprint across the globe, presenting a strategic challenge to India.

At the heart of Xi's vision for China's future was a two-stage plan he has put forward to achieve China's second centennial goal of becoming a "fully developed nation" by 2049 — the 100th anniversary of the founding of the People's Republic. The first stage — from 2020 to 2035 — aims at domestic transformation by realising the 'socialist modernisation'. The socialist modernisation, he has reiterated would be modelled on socialism with Chinese characteristics. The second stage — from 2035 to 2045 — aims for a more global agenda to become "a global leader in terms of comprehensive national power and international influence." This two-pronged vision, that sums up broadly as the 'Chinese Dream', was packaged as a panacea to all the Chinese problems, a remedy which can be exported by him to other parts of the world.

A critical feature of his address was the centrality of the role of CCP in its overall political system. He asserted that "the defining feature of socialism with Chinese characteristics is the leadership of the Communist Party of China; the greatest strength of the system of socialism with Chinese characteristics is the leadership of the Communist Party of China; the Party is the highest force for political leadership." In other words, he hinted that there will be no substantial political reforms and the nature of one-party political system will be more or less retained.

China's disapproval for 'western models of liberal democracy' is not new and Xi's address attested the disapproval. What was significant was the conscious attempt made by Xi to export what could be termed as the 'Chinese model of governance' to other developing countries. Moreover, it "offers Chinese wisdom and a Chinese approach to solving the problems facing mankind." The fact that China was not just confronting the 'West' on its own but now was ready to provide the 'Chinese alternative' came out emphatically from the address. This was a prominent ideational angle of China's 'international ambitions'.

Though Xi had attempted to project himself as a responsible leader and China as a responsible global by power participating in various multi-lateral forums, China under Xi has displayed periodic proclivity in confronting the established international rules and norms and existing security arrangement when it adversely affected its interest. China's rejection of the United Nations Convention on the Law of the Sea (UNCLOS) tribunal's ruling in the South China Sea was an excellent example of a belligerent China flouting international norms to suit its interest. This selective approval of international norms by China suggested that Beijing would respect the present order only to the extent that it suits its interests and would further re-order it that could satisfy its goal.

China's military modernisation was a significant highlight of Xi's address to the Congress as was the employment of hard power with the aim to realise domestic ideological goals initially, and then to further export it globally. Xi's emphasis on Chinese People's Liberation Army (PLA) and the military might, in his entire speech, unambiguously conveyed the significant role he attributed to the Chinese military. He announced that the PLA's focus will be on realisation of the 'Chinese Dream' for which it must develop "a new military strategy under the new situation" while national defence and military modernisation will be promoted. Xi assured that "by the end of the first stage in 2035, modernisation of our national defence and our forces will be basically completed"; and by the time the second stage comes to a full, China will be "fully transformed into a first-tier force." This ambitious build up plan is undoubtedly intended to make China a full military power, observing directly that the "military is built to fight" and that it should concentrate on "winning wars".

THE GEOPOLITICS OF CHINA'S MILITARISTIC RISE

China's rise has supported a decade of sustained growth in Asia, but also placed unprecedented stress on the global balance of power and security order. Beijing's modernisation of the PLA over the past two decades, coupled with its attempt to change the status quo in Asia's strategic fault lines, has brought China to the forefront of any discussion on India's ability to defend itself and its interests.

Notwithstanding its intentions, China's rapid rise and its growing military profile has suddenly transformed the threat matrix for India. China's economic transformation has given it the capability to emerge as a major military power. In 2017, Beijing's total defence budget for the year was $152 billion, up from $146 billion the previous year, an increase of 7 per cent. And this is when vital elements of the Chinese military build-up, including cyber warfare and space capabilities (as well as foreign procurement) were not included in the announced budget. The bulk of the increased defence spending will go to the Chinese Navy, Air Force and the Second Artillery Corps, which runs the strategic nuclear forces.

This unprecedented military rise of China has created a unique geopolitical situation for India. For the first time in its independent history, the emergence of a great military power at its immediate frontiers now appears imminent. Both during the times of British India and the Cold War, India remained relatively insulated from the security and foreign policy challenges of being a 'great power neighbour' because of its geography as well as the existence of territorial buffer zones. China's march towards being a great power and the ongoing transition of power in Asia has punctured that sense of relative security — unlike other great powers of the past New Delhi has encountered, China impinges directly on India's geopolitical landscape in multiple ways. The rise of China has only exacerbated its intensity.

First, the Sino-Indian border dispute continues to fester. India-China border dispute is not only the largest territorial dispute in Asia but is also one of longest running conflicts in the history of Post-World War II Asian politics. The two nations sharing a 2520-mile-long border are embroiled in a contest for over 47,000 sq mile of Himalayan territory. In October 1962, they fought a war across the Himalayan frontier in which India was comprehensively defeated. But even after 50 years of the border war, India and China have not been able to amicably resolve the dispute. Negotiations on the border dispute did begin in 1981 at vice-ministerial level and a total of eight rounds of bilateral meetings took place until 1987. In 1988, a Joint Working Group (JWG) was constituted to expedite the resolution of the conflict. By 2003, the JWG had met 14 times. In 2003, special representatives were appointed by the two governments "to explore from the political perspective of the overall bilateral relationship the framework of a boundary dispute." Fifteen rounds of talks have taken place between the special representatives so far. If, on one hand, there is an increasing feeling in India that negotiations have dragged for too long, frequent and strident Chinese claims about the Line of Actual Control in India's Northern sector of Ladakh and its North East have become a norm rather than an exception. The year 2017 was an exceptional year in India-China confrontation on the border as it suggested that not only the dispute is becoming intense but also expanding. The recent Doklam standoff represents the first confrontation between the two Asian giants in this area of the Himalayas since the clashes at Nathu La and Cho La in 1967. The Doklam standoff was unique, it revolved around territory disputed between China and Bhutan, and not China and India. The Indo-Sino border in this sector had been bereft of any major incidents and relatively quiet since the alignment of the Sino-Indian border in Sikkim is broadly accepted by both sides. But it now seems that the location of the disputed China-India-Bhutan trijunction border will likely remain a source of contention in the years ahead.

Second, the China-Pakistan 'axis' has always been a source of great consternation for New Delhi. This nexus between Islamabad and Beijing has only grown stronger in recent years. Not surprisingly, recent revelations about China's shift away from a three-decade-old cautious approach on Jammu and Kashmir, its increasing military presence in Pakistan, planning infrastructure linking Xinjiang and Gwadar, issuing stapled visas to residents of Jammu and Kashmir, and supplying nuclear reactors to Pakistan — all confirm a new intensity behind China's old strategy of using Pakistan to secure its interests in the region. The real concern for India however is the number of projects that China has undertaken in these areas; and that footprint is likely to increase much larger. Meanwhile, America's relative decline and the prospective withdrawal of forces from Afghanistan has only tightened the strategic embrace between these 'all-weather friends.' India's "strategic encirclement," which began in 1960s, only appears to be gaining momentum with China's rise. Billions of Chinese dollars now being invested in the China-Pakistan Economic Corridor (CPEC) suggest that this encirclement will continue to strengthen.

Third, strategic encirclement from the North has now been accompanied by a maritime encirclement. For the first five decades of India's independence, her geographical advantage in the Indian Ocean and its limited interests in the East facilitated her lackadaisical approach to maritime security in the Indo-Pacific region. China's forays into the Indian Ocean has left New Delhi concerned with the shifting maritime balance of power. In the last one decade, China has developed naval facilities in Myanmar, Sri Lanka and Pakistan; and is even planning to build naval infrastructure in Seychelles. Though the Indian National Security Advisor has tried to allay the fears engendered by the "string of pearls" theory, the Indian strategic community remains wary of China's ultimate intentions. Indian Navy is particularly alarmed by China's growing naval presence in the region. China's anti-piracy operations in Gulf of Aden and other out of area operations have also raised hackles in India. But the rivalry also extends to waters beyond Malacca. If for China, Indian Ocean is not an Indian lake, New Delhi's imperative is to contest impressions in Beijing that the waters east of Malacca automatically fall under latter's sphere of influence. India's naval engagement in the East, therefore, has also been a reaction to China's expansion in the Indian Ocean Region. The turf war between the two navies, as both nations further prosper and seek greater role in regional dynamics, is only set to grow.

Geopolitical frictions notwithstanding, Beijing is also extremely reluctant to accept India's rise in the international system and to accommodate India in global regimes and institutions as an equal. China remains the only major power in the world that refuses to discuss nuclear issues with India for fear that this might imply a de facto recognition of India's status as a nuclear power. It continues to insist on the sanctity of the UN resolution 1172, which calls for India (and Pakistan) to give up its nuclear weapons programme and join the Nuclear Non-Proliferation Treaty (NPT) as a non-nuclear weapon state. A large section of China's political and military elite views India's nuclear tests in 1998 not as an attempt by India to address its security concerns but rather an attempt by the US to contain China in so far as the US 'allowed' India to go nuclear. China's reluctance to accept New Delhi as a nuclear power was also evident in its efforts to scuttle the Indo-US nuclear deal at the Nuclear Suppliers Group (NSG) in 2008. Though, under American pressure, China hesitatingly agreed to the India-specific exemption at the NSG, it has in recent years repeatedly tried to sabotage India's efforts to join the multilateral grouping, which controls the global trade in nuclear material and technology. However, this is also reflective of China's long-held view against India's inclusion in the United Nations Security Council (UNSC). Except China, all other veto wielding P-5 nations have in principal accepted India's candidature as a permanent member of the UNSC. Beijing however has constantly tried to undermine this consensus by putting extraneous conditions on UNSC's expansion.

Therefore, managing China's rise is a security and foreign policy priority for India. However, the question of 'how should India manage China's rise' brooks no easy answers. The debates around this issue are highly variegated. More so because the current transition of power in Asia has presented India with stark choices, a situation which New Delhi's political elites have long wanted to avoid. That avoidance seems no longer possible as the military implications of China's rise are fast becoming apparent. The 73-day Doklam standoff between the militaries of India and China in 2017 brought this challenge into sharp relief. Understanding the change in Chinese military posture is now an imperative that can no longer be avoided.

CHINA'S MILITARY POWER

Given the atmosphere of suspicion and distrust that so often characterizes U.S.-China relations, it is vitally important that Chinese foreign policy and military capabilities be calmly and carefully assessed. Unfortunately, images of China as a potential threat tend to dominate in public discussions of China policy. Negative images of China stem in part from memories of the Tiananmen massacre that still loom large in the minds of most Americans.

The alleged spy scandals and accusations of theft of American nuclear secrets are also factors. China is widely seen as taking a hard line in its relations with the U.S. on such issues as human rights and arms sales. Although Chinese military capabilities have improved recently, these advances are modest, and China will remain a weak military power for a long time.

Despite the worst-case scenario painted by the Cox report two years ago, China remains a small nuclear power with only minor capabilities. There is no evidence that it has tested—let alone integrated—any stolen American technology into its nuclear forces. China has only about 20 Inter-Continental Ballistic Missiles (ICBMs)—each armed with only a single warhead—that can reach the continental United States, and its one nuclear-powered ballistic missile submarine has apparently been nonoperational for several years. In recent years China has purchased a variety of weapons systems from the Russians. Representing a significant improvement over most Chinese equipment, these weapons include advanced SU-27 fighters and SU-30 ground attack aircraft, S-300 SAM antiship missiles, Kilo-class submarines, and Sovremenny-class destroyers. China has also introduced new weapons systems of its own design, including tanks, short-range ballistic missiles, and the Song-class submarine.

China, however, continues to rely on outdated technology to equip most of its armed forces. The SU-27s and SU-30s are China's first fifth-generation, modernized combat aircraft. But most of the Chinese Air Force's combat aircraft are obsolete. China has about 30 SU-30s but relies on over 1,500 J-6 and Q-5 ground attack planes and some 700 J-7s. These designs date back to the early 1950s and 60s. Although older planes are being phased out, it will be more than a decade before China's Air Force reaches the current technological level of Taiwan's combat aircraft. The bulk of China's armored forces still features tanks based on Soviet designs from the 1950s. The Sovremenny-class destroyers are designed to attack American aircraft carriers and are far more advanced than anything else in the Chinese Navy. China has only two such destroyers, and the rest of its navy remains technologically backward. China is at least two decades away from being able to deploy a fully functional carrier with aircraft. The new Kilo and Song submarines are indeed a significant improvement for the Chinese Navy, but it will be years before China finishes replacing its older, less advanced submarines. Moreover, the Chinese armed forces continue to suffer from significant deficiencies in training and recruitment standards. The Chinese have yet to conduct a full-scale combined arms training exercise that would allow them to fully integrate the new weapons systems that they have acquired. Although worrisome, the 17.7% increase in China's 2001 defence budget is more of a political signal to the U.S. and Taiwan than an indication of substantially improving Chinese military capabilities.

Except for a brief skirmish with Vietnam over a disputed South China Sea islet in 1988, China has not resorted to the use of force since its disastrous attack on Vietnam in 1979. By and large, China has acted as a satisfied power, having increased economic ties with all its neighbours and negotiated border agreements with most neighboring countries. Only in the case of Taiwan is there a real danger of conflict. Beijing has been quite clear that it is willing to use force if Taiwan declares its independence. However, China lacks the amphibious assault capabilities it would need to land a sufficient force on Taiwan (where there are only a few, easily defended places to land troops). Taiwan's Air Force is far smaller but much more modern than China's. China could place a naval blockade on Taiwan or use its growing arsenal of missiles to try to coerce Taiwan into surrendering, but neither approach would guarantee success. Although China's M-9 and M-11 missiles look threatening, they lack the precision needed to knock out all of Taiwan's defenses, and China's submarine force is still in the early stages of modernization. A military and economic siege would take months to succeed. The cost to China itself would be immense, and the U.S. would have plenty of time to consider how to react. In sum, impressions of the Chinese threat are exaggerated, with respect to both China's capabilities and its intentions.

Problems with Current U.S. Policy

Key Problems

- Washington is moving away from its policy of deliberate ambiguity toward Taiwan's defenses. This limits future U.S. options and increases the possibility that the United States and China will stumble into a crisis.
- U.S. perceptions tend to exaggerate the extent of Chinese capabilities.
- U.S. policy on TMD and NMD has the potential to be destabilizing.

The main problem with current China policy is the growing tendency in the U.S. to overestimate Chinese military capabilities and China's potential threat to U.S. national security. Current plans to proceed with National Missile Defence (NMD) and Theatre Missile Defence (TMD) systems are largely based on this overestimation of the China threat. Given that NMD currently enjoys a fair amount of support on both sides of the aisle in Congress, it is likely to be implemented in some form. The Bush administration contends that the capabilities of NMD will be sufficient to provide protection from "rogue" states but modest enough to not threaten the Russians and Chinese. From the Chinese perspective, however, NMD represents a substantial threat to its national security. Chinese officials argue that Washington has greatly exaggerated the rogue state threat, and there is widespread suspicion that NMD's real objective is to neutralize China's nuclear deterrence capability.

Indeed, the proposed NMD system would be more than adequate to eliminate any deterrence credibility from China's meager ICBM force. This would leave China without any second-strike capability in the event of a confrontation with the United States.

If the U.S. proceeds with NMD, then China will likely decide to improve its own nuclear capabilities. One option for China would be to increase its arsenal of missiles in an attempt to overwhelm any missile defence the Americans build. China could also upgrade its missiles with multiple-entry warheads, thereby increasing the number of warheads aimed at the United States. It might even do both. However, any plan by China to increase the size or capability of its nuclear forces would likely also increase sentiment among U.S. policymakers that China is indeed a potential threat to America's security. Thus, the deployment of NMD could easily trigger a series of events that would trap the U.S. and China in a classic security dilemma of mutual misperceptions.

Extending a missile shield to Japan and Taiwan may also be destabilizing. Washington regards TMD as necessary in northeast Asia to defend Japan (and U.S. forces stationed there) against a North Korean missile threat. A TMD system could also help Taiwan resist a potential attack from China. (See Missile Defence and China by Wade Huntley and Robert Brown, FPIF, January 2001.) Beijing, which sees TMD as a threat to its territorial integrity, argues that such a system would encourage Taiwanese independence and otherwise foster the political separation of Taiwan from mainland China.

China's most obvious response would be to increase the number of its battlefield missiles, so it could overwhelm any Taiwanese missile defence system. Less obvious to many American observers is that China is also concerned about TMD in Japan. Within China's military, TMD is seen as a potential first step in the remilitarization of Japan. Far from creating greater stability in the region, TMD systems in East Asia may set off an arms race.

Arms sales to Taiwan also remain problematic. The Taiwan Relations Act (TRA) commits the U.S. to offer arms for Taiwan's self-defence. Over the past decade the U.S. has sold Taiwan 126 F-16s as well as Patriot antimissile systems, eight Knox-class frigates, seven Perry-class frigates, M-60A3 tanks, and electronic equipment. Combined with arms purchases from France, these sales have substantially improved Taiwan's defence capabilities. The Taiwanese government is currently seeking further arms purchases from the U.S., including four Aegis-class destroyers, designed to provide air defence for Taiwan's Navy. Other items reportedly on the list include submarine hunting aircraft, missiles, AIM-120 air-to-air missiles, ship-to-ship missiles, antiaircraft missiles, and submarines.

The Aegis-class destroyers have come to assume enormous symbolic value as a litmus test of the degree of U.S. political support for Taiwan. From both the Chinese and Taiwanese perspectives, any sale of Aegis destroyers would signal that the United States is moving closer to a de facto military alliance with Taiwan, rendering Washington a potential enemy in Beijing's eyes. Ironically, for all the controversy over the proposed sale, the Aegis is not necessarily the best military choice for Taiwan. These ships will do little to counter China's newer submarines, which represent Taiwan's primary threat. Taiwan would be better off buying antisubmarine weapons, which are also less politically offensive to Beijing.

Worst-case scenarios and ideological considerations are pushing the U.S. in the direction of providing Taiwan with more than is necessary for its defence. This creates a negative reaction in China and reinforces Beijing's perception of the U.S. as a potential enemy. China, in turn, is taking a more hard-line stance toward the U.S.—thereby confirming Washington's suspicions of Beijing.

Washington is also moving away from its traditional policy of deliberate ambiguity toward a more clear-cut commitment to Taiwan's defence in advance of any actual crisis. This limits future U.S. options and increases the possibility that the United States and China will stumble into a crisis that neither country wants or desires. This is especially worrisome in light of renewed congressional pressure to end or sharply curtail military exchanges between the U.S. and China. These exchanges have come under criticism, because they are perceived by some as rewarding China, despite its bad human rights record, and because the exchanges have not produced as many positive results as had been hoped. However, mutual misperceptions about military capabilities and intent are most likely to occur in the absence of communication. The April 2001 spy plane controversy, for example, was aggravated by a lack of trust on both sides. If the Bush administration decides to end the exchange program, there is a risk of fostering even greater mistrust between the two powers and increasing the chance of more dangerous incidents in the future.

CHANGING DOCTRINE AND CAPABILITIES OF CHINESE MILITARY

Since the 1990s, the PLA and its supporting air and naval arms have made impressive strides. Two events played a catalytic role in modernising the Chinese military of today — the first was the Persian Gulf War of 1990-91 and the second was the Taiwan Straits Crisis of 1995-1996. The first event is most pertinent for China's quest to acquire the strength and flexibility to execute combined arms warfare. A centralised military command structure for most of PLA's history was much too inflexible and unsuited for the conduct of future wars. This has undergone a significant shift since 2015 with the introduction military reforms by President Xi Jinping. In this regard, China has made good on the relative tranquillity it has enjoyed since late 1970s and developed a range of conventional capabilities. The consequence of this modernisation is greater assertiveness in regional disputes.

Massive military expenditures sustained by Chinese economy in the last 15 years have allowed the PLA a fair amount of defence modernisation, accumulating capabilities which are generally associated with the revolution in military affairs. Consequent doctrinal changes accompanied Chinese military thinking with its emphasis on "local wars under informationalisation." Elsa Kania argues in her chapter that the PLA has made a focussed attempt for the advancement of new forces and capabilities for information warfare. In particular, the restructuring and integration of Chinese space, cyber, electronic, and psychological warfare capabilities to create the Strategic Support Force. Additionally, the focus on mobility has allowed China to operationalise its military doctrine of "revitalised war zone strategy" in which her enormous reserves could be forced into action at very short intervals. This strategy is combined with doctrinal precept of "active defence", embodying pre-emptive military strikes with "superior concentration of firepower" in order to "destroy the opponent's retaliatory capability."

Alongside these doctrinal changes, the PLA is now going full steam ahead with technological force modernisation so that China can successfully pursue a military campaign that meets the demands of 21 century warfare. PLA's ground combat equipment has improved tremendously and it now fields a variety of capabilities. Richard A. Bitzinger's chapter covers the wide gamut of capabilities that the PLA has accrued over the years and its impact on Chinese assertiveness.

If the PLA has undergone massive transitions, the People's Liberation Army Air Force (PLAAF), too, has witnessed significant improvements in its capabilities through investments in tactical aviation. Changes in the PLAAF's fighter fleet have been evident since the 1990s. The Chinese Air Force started acquiring a small number of fourth-generation fighters in 1996. Since the mid-1990s, and for a decade and a half thereafter, the PLAAF's numbers swelled to 30 percent of the force. By 2015, the size increased to roughly 51 percent of the fighter fleet of the PLAAF and will grow further to 62 percent by the current year. An estimate notes that the Chinese fourth-generation fighter fleet increased from 383 to 736 jets between 2010 to 2015, representing a 92 percent jump in fighter air combat power. Today, China operates roughly 1,200 short-range fighters.

Operationally active in the PLAAF's fleet are approximately 400 J-7 fighters, a reasonably effective aircraft. Yet the J-7 fighter strength will decrease in numbers, replaced with more advanced fourth-generation jets. The PLAAF's current fleet strength stands at approximately 1977 aircraft. It is also driven to developing stealth capabilities for a segment of its fighter fleet, testing a number of J-20A operationally and undertaking flight tests of a second stealth type in the form of the J-31. Stealth technology will be core component in the transformation of the PLAAF from a predominantly territorial airforce to one conducting both defensive and offensive operations. The induction of the J-20 A will present a fundamentally different threat compared to the Russian Sukhoi 27/30 derivates that form the mainstay of Chinese airpower. While the size of the Chinese Air Force is important, the strength of the PLAAF lies in its establishment of a dense air defence network. Defending Indian airspace from any future PLAAF challenge with the proliferation of aircraft like the J-20A, presents a challenge the Indian Air Force (IAF) has few answers to numerically or in terms of capability. The PLAAF has the first mover advantage over the IAF, according to Arjun Subramaniam, with its superior space and information warfare assets coupled with its standoff weapons capability and superior multi-layered air defence systems.

Similarly, China's growing naval capability has resulted in an impression that Beijing not only seeks primacy in near seas but naval dominance in far flung areas. The naval expansion of the PLA continues apace through its Anti-access and Area Denial (AAAD) capabilities. The Chinese navy has made progress in both the surface and subsurface segment of its fleet. The People's Liberation Army Navy (PLAN) has procured 12 Russian-made Kilo Class conventional submarines since the mid-1990s, and added four indigenously developed submarines. These include a Jin Class 'Type 094' nuclear-powered ballistic missile submarine (SSBN) and a new Shang Class 'Type 093/

093' nuclear attack submarine (SSN). The latest addition to the PLAN is the SSN classified Song Class 'Type 039/039G'. Each of the Jin Class submarines will be equipped with 7,400-kilometre range JL-2 nuclear-armed submarine launched ballistic missiles (SLBMs). Significantly, advances in the submarine arm of the Chinese are a by-product of Russian designs. The Chinese navy's surface fleet has also witnessed improvements. The latest addition is the first Chinese aircraft carrier *Liaoning* 'Type 001' design vessel to the PLAN's surface fleet. It is a conventionally powered carrier with a displacement of approximately 60,000 tonnes. A second carrier, the *Shandong,* is under construction and a third carrier is planned. The air wing of the *Liaoning* could potentially consist of a combination of 36 fixed and rotary wing aircraft, including 24 J-15 fighters, six anti-submarine warfare helicopters, four airborne early warning helicopters, and two rescue choppers. China expects to induct four to six aircraft carriers. The current and follow-on *Shandong* carrier might be limited by operating range, though not so, if reports are to be believed. The PLAN's long-term ambitions include the acquisition of nuclear-powered carriers, resulting in two carrier strike groups operating in the Western Pacific and an additional two groups in the Indian Ocean. The potential Chinese nuclear-powered carriers will inevitably use electromagnetic catapult systems for the launch of carrier-based fighter aircraft. Notwithstanding an absence of experience in operating carriers, the PLAN's introduction of aircraft carriers provides additional weight to the Chinese navy's surface warfare and force projection capabilities. The Indian Navy, on the other hand, is floundering according to RADM (Retd.) Sudarshan Shrikhande, with its limited resources being squandered on 'symbolic aircraft carriers' and placing ship building orders for specious reasons like keeping yards, which alone do not make a strong argument for poor platform choices or the lack of anti-submarine helicopters.

China's military modernisation has also resulted in the proliferation of military technology in the region, enhancing the military capabilities of a number of states, including

Pakistan. Pakistan's indigenous Unmanned Aerial Vehicle, the 'Shahpar', bears a striking resemblance to the Chinese CASC CH-3. The co-development and production of the JF-17 in significant numbers for the Pakistani Airforce has a cascading effect on India's conventional deterrence.

IMPLICATIONS FOR INDIA

India's loss in the 1962 war against China had for the first time exposed serious deficiencies in post-independent India's defence posture and capabilities. As a result, New Delhi made a sustained effort to build its defence forces. Much of the focus went to the Army and the Air Force, as New Delhi realised the "reality of having to make defensive arrangements along a vast frontier."

By late 1963, a new defence plan was formulated and India decided to increase its defence expenditures from 2 percent of GDP to about 5 percent. Under this defence plan, 10 mountain divisions were raised along the Himalayan frontier.

India also upgraded its Air Force by procuring MIG fighters from the Soviet Union and advanced radar systems from the US. Long neglected, the Indian Navy finally started receiving some attention but its role in any conflict with China was considered miniscule.

For long afterwards, India's approach was to ensure that a repeat of 1962 could be avoided by putting up a resolute defence against any aggression from the Chinese forces. Defending the mountain passes in the border was the sole focus. As an inadvertent result of India's wars with Pakistan in 1965 and 1971 and consequent military modernisation of its defence forces, India's deterrent capability vis-à-vis China automatically increased.

By mid-1970's, India assessments of Chinese threat was reduced to Beijing's support for insurgencies in India's Northeast and military equipment to Pakistan. If India's military modernisation had created a deterrent, infirmities in China's military capability became quite evident during its war with

Vietnam in 1979. By early 1980s, analysts predicted that the Indian Army was enjoying an "advantageous" position against China to the extent that it could make "incisive thrusts into Tibet across the Chinese borders in the North." Chinese threat in the Indian Ocean was also miniscule. China's limited naval capability ruled out any sustained involvement in the Indian Ocean. India's naval attitude was also largely defensive. India's naval strategy towards the end of the Cold War was essentially one of creating a *"cordan sanitaire"* around India's waters.

Such defensive strategy however is now under serious question, especially with the modernisation in Chinese military. In the last one decade, there has been a growing realisation in the Indian military establishment that on the face of growing Chinese military power, a defensive strategy will not survive. All the three services therefore have adopted certain offensive components in their war-fighting strategies. The Indian Army, with the development of two mountain strike corps, now intends not only to withhold any Chinese conventional thrust but also to take the offensive into the Chinese territory.

Brig. Arun Sahgal's contribution in this primer however brings to fore the Chinese challenge in the Tibet Autonomous Region and limitations of the Indian Army offensive aspirations.

The Indian Air Force similarly has now placed its most advanced air assets along the Line of Actual Control (LAC). The Navy, on the other hand, has been arguing for economic strangulation of the Chinese economy by attacking China's sea lines of communication in the Indian Ocean, in case of hostilities along the land frontier.

Lt. Gen (Retd.) Narasihman argues that the three services operational and strategic deficiencies originate from an incoherent grand strategy and any offensive makeover remains uncoordinated at the highest levels. First, the lack of progress in adopting a capability-based approach versus the existing threat-based approach reflects the determination of bureaucratic interests in the individuals service branches to preserve their own interests, rather than maximise combat performance efficiency. Any integrated war fighting capability is dependent on individual services maintaining capabilities in their core competencies. All three services currently continue to operate in silos with number-based calculations versus capability-based approaches is a reflection of bureaucratic interests in the individuals service branches to preserve their own interests, rather than maximise combat performance efficiency. Given the constant referencing by the armed forces of the two-front war scenario against Pakistan and China, maximising the combat potential of limited assets available due to limited logistical availability or delays in modernisation will help services fill capability gaps. An ongoing research at the Observer Research Foundation based on quantitatively examined time-series data constructed from ten IISS *Military Balance* volumes from 2008-2017, depicts a depressing force ratios heavily in favour of the adversary, in this case China and of course Pakistan. Figures are reflective of China's spend of 3.2 times more than India on defence.

Even when the Indian defence establishment recognises the need to counter PLA modernisation and adopt the operational concepts of "informationised warfare", which has become the PLA's key operational concepts, there exists a broader ambivalence regarding force integration among the three Indian services. There is little evidence to suggest that any of the three services have adopted a capability-based approach versus the previous threat-based approach. The Indian Army is still in the process of raising the Mountain Strike Corps to further add manpower to its standing strength of 1.18 million men. The Indian Air Force continues to press for 42-45 fighter squadrons to deter a two-front war while the Indian Navy wants to eventually operate 200 ships, including three aircraft carrier groups. Although there are plausible reasons for each of these demands individually, there is little to align these goals with a broader strategy shared among the three services. Arzan Tarapore's chapter covers the doctrinal concept known as Multi-Domain Battle (MDB) designed to evolve the concept of joint war fighting, by more deeply integrating operations in the three traditional domains of battle — land, sea, and air — alongside the two, and by analysing how the Indian armed forces are far away from adopting the concept of jointness and how other increasingly essential domains of cyber and space remain missing.

And finally, do nuclear weapons have a role in the Sino-Indian dyad? S. Paul Kapur and Diana Wueger argue that nuclear option provides India an import measure of insulation and protection against an increasingly coercive China.

The aim of this primer is to assess India's current military's effectiveness and combat potential vis-a-vis China. While there are no easy answers or simple formulas for the assessment of Indian military effectiveness, it is vital to understand how the changing capabilities, doctrines and tactics of the Chinese military impacts the effectiveness of India's conventional military deterrent. Given that China is unlikely to shift strategies away from relying on coercion and manipulating risk to achieve its territorial objectives, observing its military modernisation and development of power projection capabilities will influence the trajectory that characterises the Indian defence establishment's strategy to counter the kinetic and geographic components of China's growing capabilities. China's lack of any combat experience for more than 30 years and or experience in conducting joint operation in 'far seas' or on land will remain a short-term advantage Indian military develops effective counters against.

India's military effectiveness must be located at all the three levels of military activity: the strategic, the operational and the tactical. While overlapping, each is characterised by different actions, procedures and goals. This primer emphasises the operational approach, underlining the importance of doctrines, tactics, combined arms, inter-service systems and their proper utilisation on the battlefield, and makes a break from the narrative of observing capabilities centred on new military hardware as it is introduced in-service. If this primer succeeds in generating an honest debate on the military challenge China poses to India, it would have served its purpose.

CHINA'S MILITARY MODERNIZATION: IMPLICATIONS FOR THE REGION

China has been steadily building up its strategic and conventional capabilities since the 1990s. Eighteen years ago, experts say, China had a "bare-bones" military: basic capabilities, but nothing sophisticated or top-of-the-line. But two decades of double-digit spending increases have changed that picture. China says its 2008 defence budget is $61 billion, though the Pentagon has historically challenged Beijing's reported figures.

In its annual report to Congress, the U.S. Defence Department estimated China's total military-related spending for 2007 was between $97 billion and $139 billion, as compared to $52 billion reported by China.

All that spending has gone to building a sophisticated, modern military: a large, increasingly capable submarine fleet, an air force stocked with Russian warplanes, and technical strides which have improved China's ballistic missile arsenal, as well as satellite surveillance, radar, and interception capabilities. China continues to stress that its military modernization is in line with its peaceful rise in the world.

Its latest White Paper on national defence emphasizes it will never seek hegemony or engage in military expansionism. However, this has not alleviated concerns among its neighbours and regional rivals, say experts. A CFR Independent Task Force report (PDF) in 2007 on U.S.-China relations noted that many of China's neighbours and potential adversaries were making adjustments to their own defence plans and expenditures to balance China's growing military capabilities.

Japan

Japan and China compete over a host of issues, from regional security to international trade to access to energy. The two countries have a centuries-old history of conflict, including two Sino-Japanese wars that began in 1894 and 1931, and a bloody Japanese occupation of China during World War II. As this Backgrounder points out these animosities surface in recurring cycles, often involving Chinese anger over Japan's perceived lack of contrition for wartime crimes. But concrete territorial and economic issues also aggravate the relationship, including Japan's close alliance with the United States, trade frictions, and ongoing disputes over ownership of various islands in the East China Sea.

In 2007, China and Japan ranked third and fifth respectively in national defence expenditures (PBS), both spending only a small fraction of the U.S. budget even after adjusting for gross underreporting by Beijing. China's military modernization fuels Japanese fears that China will use its growing economic leverage and military prowess to throw its weight around and dominate the region. Tanaka Akihiko of the University of Tokyo, speaking at a December 2008 CFR symposium on U.S.-Japan relations said China's growing military forces might change the balance of power in East Asia, which "would necessitate for Japan and the United States to readjust its force structure and other military management."

Japan has significantly upgraded capabilities over the past 15 years, deploying the Aegis radar and accompanying missile systems for its navy and warplanes armed with advanced air-to-air missiles for its air force. Since 1998, when a North Korean missile test violated Japanese airspace, Toyko has been working in partnership with the United States to develop theater missile defences which have obvious application in the event of any conflict with China.

Over the past decade the U.S.-Japanese security alliance has been strengthened through revised defence guidelines, which expand Japan's noncombatant role in a regional contingency, allows for the deployment of an X-Band radar system in Japan as part of a missile defence system, expands bilateral cooperation in training and intelligence sharing, and allows a nuclear-powered U.S. aircraft carrier in the Yokosuka Naval Base. In September 2007 Japan joined a multinational naval exercise with the United States, Australia, Singapore, and India in the area west of the Malacca Straits.

The exercise reinforced the U.S.-led campaign of strengthening security ties among its democratic allies and "the strategic countering (PDF) of Chinese military power," argues a December 2008 U.S. Congressional Research Service report. In 2005, a joint statement by U.S.-Japan Security Consultative Committee 2005 for the first time included Taiwan as a common strategic objective where the parties would "encourage the peaceful resolution of issues" through dialogue.

Though Japan's foreign affairs ministry said this did not change the country's position on Taiwan, many experts believe the shift indicates that Japan is increasingly concerned with China's growing military capabilities.

Taiwan

It is the main driver for China's militarization drive and biggest concern for the United States as this Backgrounder points out. Taiwan is also pursuing modernization goals which include procurement of army attack helicopters, army utility helicopters, PAC-3 missile defence systems, fighter jets, and diesel-electric submarines, as well as transformation of the military. Relations between China and Taiwan have improved dramatically under the administration of President Ma Ying-jeou, although U.S. arms sales to Taiwan remains contentious. In its white paper on national defence, China says the United States continues to sell arms to Taiwan "causing serious harm to Sino-US relations as well as peace and stability across the Taiwan Strait." In October 2008, Beijing suspended military contacts with the United States in protest of the U.S. decision to sell $6.4 billion in defence equipment and services to Taiwan.

South Korea

It has undertaken a major modernization drive, replacing antiquated fighter aircraft, frigates, tanks, and artillery pieces with advanced systems, many of them purchased from the United States or developed in partnership with U.S. defence industries, notes the 2007 CFR report (PDF). However, most experts say South Korea's military initiatives are more in response to a possible conflict with a nuclear North Korea.A thorough look at the status of South Korea's military is contained in CFR's Crisis Guide: The Korean Peninsula.

Russia

The country is China's largest supplier of advanced military hardware as well as a potential great power rival. Moscow experienced a significant decline in its overall military capabilities during the 1990s, but buoyed by strong oil revenues in the past decade, it has been increasing its defence expenditure, in what most experts see as a sign to counter U.S. influence in the region. The 2009 defence budget was about $50 billion, a 25.7 percent increase from previous year. Fedor Lukyanov, chief editor of *Russia in Global Affairs,* told a January 2009 CFR meeting that there are limits to Russian military cooperation and arms sales to China. "We sold everything we could without making damage to Russian security," he said. CFR's Senior Fellow on Russian and Eurasian Studies, Stephen Sestanovich says Russia's relationship with China is based on the interests of some elites—those in the energy sector, the nuclear power sector, and the arms exports, that see China as an important market.

China and Russia also formed a security alliance to solve border disputes, which has grown into an important regional organization, the Shanghai Cooperation Organization (SCO), and includes Central Asian countries Kazakhstan, Kyrgyzstan, Tajikistan, and Uzbekistan. China and Russia have held a number of joint military exercises under the SCO. In October 2007, the SCO also signed a memorandum of understanding with the Collective Security Treaty Organization, a military alliance of several former Soviet states. Some analysts see the SCO as a vehicle for Russia and China to curb U.S. access to the region's vast energy supplies. But others say Russia and China have very different objectives in Central Asia. Russia wants to reassert its regional leadership there, while China seeks energy ties, note some analysts. In 2008, China and Russia resolved (BBC) their last remaining border dispute involving islands in the eastern part of the border which had seen armed clashes between the two sides during the Cold War.

Southeast Asia

Experts say Southeast Asian countries, including Indonesia, the Philippines, and Thailand, are currently calculating whether the political and economic benefits of closer ties with a strong China outweigh the military risks. Bilateral trade between China and all ten countries within the Association of Southeast Asian Nations (ASEAN) exceeded $200 billion in 2008 up from $ 190 billion in 2007.

The region is now China's fourth-largest trading partner. Despite the economic windfall, ASEAN countries want the United States to pay more attention to the new security trends in the region, experts say. While these countries are not very vocal about their fears, experts say they are nervously looking over their shoulders at China's military buildup and wondering where it's headed. Border disputes with some countries also complicate China's relations with its Southeast Asian neighbours. Vietnam and China each assert claims to the Spratly and Paracel Islands, archipelagos in a potentially oil-rich area of the South China Sea. Malaysia, the Philippines, and Taiwan also claim all or part of the South China Sea.

China's assertion of "indisputable sovereignty" over the Spratly Islands and the entire South China Sea has elicited concern from Vietnam and its Southeast Asia neighbours, according to the U.S. State Department. Vietnam has been pursuing closer military relations with the United States through joint military exercises, and sharing intelligence on terrorism, drugs, and other transnational threats. Vietnam has also hosted U.S. warships at its ports.

India

It has long-time rivalry with China over disputed borders and these two Asian giants also fought a war in 1962. New Delhi watches Beijing's military buildup closely and has undertaken military reforms of its own. It is currently building a nuclear submarine and is trying to acquire two more aircraft carriers in addition to the one it possesses.

It also launched its first unmanned moon mission in October 2008, another step in what many analysts see as a race with China in space. It has also been expanding its military cooperation with the United States. In June 2005, New Delhi and Washington agreed on a new framework for their defence relationship, including increases in defence trade, technology transfers, and joint exercises for the next ten years.

China's close military cooperation with Pakistan also concerns New Delhi. Each country helps the other to check India's power, say experts. China remains a key supplier of arms to Pakistan and in 2008, agreed to help Pakistan build two nuclear power plants.

China also supplies Pakistan with nuclear technology and assistance, including what many experts suspect was the blueprint for Pakistan's nuclear bomb. Pakistan's army has both short-and medium-range ballistic missiles that experts say came from China. According to Thomas C. Reed, a former U.S. Air Force secretary, China probably helped Pakistan test a nuclear weapon inside China in 1990. Reed adds that this weapon was most likely based on a Chinese design.

Central Asia

Several Central Asian countries— Kazakhstan, Kyrgyzstan, Tajikistan, and Uzbekistan —have forged closer relations with China as part of the Shanghai Cooperation Organization. Experts say tensions in China's western province of Xinjiang is one of the major reasons behind Beijing's eagerness to improve relations with the Central Asian states.

Xinjiang is largely made up of Uighurs, predominantly a Muslim community with ties to Central Asia, and China has been concerned that Central Asian states may back a separatist movement in Xinjiang.

Beijing also seeks energy ties in the region. Under the SCO, the countries conduct joint military exercises. Problems with their own Muslim fundamentalist groups have led these countries to assist China in its struggle against separatists from Xinjiang, say experts. However, some experts say the Central Asian states still view China and Russia as possible hegemonic powers.

'RISING CHINA' POSE A THREAT TO INTERNATIONAL SECURITY

The collapse of the Soviet Union in 1991 marked the conclusion of a bipolar political order that had defined the world since 1945. In its place emerged a global framework, largely characterised by the hegemonic ascendance of the United States of America (U.S.). The primacy of the U.S. in this unipolar system has led theorists such as Waltz to claim, 'never since Rome has one country so nearly dominated its world' (2002: 350). Assertions such as this, however, have been problematised by the rapid rise of China as a global power. Increasingly, contemporary China is being re-conceptualised as a realistic economic, political and military counterbalance to U.S. hegemony. For much of the world, this perception has led to growing anxiety that the rise of China poses a significant threat to international security. This essay, however, will dispute this claim, arguing that China's potential as a threat to international security is consistently exaggerated and a relatively benign rise is entirely possible. This will be done by first establishing the ways in which the current rise of China is viewed as a threat to international security by many states and individuals. The inevitability of China 'rising' to achieve hegemon status will next be critiqued, as well as current perceptions regarding emerging Chinese foreign policy. Next, the importance of China's economic integration with the rest of the world will be highlighted. Lastly, the likelihood of a more powerful China leading to regional insecurity, particularly surrounding relations with Taiwan, will be examined.

For numerous states, the sustained military, political and economic ascension of China is increasingly viewed as a likely threat to international security. The rapid pace in which China has managed its societal transformation is arguably without historical comparison. China's subsequent increase in military spending, as well as its commitment to modernising its military capabilities, is cited by many, including the U.S., as clear evidence of its growing potential to threaten international security. This concern was evident in the 2006 Quadrennial Defence Review, which cited China, of all major and emerging powers, as having the 'greatest potential to compete militarily' with the U.S. and highlighted China's ability to field military technology 'that could over time offset traditional U.S. military advantages' (2006: 29). As well as China's general military capacity, the U.S. has grown increasingly concerned over Chinese nuclear ambitions. This was highlighted in the 2010 Nuclear Posture Review Report (NPRR) which cited China's 'qualitative and quantitative modernisation' of its nuclear arsenal, as well as its relative lack of transparency, as significant factors in growing regional and international anxiety (U.S. Department of Defence 2010: V). China's strengthening military, coupled with a perceived increase in regional antagonism, has generated additional concern for international security. Regarding Chinese regional aspirations, it is the claim of many that China ultimately wished to assert a "Monroe Doctrine", throughout East Asia, excluding non-regional powers (Bowring 2010: 2). Given the continued U.S. involvement in much of East Asia, if this assessment proves accurate, the ramifications for international security would indeed be severe.

As well as China's military advancements, its economic growth has continued at an unrivalled pace. The meteoric ascent of China's economy over the last twenty-five years has transformed regional and international power dynamics (Blij 2005: 129). This very phenomena, however, has been cited as a likely cause of future international insecurity. Realists such as Mearsheimer argue that if the rapid economic growth of China continues over the coming decades, an intense security competition between the U.S. and China is likely to result, with a significant potential for war (2006:160). In order to more accurately assess China's capability to disrupt international security, a more reasoned analysis of China's current and potential strength as a state must be undertaken.

Threats to international security generated by China's challenge to U.S. hegemony must be viewed more soberly, particularly given the uncertainty of China's 'rise'. While China's economic growth and surge in GDP has been dramatic, its long-term continuation has been challenged by some. One study suggests that by 2015, the odds of China experiencing a significant slowdown in GDP growth rates were over 70% (The Economist 2011: 2). This makes assertions on the inevitability of war, generated by an economic rivalry between the U.S. and China, increasingly problematic.

Additionally, while China has indeed experienced an unprecedented surge in national GDP, wealth disparity continues to impede the state's development. The decision of Chinese leadership to identify inequality as one of the greatest political challenges currently facing its society (Klein 2008: 07:33), clearly demonstrates the continued uncertainty surrounding China's rise. Similarly, growing anxiety surrounding China's military spending must also be properly contextualised, particularly given the continued dominance of the U.S. military.

In 2009 the U.S. military spent over USD $738 billion, whereas estimates of China's annual military budget range from USD $69.5 billion to USD $150 billion (Thomson 2010: 87). Additionally, China's potential nuclear threat, while growing, is still comparatively small and vulnerable when viewed alongside that of the U.S. China's nuclear stockpile is currently between a tenth and a hundredth the size of the U.S. arsenal (Glaser 2011: 91). These figures suggest that, despite China's military modernisation attempts, any military exchange between the two states would be hugely asymmetrical. The continued pre-eminence of the U.S. military will be a significant factor in the potential of a growing China to disrupt international security. China, fully aware that an increase in bellicosity can be challenged by the U.S., with overwhelming force, will attempt a peaceful transition to great power status. This is further apparent through an examination of China's current foreign policy.

An analysis of China's foreign policy suggests that its growth in power and influence will present a minimal threat to international security. Among those who claim that a rising China constitutes a significant risk to international stability, comparisons are often drawn between current U.S./China friction and the Cold-War relationship between the U.S. and the U.S.S.R. This, however is misleading. The Cold-War was essentially a conflict of incompatible ideologies. While the capitalist U.S. model advocated individual freedoms, the free market, and political and civil rights; communism sought to promote class equality and an emancipation of the working class (Brady and Said 1993: 591). Crucially, both models were expansionist in nature, ensuring tensions between the two superpowers would escalate in the post-WWII years. This ensuing conflict would play a dominant role in world politics, with both superpowers transforming global security into a zero-sum game (Bisley 2007: 233). The relationship between contemporary China and the U.S. is vastly different, with a far greater likelihood of non-zero-sum solutions arising to emerging problems. Jisi argues that China currently has little interest in transforming itself into a hegemon, viewing its core interests as security, sovereignty, and development, as well as the elevation of its people's living standards (2011: 5).

This challenges the assertions of offensive realists, who claim that achieving hegemon status within the global system is a state's ultimate goal (Mearscheimer 2001, cited in Snyder 2002:152). Concern over the rise of China often stems from fears that an increase in parity between China and the U.S. will trigger an accelerated security dilemma between the two states. Hertz contends that the security dilemma is an unavoidable condition that results from the anarchical nature of the international system, whereby the defensive security measures of a state can cause a perception of hostile intent by other states (1950, cited in Burke 2007: 148). This can lead to a military build-up in response, resulting in an overall loss of security and increase in anxiety for all states. Given China's primarily domestic focus, as opposed to the expansionist grand strategy of the Soviet Union, predictions of international insecurity resulting from an emerging security dilemma seems exaggerated. This is made further apparent with an examination of the economic interconnectedness that exists between China and the rest of the world.

The continued economic benefits of a rising China for the rest of the world, will largely mitigate any potential threat it poses to international security. A key determinant in the likelihood of international hostilities resulting from a growth in China's status, is China's current position in the world economy. Unlike the rise of the Soviet Union, which was characterised by confrontation and autarky, China has opted for global integration through its own form of capitalism (Jacques 2005: 1). China's entry into global economic institutions, such as the World Trade Organisation (WTO), represents an encouraging development in international security. Liberal theory suggests that the creation of institutions and regimes, such as the WTO, are crucial in blunting the more destructive features of international anarchy and ensuring the prevention of the security dilemma (Booth and Wheeler 2008: 139), which as previously established, is a crucial component in the increase of international insecurity. The economic inter-dependence that exists between China and the rest of the world has hugely increased the potential costs of war, while decreasing its probable gains. This is apparent by observing growing trade between China and other states. Between 2000 and 2005, Chinese imports from the U.S. climbed from USD$16 billion to USD$42 billion, while Chinese exports to the U.S. rose from USD$100 billion to USD$243 billion (Hufbaur, Wong and Sheth 2006: 4). As well as the U.S., China has economically integrated itself with large areas of the globe. States that have recently forged closer bonds with China include Australia, which currently experiences unprecedented and growing economic ties with the rising power (Taylor 2005: 193), and the European Union (EU), which has considered lifting its twenty year arms embargo of China in the hopes of guaranteeing more lucrative trade deals (Cendrowicz 2010: 2). Despite global economic integration contributing to a more benign rise of China, some fear that China's demand for resources may trigger conflict with other great powers. Bijan suggests that this is unlikely, as China, through efficiency, alternative energies, and conservation, hopes to develop non-zero sum measures to transcend resource scarcity (2005: 22). Even if this is possible, however, many contend that the true threat to international security lies in China's dealings with other regional powers.

Despite alarmist claims to the contrary, the growth of China is unlikely to jeopardise the security of other regional states. When describing the rise of continental powers, Napoleon famously said, 'the policies of such states are inherent in their geography' (cited in Kaplan 2010: 23). This is certainly true regarding the rise of contemporary China. Whatever China's true regional ambitions are, an observation of the East Asian alliance system indicates the improbability of a Chinese "Monroe Doctrine" in the near future. With direct economic and political contestation from both India and Japan, both key allies to the U.S. (Power 2006: 32), any attempt to supplant the U.S. as a regional hegemon, seems increasingly unlikely. Nye states that a more probable scenario for East Asia is one in which the U.S., Japan, Australia, India, and others, from a position of strength, engage China and incentivise it to engage more responsibly with the regional community. By again contrasting the rise of China with that of the Soviet Union, likely regional developments are better able to be ascertained. While the Soviet Union was believed to be a 'highly revisionist state bent on radically overturning the status quo' (Glaser 2011: 85), virtually no evidence suggests China shares these qualities. This highlights the reasonable probability of avoiding war within East Asia, as China continues to rise.

Finally, the maintenance of the regional status quo seems increasingly likely, given the direct advantage to China of a significant U.S. naval presence in East Asia. Strategic analyst Khalid R. Al-Rodhan argues that the U.S. naval dominance of

East Asia serves China strategically by providing security against terrorism and smuggling, maintaining the balance of power by preventing Japanese militarisation, and contributing to general stability (2007: 52). The fact that the U.S. East Asian naval presence allows China to better focus on domestic matters, strongly suggests that peace can be maintained regionally, as China continues to strengthen. Despite these positive developments, virtual unanimity can be found among those concerned with China's rise, when focus is placed on the volatility that exists between China and Taiwan.

Despite the severe risk to international security presented by China and Taiwan's fractious relationship, the chances of a peaceful resolution are greater than the alternative of war. Tensions between China and Taiwan, resulting from Taiwan's uncertain international status, have been regularly identified as having the potential to cause massive international instability, and until this point have been dealt with by a combination of legal manipulation, complex diplomacy and a detachment from political realities (DeLisle 2000: 35).

Despite the situation's current failure to escalate into internecine conflict, fears are growing that the rapid rise of China may manifest into revisionism of Taiwan's status, triggering hostilities. Given its potential to entangle the U.S. and China in large scale war, the Taiwan Strait is viewed by many as one of the most dangerous areas on Earth. (Mandelbaum 1998/99: 31). Some contend, however, that while potentially grave, the Taiwan situation shows signs of stability.

Johnston identifies potential processes between China and Taiwan such as noncooperation and conflictual actions, as well as an escalation of 'malign reciprocation' (2003: 50), as indicators of an emerging security dilemma. The failure of this situation to so far occur should be grounds for guarded optimism. Currently the vast majority of Taiwanese citizens favour either unification with the Chinese mainland, or maintenance of the present status-quo (Chang and Wang 2005: 42).

This, combined with an improvement in cross-straight relations and institutional cooperation since the 2008 electoral victory of the Kuomintang Party in Taiwan (Bitzinger and Desker 2008: pg106), should provide additional hope among proponents of peace. Lastly, given that Taiwan's naval power is still technologically superior to China's, it is predicted that even without direct U.S. assistance, were diplomacy to collapse, China would be unable to invade Taiwan for at least ten years, *if not considerably longer* (O'Hanlon 2000: 53, my emphasis). These factors, when viewed in concert, suggest a high probability for future peaceful negotiations of the Taiwan situation, despite the strengthening of China.

This essay has sought to challenge the claim that a rising China poses a significant threat to international security. The relatively sudden propulsion of China to great power status, through the exponential growth of both its military and economy, has generated considerable anxiety among numerous states.

Some contend that as China grows, its contestation with the U.S. for hegemon status may escalate into large-scale warfare. These concerns, however, seem less credible when a realistic comparison of China and the U.S. is undertaken. While the accelerated growth of China's GDP is indeed enviable, current problems concerning its wealth disparity has the potential to cripple further developments.

Additionally, while China and the U.S. are approaching overall economic parity, a huge military asymmetry remains. This will almost certainly inhibit more severe forms of bellicosity from China as it continues to strengthen. Those who fear an emerging Cold War between the U.S. and China consistently fail to comprehend how vastly different the structure of the Chinese state is to that of the former Soviet Union.

While the U.S.S.R was largely defined by its confrontational foreign policy and economic isolationism, contemporary China presents an inversion of this grand strategy. By prioritising domestic issues over expansionist foreign policy, as well as a direct economic engagement with the global community, China has forged strong and lasting financial links with other powerful states, which should prevent an escalation of any emerging hostilities.

Despite continued concerns over China's regional ambitions, the strength of the U.S.'s alliance system within East Asia, seems likely to pressure China's acceptance of the regional status-quo for some time to come. Lastly, given the potential for a rapid and irreversible acceleration into a large-scale conflict, the situation involving Taiwan's status does constitute a credible threat to international security.

However, given the apparent lack of will from either China, Taiwan, or the U.S. to disrupt the political equilibrium, coupled with indicators that suggest China is not seeking overall regional revisionism, the risk to international security seems manageable. While uncertainties regarding the future of China are legion, the peaceful integration into the international order of a strengthening and influential China is entirely possible. Through interaction and increased inter-dependence, the peaceful rise of China can be assured.

7

Strategy for Weapons and Equipment Development in India and China

The weapons development strategy is dictated by the realpolitik of politics, economics, national defense and science and technology. These situations suggest comprehensive ideas for the development of weapons. Weapons development hinges between the needs of combat and military construction, and what is possible economically and in science and technology. At the same time it is also determined by a country's political system, its national defense strategic policies, and its fundamental appraisal of the international condition. Thus, different countries have different weapons development strategies.

China is a socialist country and a part of the Third World. This is the political basis from which China formulates its national defense development strategy. China espouses a foreign policy of independence and self-determination.

It is against all expansionism and aggression. It supports all struggles and movements for justice. China, together with the rest of the Third World, is a major force for the preservation of world peace. This demands that China have the necessary military strength and an appropriate weapons development program to defend itself against outside aggression.

It also demands that it have the ability to completely protect its territory and rights, to protect its country's unity, legitimate rights, interests and self-respect, to prevent the breakout of world wars and to protect world peace. China is a country that is still economically, scientifically, and technologically undeveloped. This in itself imposes a limit on the amount of money it can possibly commit to weapons development and makes it even more impossible for it to be involved in an arms race. Thus, the development of China's weaponry must be based on the needs of national defense and military construction and economic strength, the level of potential in construction and its economic strength, the level of potential in the development of its science and technology, and the independent, self-determining and self-reliant road it takes toward developing weaponry.

In the near future, our actions must be firmly directed toward transforming our present weaponry, so that our military weapons will be improved by the end of the century and they will have the ability to meet the demands of a localized conflict. We must also face the future by developing weapons systems for our country, striving to reach world advanced standards in weapons in the next century and carrying out the modernization of our weapons. In order to realize the objectives of the above-mentioned weapons development strategy, our military must develop suitable strategic nuclear weapons and tactical nuclear weapons, strengthen its research for precision-guided weapons and electronic and technological equipment, and work even more toward modifying various conventional weapons.

Strategic nuclear weapons are not only a combat tool of immense destructive power; they also serve as powerful deterrents and an anti-deterrent force.

After our country had successfully exploded its first atomic bomb on October 16, 1964, it went on to successfully explode its first hydrogen bomb in June 1967. With every step China takes in the development of its strategic nuclear weapons, the strength of world peace is also increased by those steps. China's development of its limited nuclear capability is completely for the purpose of defense, for breaking up the nuclear monopoly and nuclear threats of the United States and the Soviet Union, and for preserving long-lasting world peace.

To win time for the world to stabilize within this nightmarish nuclear situation and to provide our socialist modernization greater security in the international environment, to completely destroy the nuclear blackmail of the U.S. and the Soviet Union, to strive for the thorough destruction of nuclear weapons, to proceed toward preventing a world from exploding into war, and to increase the strength for world peace over war so that China and Third World countries can play a greater role in international affairs, China must continue to develop proper strategic weapons and move toward upgrading their precision, lessening their weight, and increasing their mobile combat capability.

Field tactical nuclear weapons are an effective antipersonnel weapon. The extent of their destructive area is above 300 km.

This weapon not only has the superior tactical technical capabilities of long range, fast firing rate, high accuracy, and great destructive power, but it could also be used as a surprise weapon in major field operations to strive for and grasp the field initiative. In its tactical use, in an offensive situation it could directly break up the effective fire power of the enemy and destroy the defense points of the enemy from a distance, or it could attack the depth defenses of the enemy and cut off the enemy's retreat. In a defensive situation it could attack the enemy rear echelon troops, stop the continuous assault of the enemy, and defend against the enemy making a direct deep push.

Coordinated and complementary field tactical nuclear missiles used with various other conventional weapons systems could give the military greater military benefits and battlefield power. In a situation where, temporarily, no global wars are being fought, localized wars will be the major forms of combat for a period of time. In localized wars, the possible use of field tactical nuclear weapons by the enemy cannot be dismissed. Thus, China appropriately and within reason must develop field tactical nuclear weapons in order to further break down the various kind of nuclear threats of the hegemonists and restrain the use of field tactical nuclear weapons by the enemy.

After the implementation of the strategical changes in the guiding ideologies of military construction, the serious research of various weapons systems for localized wars will become the major tasks of our country's weapons system development for a period of time. The effective use in recent years of conventional precision-guided weapons in several localized combat theatres of operations has been followed with general interest by various countries around the world. Our national socialist characteristics have also determined that the major combat form of our military will hereafter still be that of defending our national territory. In a defensive war, the major missions assumed by our military will be defending against the enemy's surprise air attacks and stopping a mass invasion by the enemy's tanks. In our military's conventional arms buildup, the development of different precision-guided weapons for anti-air and antitank defense will be of special importance.

The level of modernization of our weapons directly corresponds to how sophisticated our electronic technology is and this will have a direct impact on victory or defeat in modern warfare. After our forces are equipped with a large quantity of electronic equipment and computers, not only will the electronic command, control, communications and information systems (C3I) within our combat and control become highly automated, and simple platforms and partial electronic equipments of warfare like reconnaissance and antireconnaissance, jamming and antijamming, destructive and antidestruction devices be completely transformed for "electronic wars;" they will also allow electronic technology to spread and permeate into all of the other weapons systems until it becomes the mainstay of our modern weaponry.

The energetic development of our country's military use of electronic technology is of utmost importance to upgrading the modernization level of our military weapons and closing the weapons gap with advanced countries.

For a long time, our military had summarized a complete set of combat methods and experience on how to gain victory with inferior equipment over a superiorly equipped enemy. Facing a strong opponent, our military would be inferior in terms of weapons. Our country's economic strength is still very weak, our science and technology is still not very developed and compared to a strong enemy, the gap in our weapons will be difficult to overcome immediately.

After our country implemented the strategic change of "transferring the work emphasis towards economic construction," there has been little possibility that military expenditures will be increased greatly and also little possibility that more money will be forthcoming for the research of sophisticated weapons. Thus, we must begin exploring new ways to develop weapons that possesses Chinese characteristics.

On the one hand, we can track the development of global high technology, build a good technological reservoir, and actively research new weapons systems in order to lay a foundation to close the gap with the advanced standards in foreign countries. On the other hand, we can use what we currently have and what high-technology results we have already achieved to change the low-tech conventional weapons system in our military, and upgrade the tactical technological capability of our present weapons so that with these slightly improved low-tech weapons systems we can still win a victory over our enemy's hi-tech weapons.

A weapons development strategy is an important component of our national defense development strategy.

In the historical situation where our guiding ideology for military buildup is undergoing grave strategic changes, the somber formulation of a military weapons development strategy, the development of military weapons in a planned, focused, and measured way, and the acceleration of the pace of development of our military weapons will all have practical and long term impacts on encouraging our military's modernization and standardization.

WEAPONS OF MASS DESTRUCTION INDIA

Ballistic Missiles

a. Prithvi I - Army Version (150 km range with a payload of 1,000kg)

   Prithvi II - Air Force Version (250 km range with a payload of 500kg)

   Prithvi III - Naval Version (350 km range with a payload of 500kg)

b. Dhanush is a System consisting of stabilization platform and missiles and can fire either the 250Km or the 350Km range missiles.

   Then the following year in December the missile's 350Km version was tested from the INS Rajput and hit the land based target

c. The Agni Missile system comprises of Agni I, Agni II and the Agni III 1500 Agni I uses the SLV-3 booster (from India's Space Program) for its first stage and a liquid-fueled Prithvi for its second stage.

d. On the other hand India's Agni II missiles have a range of the 1500 to 2500 kilometres. Unlike the Agni I, the Agni II has a solid-fueled second stage. India has also tested the Agni III IRBM with a range between 3000 and 5500km kilometres which has two stages. With a normal payload of 1000kg it can travel 5000km

e. The Surya-1 and -2 will be classified as strategic weapons, extending the Indian nuclear deterrent force to targets around the world. India currently is limited by the range of the Agni-3 missile.

   The Surya-1 will have an expected range of 6000 - 10,000 km. It reportedly has a length of 40 m and a launch weight of 80,000 kg (some reports indicate as much as 275,000 kg. As the missile has yet to be developed, the payload and warhead are as yet unknown. It is believed to be a three-stage design, with the first two stages using solid propellants and the third-stage using liquid. The first test flight is expected in 2009, but there may be delays. The Surya- is a longer-ranged variant of the Surya-1. It has a reported range of over 20,000 km.

f. The Shaurya missile is a short-range surface-to-surface ballistic missile developed by DRDO of India for use by the Indian Army.It has a range of 600 km and is capable of carrying a payload of one-tonne conventional or nuclear warhead.The Shaurya missile provides India with a significant second strike capability.

g. Sagarika is a nuclear capable submarine-launched ballistic missile with a range of 750 km. This missile has a length of 8.5 meters, weighs seven tonnes and can carry a pay load of up to 500 kg

CRUISE MISSILES INDIA

a. Nirbhay is a long range, subsonic cruise missile being developed in India. The missile will have a range of 1000 km and will arm three services, the Indian Army, Indian Navy and the Indian Air Force.

b. India has acquired around 200 3M-54 Klub for arming Talwar class frigate, Shivalik class frigate, Kolkata class destroyer and Sindhughosh class submarine The Russian 3M-54 Klub is a multi-role missile system developed by the Novator Design Bureau(OKB-8) with a range of 250Km-300Km and a average speed of .8 Mach with a maximum of 2.9 Mach

c. Popeye II, an air launched cruise missile capable of carrying nuclear warheads with a range of 80 Km can be launched from planes was given to India along with missile defence radars in a deal.

   The exact number transferred to India is unknown, but possibly 20 missile to perhaps 50 missiles could have been given with possibly more being built in India.

d. India has Soviet P-70 Ametist submarine-launched cruise missiles.

The missiles can carry nuclear warheads and have a range of 50-65Km.

e. The P-270 Moskit is a Russian supersonic ramjet powered cruise missile capable of being launched from land and ships. India has most probably bought both land and ship variants which have a range of 120km.

f. Akash is India's medium range surface-to-air missile defense system The missile can target aircraft up to 30 km away, at altitudes up to 18,000 m.Akash is said to be capable of both conventional and nuclear warheads, with a reported payload of 60kg. Akash can be fired from both tracked and wheeled platforms.

NUCLEAR SUBMARINES

According to some accounts India plans to have as many as 20 nuclear submarines capable of carrying missiles with nuclear warheads. The Advanced Technology Vessel (ATV) is a Nuclear Powered Ballistic Missile Submarine being constructed for the Indian Navy at Visakhapatnam, India The ATV is an SSBN and will be armed with the ballistic missiles.

Once it is completed, it can be equipped with 6-8 nuclear capable Dhanush,Sagarika or Agni SLBM ballistic missiles and upto 12 BrahMos cruise missiles. It is also to be fitted with an advanced sonar system. The second and third submarines of the class may incorporate the Nirbhay as well. As of July 2007, the Sagarika missile as well as Dhanush had undergone three successful tests each. The ATV is to be unveiled on January 26, 2009 but trials will start later that year while induction is planned for 2010.

The INS Sindhuraj, INS Sindhuvir, INS Sindhuratna, INS Sindhushastra, INS Sindhukesari and INS Sindhuvijay are capable of launching 3M-54 Klub and BrahMos nuclear-capable cruise missiles. India bought 10 Kilo class (in India known as Sindhughosh Class) submarine of which 6 have been refitted by the Russian Navy so that the they can launch cruise missiles such as nuclear capable BrahMos and 3M-54 Klub's 3M-14E variant.

The Submarine version of the BrahMos has been tested from static, underwater test stands in Russia and from the INS Sindhuvijay. As the Sinduvijay is similar to the other refitted submarines the test is considered a success.

AGNI MISSILE TESTING IN INDIA

On 19 February 1994 Agni took its third test flight at the Indian missile test range at Balasore, this time successfully with its range extended to 1200 km. The third flight marked the end of the first phase of Agni development program. The program went into a period of dormancy while the new Agni II began development, a longer range version that replaced the liquid fuel upper stage with a solid fuel version to make an all solid fuel missile India became a nuclear weapon state in reality in May 1994, though most observers thought that this milestone had been passed years before. It was then that India completed its development of a fully combat ready system for delivering nuclear weapons by successfully conducting acceptance tests. The ARDE developed bomb case, and the TBRL developed implosion system were mated with a modified Mirage 2000 and successfully test dropped at Balasore. The bomb, complete except for its plutonium core, was fuzed for an airburst and released over the ocean. If it been required due to national crisis, no doubt the system could have been pushed into service at an earlier date as a stop gap, but in May the fully mature reliable and safe system entered service. India now had an arsenal of at least a couple of dozen operational nuclear bombs.

The years 1995-1996 proved to be watershed in the history of South Asia, and in nuclear proliferation efforts world-wide. The Non-Proliferation Treaty (NPT) came up for review and extension in 1995. Since its original drafting in 1968 the NPT had steadily gained adherents until by the mid-90s the vast majority of states in the world had signed it (by 2000 only 4 states out of 191 had not signed it - with India and Pakistan being half of the four). India had endorsed the NPT in principle, but had refrained from signing because it objected to the establishment of "legitimate" nuclear weapon states limited to the 5 nuclear armed nations then in existence. The NPT committed these nuclear states to good faith efforts at eliminating their arsenals but in the nearly 30 years since no effort in that direction could be discerned. India refused to sign the NPT unless the nuclear states committed themselves to a specific timetable to accomplish disarmament, an approach they unanimously refused to consider. As the NPT extension date approached the nuclear states began pressing for making the NPT permanent so that it would never expire again, while the non-nuclear signatories to the treaty began insisting on a firmer commitment to arms limitation from the nuclear powers in return. In lieu of an actual disarmament commitment, the nuclear powers pushed two treaties that provided for restrictions on specific proliferation activities - the Comprehensive Test Ban Treaty (CTBT) to prohibit all nuclear tests, and a treaty to cut-off the production of fissile materials for weapons. Neither of these treaties would seriously inconvenience the states already possessing extensive stockpiles of tested weapons, but they would have serious effects on states with less well developed arsenals - like India.

This situation presented India with the worst of all worlds. They found themselves under intense pressure, particularly from the U.S., to assent to these treaties which would lock them in to a permanent status of a "second tier state", sharply constrain or wholly foreclose their nuclear capabilities developed at great expense and now at a stage of advanced development, while exacting a negligible price from the nuclear weapon states. To add further insult, two of the nuclear states - China and France - embarked on a new round of nuclear tests to add still more sophisticated designs to their arsenals before the CTBT shut down all testing. The dilemma was strongly reminiscent of the 1980s when developing international restrictions on ballistic missile technology induced India to push ahead with its missile program before the door could be shut on them. The new international push for limiting the spread of nuclear weapons (but not reducing those already held by the major powers) created pressure in India to breakout of its closet status, test its new weapons, and openly deploy them.

The linkage between U.S. pressure on the NPT and India's decision to move ahead aggressively on its strategic programs seems to have been quite direct. The full court press for the NPT began in January 1995, PM Rao responded by meeting with Chidambaram and authorized him to prepare to conduct a series of tests, including a hydrogen bomb test device and sub-kiloton devices to provide data for post-CTBT weapon simulations. Rao even specified that the scientists should be ready to conduct a test on 10 days notice, after the Prime Minister's decision to do so. Later, on 13 April 1995, Rao authorized 6 billion rupees for the development of the Agni II. Kalam was directed to intensify work on setting up a sophisticated command and control system for India's nuclear weapons, and to build additional weapon storage sites around the country (up to that point they nuclear components for weapons were all stored at BARC in Trombay).

It was after Rao's meeting with him that Chidambaram authorized Satinder Kumar Sikka at BARC to begin the development and preparation of a thermonuclear test device - a hydrogen bomb. BARC had developed some designs for thermonuclear weapons in the 80s, but these had languished without any serious effort to move forward with device fabrication although important work in the basic physics and in producing many of the essential materials like enriched lithium-6 and tritium provided a sound foundation. Sikka began developing a new design — a sophisticated one intended for deployment on ballistic missiles (with a weight thus limited to 1000 kg) and using a boosted fission bomb primary.

The NPT extension passed overwhelmingly on 11 May, four days later on 15 May China conducted another nuclear test, and the next day PM Rao announced that India was considering deploying the Prithvi missile in the near future. In August K. Santhanam, DRDO's chief technical adviser, was appointed mission director for the planned test series. That month U.S. intelligence satellites observed water being pumped out of the test shafts at Pokhran, which had become flooded in the intervening years. Construction also began on a new shallower test shaft.

In October 1995, 20 pre-production models of the initial Prithvi SS-150 (with a 150 km range) were secretly delivered to the Army to form the 333rd Missile Regiment based in Secunderabad. At this time the Prithvi was not yet equipped with a nuclear warhead.

Rao had never actually authorized tests though, simply preparations for them to keep his options open. Unlike in 1974, PM Rao conducted an extensive series of reviews to determine involving political, foreign policy, and economic advisers (but, in keeping with long-standing Indian practice, not the military) in addition to the nuclear scientists and engineers to determine whether tests should be conducted. Although the nuclear scientists, and members of the "strategic enclave" (like Sundarji and Subrahmanyam) strongly advocated tests, the net result of the reviews were negative, by the fall Rao had decided not to conduct tests.

The principle reason for not testing were again economic, Rao recognized the principle source of China's international clout was its economic strength and that India needed to focus its energies on its economy to compete. Thus when the news that the U.S. had detected test preparations broke in the press in December, actual tests were no longer under consideration and test devices had never been transported to Pokhran. The shift of Indian public opinion towards favouring tests is illustrated by an *India Today* survey of 2000 adults on 5 December 1995 showing that 62 percent of the respondents would approve if India exploded an atom bomb to develop its nuclear weapons capability.

The disclosure created a storm of controversy booth inside and outside of India. Pres. Clinton called PM Rao soon after the disclosure to ask him not to test. Rao responded that India would not act "irresponsibly" but gave no other assurances. On 18 December the government declared that it would not succumb to external pressure, but the next day Foreign Minister Pranab Mukherjee denied that tests were planned.

But Rao's term in office was drawing to a close. Elections were held in April-May 1996, and the Congress Party was voted out of office. The balance of power in the Lok Sabha was indecisive - the BJP won the largest seats with 186. Congress and its allies won only 138 seats, and the National Front took 113 and remaining 95 split among smaller parties. A governing coalition required 273 seats and it was not clear what part could assemble a sufficiently large coalition. Since the BJP had gained the largest share of seats President Shankar Sharma asked the BJP led by Atal Behari Vajpayee to form a government on 15 May. Vajpayee was faced with the challenge of marshalling at least another 75 votes within 15 days to win a vote of confidence and remain in power.

Vajpayee had supported open nuclearization of India for 30 years, since the first Chinese nuclear test, as had the BJP for its entire existence, and as had its predecessor, the Jana Sangh before that. One of the planks in the campaign platform for the BJP had been "to exercise the option to induct nuclear weapons". So it should have been to no one's surprise that one of the first actions taken by Vajpayee upon taking office would be to set in motion the test operations that Rao had ordered to be made ready. That it appears to have actually been *the* very first issue acted upon by Vajpayee though is notable.

According to Chengappa, Vajpayee's attempt to order nuclear tests was delayed until the day after his inauguration due to problems in contacting Abdul Kalam to receive the order. Three test devices were brought to Pokhran and emplaced in the test shafts:

- a lightweight pure fission bomb (12 kt);
- a boosted fission bomb; and
- a sub-kiloton experimental test device.

The site preparations at Pokhran came within about a day of being completed, when it became apparent that Vajpayee's government was not going to be able to win the upcoming vote of confidence. Although he had the authority to order the test, Vajpayee recognized that it would be improper to saddle a successor government with dealing with the consequences of a test with which it had no involvement. So Vajpayee rescinded his authorization until after the vote was held. On 28 May the BJP lost the vote of confidence and Vajpayee's government was dissolved. Vajpayee's aides felt that without the one day delay in locating Kalam the tests would have been conducted in 1996. Within several months information about Vajpayee's initial authorization of nuclear tests leaked out, and although it did not become widely known this was undoubtedly picked up by U.S. intelligence - making the later admission of "surprise" by the U.S. when Vajpayee took office in 1998 and conducted tests soon after difficult to justify. The delay in testing brought about the hesitance of Rao and Vajpayee was actually a boon to the weapons scientists. The thermonuclear device was not ready yet, and the delay gave them time to prepare additional devices - two sub-kiloton experiments, and a boosted fission device using reactor-grade plutonium to enable India to draw upon its very large inventory of power reactor produced material if desired.

EQUIPMENT AND TECHNOLOGY OF CHINA

In their various campaigns, the Chinese armies through the ages, employed a variety of equipment in the different arms of the army. The most notable weaponry used by the Chinese consisted of crossbows, rockets, gunpowder weapons, and other "exotic weapons", but the Chinese also made many advances on conventional iron weapons such as swords and spears that were far superior to other contemporary weapons.

Crossbow

The crossbow, invented by Chinese in the 7th century BC, and by Greeks in the 5th century BC, was considered the most important weapon of the Chinese armies. The mass use of crossbows allowed Chinese armies to deploy huge amounts of firepower, due to the crossbow's deadly penetration, long range, and rapid rate of fire. As early as the 4th century BC, Chinese texts describe armies employing up to 10,000 crossbowmen in combat, where their impact was decisive. Crossbow manufacture was very complex, due to the nature of the firing bolt. Historian Homer Dubs claim that the crossbow firing mechanism "was almost as complex as a rifle bolt, and could only be reproduced by very competent mechanics. This gave an additional advantage, as this made the crossbow "capture-proof" as even if China's barbarian enemies captured them they would not be able to reproduce the weapon.Crossbow ammunition could also only be used in crossbows, and was useless in the conventional bows employed by China's nomadic enemies.

In combat, crossbows were often fitted with grid sights to help aim, and several different sizes were used. During the Song Dynasty, huge artillery crossbows were used that could shoot several bolts at once, killing many men at a time. Even cavalrymen were sometimes issued with crossbows. It was recorded that the crossbow could "penetrate a large elm from a distance of one hundred and forty paces". Repeating crossbows were introduced in the 11th century, which had a very high rate of fire; 100 men could discharge 2000 bolts in 15 seconds, with a range of 200 yards. This weapon became the standard crossbow used during theSong, Ming, and Qing dynasties.

Gunpowder weapons

As inventors of gunpowder, the Chinese were the first to deploy gunpowder weapons. A large variety of gunpowder weapons were produced, including guns, cannons, mines, the flamethrower, bombs, and rockets. After the rise of the Ming Dynasty, China began to lose its lead in gunpowder weapons to the west. This became partially evident when the Manchus' began to rely on the Jesuits to run their cannon foundry, at a time when European powers had assumed the global lead in gunpowder warfare through their Military Revolution.

Guns and cannons

The first "proto-gun", the fire lance, was introduced in 905 AD. This consisted of a bamboo or metal tube attached to a spear filled with gunpowder that could be ignited at will, with a range of five metres. It was capable of killing or maiming several soldiers at a time and was mass-produced and used especially in the defense of cities. Later versions of the fire lance dropped the spear point and had more gunpowder content.

Traditionally interpreted as a wind god, a sculpture in Sichuan was found holding a bombard, and the date must be as early as AD 1128 These cast-iron hand cannons and erupters were mostly fitted to ships and fortifications for defense.

Cannon were used by Ming dynasty forces at the Battle of Lake Poyang. Ming dynasty era ships had bronze cannon. One shipwreck in Shandong had a cannon dated to 1377 and an anchor dated to 1372. From the 13th to 15th centuries cannon armed Chinese ships also traveled throughout south east Asia.

Bombs, grenades and mines

High explosive bombs were another innovation developed by the Chinese in the 10th century. These consisted largely of round objects covered with paper or bamboo filled with gunpowder that would explode upon contact and set fire to anything inflammable. These weapons, known as "thunderclap bombs", were used by defenders in sieges on attacking enemies and also by trebuchets, which hurled huge numbers of them onto the enemy. A new improved version of these bombs, called the "thunder-crash" bomb, was introduced in the 13th century; it was covered in cast iron, was highly explosive, and hurled shrapnel at the enemy. These weapons were not only used by Song China, but also its Jur'chen and Mongol enemies. In the history of the Jur'chen Jin dynasty, the use of cast-iron gunpowder bombs against the Mongols is described.

By the time of the Ming Dynasty, Chinese technology had progressed to making large land mines, many of them were deployed on the northern border.

Flamethrower

Rockets

During the Ming dynasty, the design of rockets were further refined and multi-stage rockets and large batteries of rockets were produced. Multi-stage rockets were introduced for naval combat. Like other technology, knowledge of rockets were transmitted to the Middle East and the West through the Mongols, where they were described by Arabs as "Chinese arrows".

Infantry

In the 2nd century BC, the Han began to produce steel from cast iron. New steel weapons were manufactured that gave Chinese infantry an edge in close-range fighting, though swords and blades were also used. In addition, the Chinese infantry were given extremely heavy armor in order to withstand cavalry charges, some 29.8 kg of armor during the Song Dynasty. Unclear reference.

Cavalry

The cavalry was equipped with heavy armor in order to crush a line of infantry, though light cavalry was used for reconnaissance.

However, Chinese armies lacked horses and their cavalry were often inferior to their horse archer opponents. Therefore, in most of these campaigns, the cavalry had to rely on the infantry to provide support. Between the Jin and Tang dynasty, fully armoredcataphracts were introduced in combat. An important innovation was the invention of the stirrup. From early Indian invention, which allowed cavalrymen to be much more effective in combat; this innovation later spread to East north and west via the nomadic populations of central Asia and to west by the Avars.

However, some believe northern nomads were responsible for this innovation. Some authors, such as Lynn White, claim the use of the stirrup in Europe stimulated development of the medieval knights which characterized feudal Europe. However, this thesis was disputed in the Great Stirrup Controversy by historians such as Bernard Bachrach, although it has been pointed out that the Carolingian riders may have been the most expert cavalry of all at its use.

Chemical weapons

During the Han Dynasty, state manufacturers were producing stink bombs and tear gas bombs that were used effectively to suppress a revolt in 178 AD Poisionous materials were also employed in rockets and crossbow ammunition to increase their effectiveness.

Logistics

The Chinese armies also benefited from a logistics system that could supply hundreds of thousands of men at a time. An important innovation by the Chinese was the introduction of an efficient horse harness in the 4th century BC, strapped to the chest instead of the neck, an innovation later expanded to a collar harness.

This innovation, along with the wheelbarrow, allowed large-scale transportation to occur, allowing huge armies numbering hundreds of thousands of men in the field.

Chinese armies were also backed by a vast complex of arms-producing factories. State-owned factories turned out weapons by the thousands, though some dynasties (such as the Later Han) privatized their arms industry and acquired weapons from private merchants.

Rations

During the Han dynasty, Chinese developed methods of food preservation for military rations during campaigns such as drying meat into jerky and cooking, roasting, and drying grain.

Command

In early Chinese armies, command of armies was based on birth rather than merit. For example, in the State of Qi during the Spring and Autumn Period (771 BC–476 BC), command was delegated to the ruler, the crown prince, and the second son. By the time of the Warring States Period, generals were appointed based on merit rather than birth, the majority of whom were talented individuals who gradually rose through the ranks.

Nevertheless, Chinese armies were sometimes commanded by individuals other than generals. For example, during the Tang Dynasty, the emperor instituted "Army supervisors" who spied on the generals and interfered in their commands, although most of these practices were short-lived as they disrupted the efficiency of the army.

STRATEGY FOR WEAPONS AND EQUIPMENT DEVELOPMENT

Weapons are tools used to carry out armed conflicts. It is an important component of the military's combat power. It is the major element that determines the success and failure of a war. The development of modern weaponry, contained and controlled by national defense science and technology and national defense economic realities, have affected a succession of military scientific theories.

The Development of Modern Weaponry and National Defense Science and Technology

On June 7, 1981, the Israeli Air Force sent out 14 aircraft and bombed a nuclear reactor 20 km southeast of the Iraqi capital of Baghdad. "The bombs landed precisely on the main building where the nuclear reactor was located."

On May 2, 1982, during the Falklands War between England and Argentina, England's SSN Conqueror fired two wire-guided TIGERFISH torpedoes and sank the only 13,000-ton large cruiser, General Belgrano, in the Argentina Navy. Two days later, the Argentina air force flying the French manufactured SUPER ETENDARD fighters needed only one EXOCET AM39 air-to-ship missile to sink the large, superbly equipped and costly ($200 million) SHEPHERD class destroyer from a distance more than 45 km away. On May 25, Argentina sank the British Navy's 18,000-ton troop transport, an ATLANTIC SEA TRANSPORT [Daxiyang Yunsongze] class ship.

In June 1982, in the air battle above Syria's Bekka Valley, the Israeli Air Force won an important battle by using all types of jamming methods and precision-guided weapons like air-to-surface missiles and television and in 2 days completely destroyed all the surface-to-air missile sites in the Bekka Valley. In the surprise attack on Grenada on October 25, 1983, the United States used many surveillance methods and sent out an E-2C high-altitude, early-warning aircraft with antijamming capability, and hi-tech F-15s and F-16s, which had been remodeled and equipped with infrared sighting equipment, laser-guided bombs, and radar-guided self-seeking air-to-surface missiles, to achieve its predetermined military objectives with very little cost.

During the military conflict over the Gulf of Sidra between the United States and Libya between March 24-25, 1986, and in the air attack on Libya by the United States on April 15, the United States used hi-tech weapons such as laser-guided bombs, "Rockeye" cluster bombs, TRIDENT radar-guided, self-seeking air-to-surface missiles and for the first time, used its high speed antiradiation missile "HARM" as well as other hi-tech equipment such as new infrared sighting equipment.

The United States lost only one F-111 fighter-bomber and in turn sank and seriously damaged two Libyan cruisers, destroyed one missile launching site, destroyed about 5 to 12 Soviet made MIG-23s and 3 to 5 IL-76 transports, and achieved combat successes on 5 predetermined targets.

Since the 1980s, several local area conflicts have vividly shown, and people have clearly understood even before the smoke cleared, that modern weapons have assumed some new characteristics under the impetus given them by the advances made in national defense science and technology.

One is electronics. With the development of microelectronics, computers, satellite communications, lasers, and other technologies and greater improvements seen in communications, navigation, radar, telemetering, remote control, remote sensing, and modern electronic command, control, and communications systems because of electronics and the radio, various kinds of weapons systems are extensively using electronic equipment and technology.

From the perspective of the cost accounting of weapons systems, the percentage of the costs of the electronic equipment within each of these weapons systems is relatively sizable. In aircraft, it is 33 percent; in missiles, 45 percent; in space vehicles, 66 percent; in military vessels, 22 percent; and in combat vehicles, 24 percent.

Electronic equipment has already become an indispensable component of modern weapons systems. It has also become the nerve center of modern weapons systems. With the development of the fifth generation of computers, artificial intelligence, and robotic technology, it is possible that troops could be equipped with simple artificial intelligence weapons systems in the future.

Second is the change in guidance systems. Since the 1950s, along with the development and discovery of new technologies like wireless, television, infrared, laser, microwave, inertia guidance, photoelectricity, acousto-electronics, sensors, and precision measuring and automation, precision-guided weapons systems (cruise missile, surface-to-air missile, air-to-surface missiles, air-to-air missiles, surface-to-surface missiles, ship-borne missiles and antitank missiles) have appeared along with terminal precision-guided weapons warheads for guided artillery shells, guided bombs, and guided torpedoes. The guidance system changes in these weapon systems have greatly increased their capabilities for automatic searches and identification and attack, and have increased tenfold the precision of these weapons systems, to the point of near perfect accuracy.

Third is covertness. Weapons are tools for the destruction of the enemy but at the same time, they are also the major target of offensives by the enemy. The new technological revolution has searched for and provided advanced equipment, ways, and methods for the modern battlefield, and together with troops, weapons have now become a serious threat.

In the history of combat, to increase battlefield survivability of weapons, man has thought of many kinds of decoys and camouflage. With the development of invisible light technology (like infrared, ultraviolet, laser, microwave, and others), surveillance technology and various anticamouflage technology, original camouflage mechanisms have lost a great deal of their effectiveness.

To increase their battlefield survivability, weapons systems have begun moving toward the direction of concealment. "Concealment" is the use of various types of scientific technology to decrease detection by radar, infrared, photoelectricity, and weapons sighting systems. It is the adoption of a specialized technology through systems research and design.

Major "concealment" methods include:

- Having the weapons system's structural distribution and design be scientifically rational and still be able to decrease the effective reflecting surfaces of radar, electromagnetic spectrum, and laser.
- Decreasing infrared radiation and the noise level of engines within the propulsion system in the weaponry.
- Selecting coatings that will absorb and shield radar waves and infrared radiation as well as effectively reduce radar reflecting surfaces. For coating on surfaces of the weaponry, new wave-absorbing structured materials made of composite materials and electromagnetic spectrum "absorbing material" are now being selected. There is also the use of different kinds of concealment technology and use of different methods for different weapons systems, such as missiles, aircraft, ships, tanks, vehicles, and artillery. The U.S.'s B-1B bomber is a weapons system that uses rather advanced stealth technology. Structurally, it uses swing-wing. The outer shape of the body and wings are designed for radar reflecting surfaces. It uses a turbofan engine and a bypass culvert that dispenses the mixed hot and cold air to decrease the heat radiation strength of the jet. It uses the radioactive isotope polonium 210 and curium 242 as well as ferrite as its surface coating. Cover coating the aircraft surface with these substances decreases the

> radar reflecting surfaces and will furthermore absorb and shield radar, electromagnetic spectrum, and laser radiation. From what we have seen in localized wars during recent years, covert technology has raised the survivability of weapons systems in close concealed contact with the enemy and in surprise attacks. It has also played a role in decreasing wastefulness in terms of consumption.

Fourth, focused energy, is different from radiation mass destruction weapons like chemical, atomic, and nuclear weapons. A focused- energy weapon directs energy into beam power that kills the enemy or destroys a target directly. (It is also called a directed energy or directed beam energy weapon.) The rapid rise of laser technology, particle beam technology, microwave technology, and plasma technology has provided the foundation for the creation of focused-energy technology. In recent years, there has been rapid development in focused-energy weapons, and at present, the phase of theoretical experimentation has largely been completed and has entered the prototype stage of research. According to reports, the Soviet Union is in the process of researching three kinds of high energy laser weapons for its anti-air defense. It could complete the research work for a practical model against a star wars weapon in the 1990s and deploy a small quantity of them. There is intense research going on for various kinds of tactical laser artillery and guns and the coming of directed- energy weapons in theatres of war are not far away. The combined use of these and conventional weapons systems will result in greater casualties and destruction.

War and the need for the development of weapons power are the motivations for weapons development. As long as war, an abnormal development of mankind, persists, the military will strive to find more sophisticated weaponry and suggest the need for development of weapons. With this "demand as an incentive," opposing sides, all wanting victory, will initiate national defense construction "monitors" for "military expenditures" for large investments in national defense science and technology and support for research work in the leading edge of technology and advanced weapons systems. The greatest "INVESTMENT returns" in weapons development for national security and arms superiority would be a pioneering spirit in new ideas, exploitation, and creation of new technologies. In other words, national defense science and technology could apply all kinds of new technologies to both the research of weapons and their production, thus acting as "technology boosters." In this way, the research disciplines within national defense science and technology could become the "breeding grounds" for high technology development; furthermore, the new achievements of science and technology would most appropriately find their first applications within the military.

Weapons Development and the National Defense Economy

It is common knowledge that modern warfare is not only the competition of weapons on the battlefield but is also, at the same time, an all-out competition of the total strength of the opposing side's politics, economics, military, and science and technology. During the development of weaponry, the four aspects of politics, economics, military and science and technology are completely brought into play. In today's climate of rapid development of national defense science and technology and the daily emergence of new weapons, the material base of the actual national defense economy should be not only strong but also exceptional.

- With the upgrade in the tactical and technical performances of weapons, manufacturing costs would correspondingly be also more expensive. Since the end of WWII, science and technology development has flourished. There has been a multitude of achievements in science and technology that have continuously increased weapon precision, its powers to cause casualties, and its military effectiveness. The explosive power of a small atomic bomb has the same effectiveness as 100 bombers from WWII. The fire power of today's tank is tenfold greater than that of WWII. A mission to destroy 60 percent of the equipment of a tank division would today require only 1 percent of the aircraft used 40 years ago. During the Falklands War between England and Argentina, the EXOCET missile, which cost only $200,000, fired by the Argentinean Air Force was able to sink a British SHEPHARD missile destroyer that costs $200 million. The ratio of the two costs effectiveness is 1:1,000. The precision of precision-guided bombs and artillery shells is 2 to 3 times better than that of non-guided bombs and artillery shells. However, the upgrading of weapons performance has also brought with it the consequence ofmore expensive manufacturing costs. The cost of scientific research and technical components compared to the cost of a system with microcomputer technology, new materials, and new techniques imported in great quantities would appear to be prominently greater. Each of the U.S.'s HELLFIRE antitank missile costs about $28,100 to buy, but the scientific research to produce it costs $310 million. Each of the LEOPARD-II tanks of the Federal Republic of Germany costs $3.58 million to buy, yet the scientific research cost was $360 million. The research cost of Japan's MODEL 61 tanks cost •500 million to research and develop in the 1950s, its MODEL 74 tanks cost •2.5 billion to develop in the 1960s, and the MODEL 88 tanks that currently are under research and development have a budgeted cost that could reach •25 billion. The research and development expenditures of three generations of tanks seem to have increased geometrically. According to statistics, the costs of fighters and tanks increase about tenfold every 20 years and the costs of aircraft carriers increase by tenfold every 30 years. Weapons development has come to rely more and more on the national defense economy, causing great burdens for many countries.

- The increase in weapon power has also created battlefield situations where the consumption of battlefield material and economic losses are immense. It requires a huge quantity of material reserves. The 4th Middle East War lasted only 18 days and both sides, Egypt and Israel, suffered economic losses of over $5 billion. The loss of aircraft by both sides was comparable to the combined loss in aircraft in a year by all of the participant countries during WWII. In the first 3 days after the war started, the total number of tactical missiles launched by both sides was equivalent to the combined total of all the reserves of the countries in NATO. The loss of tanks was equal to one-third the number of those in the possession of NATO countries at that time. Both sides strategic reserves and materials were exhausted a week into the war. We can infer the amount of economic loss that could be created by modern warfare from this. In the Falklands War, the English spent a total of $2.16 billion, about $1.2 million every hour. This kind of consumption, to fight one mid-size modern war, is difficult for even an economically great power to support.

In addition to the above, research and production of weapons, ammunition, technical facilities and engineering equipment all consume large amounts of metal and various kinds of nonferrous metals. They also need the support of the chemical industry and energy resources, as well as military industrial products. According to the statistics from affiliated departments at the United Nations, 15 to 16 percent of the world's copper output and 10 percent of it tin, nickel, lead, and zinc outputs are used for weapons production and toward the building of other national defense installations. The consumption of energy resources is even greater. During WWI, the consumption of fuel by each soldier for each day averaged about 6 kg. During WWII, it was increased to 20 kg for each person each day. In the several local area wars fought in recent years, the fuel consumption of each man each day increased to 90 kg. The consumption level is shocking! This not only raises problems for logistics support, it also increases the economic and energy resources burden.

- The rapid increase and shorter intervals in the updating and replacement of weaponry have sharply increased military expenditures and expenses. The advancements of science and technology have caused new weapons to emerge in an endless stream and greatly accelerated replacement and updating of weaponry. Before and after WWI, the time period for a weapons system to go from research and design, through trial tests and production to its deployment within the service required about 20 to 30 years. At present, this procedure requires only 10 to 15 years or an even shorter period. According to the analysis of a Soviet economist, Maj. Gen. Guluofu, a new weapons system for the Soviet military from research to its deployment in the services requires 10 - 15 years. Since the 1960s, Soviet missiles have already been updated three generations. The majority of its aircraft, submarines, and surface ships underwent updating long ago. Its anti-air defense missiles, radar, command equipment, communications equipment, and other equipment have also been through several generations of updating. The research of new weapons and the updating of existing weapons have greatly increased the military expenditures and expenses of every country. According to an analysis by western observers, "The world economy is already shouldering a burden of massive destructive weapons, poverty, and debt. Militarization will further sap its strength." Since the 1960s, the global expenditure for weapons has been about $14 trillion. In 1985 it was about $800 billion, in 1986 about $900 billion. Every second of every year about $1.7 million are spent. Immense military expenditures have become serious economic problems for each of the world's countries.

- The research and production of modern weapons have made even greater demands on the national defense economy and national defense industries. Since WWII, especially during the 1960s and 1970s, the unceasing discovery of new technology has led to a great revolution in weapons and military-use equipment.

In 1945, the atomic bomb appeared. The research of computers for weapons use came in 1946. In 1952, the first transistorized computer was developed. In 1953, the world's first hydrogen bomb was exploded.

In 1955, the first nuclear-powered submarine was launched. In August 1957, the first intercontinental ballistic missile was fired, and in October of that same year, the first manmade satellite was orbited.

In 1960, mankind recovered its first satellite. In 1961, the world's first manned satellite did an orbit around the earth and returned to the surface.

In 1967, the first integrated circuit was successfully developed. In 1969, man had his first landing on the moon. In 1977, the neutron bomb was researched and developed. In April 1981, the world's first spacecraft flew.

The research and production of all these new weapons and equipment and a large portion of the new technology that entered into the sphere of the national defense economy not only greatly changed the production and industrial structure of the national defense economy, it also added a series of new production and industrial sectors.

These changes helped to restructure the traditional national defense industries, moving them in the direction of technological improvement, and development of a technological reserve. The diffusion of a large quantity of high technology made it possible to turn a consuming national defense economy into a propagating field of national defense economy.

Weapons development is reliant on the development of the national economy. It also encourages the growth of national defense science and technology. Military high-technology also gave impetus to the development of the economy. Looking at this from two-dimensional space, this big "O" cycle could possibly expand further. Analysing it from a three-dimensional space, this kind of spiraling trend is perfectly suited to the objective laws of material development.

CHINA'S ARTILLERY DEVELOPMENT

Firepower is the basic element of combat strength and artillery troops are the main firepower of the army. These are the chief forces for launching a ground offensive with firepower and the main forces for air defence in the combat. In peacetime, artillery troops are important components of the conventional deterrent forces for containing war. The degree of modernization of artillery troops directly affects the coordinated fighting ability of the armed forces and affects the modernization process of national defence.

The people's artillery troops were born and rapidly grew and became stronger during the revolutionary war era. Since the founding of new China, and under the direct leadership of the Party Central Committee, the State Council, the Central Military Committee, and the Headquarters, it was through nearly 40 years of hard work by various industrial departments that our artillery weapons development has made important achievements and greatly improved our fighting capability. But owing to the disturbances of the Cultural Revolution, the limits of our national financial resources, and problems with structure and in our work, our artillery weapons at present are quite backward. Compared with the advanced level of foreign artillery, we are facing serious challenges. When looking to the future, we need to sum up the experiences of 40 years of equipment development, grasp favorable opportunities, and facilitate the development of equipment in order to strengthen the power of the "god of war."

The Historical Turning Point

Since the founding of new China, artillery weapons have experienced important changes. In the early days of the People's Republic, artillery weapons were mostly guns, vehicles, and optical instruments captured in war and made in other countries. During the period of resisting the United States and assisting Korea, we bought a number of weapons from the Soviet Union. Starting in 1953, we began to manufacture Soviet-style artillery and instruments and formed a weapons system based on Soviet artillery. Under the guidance of the policy of independence and self-reliance, in 1958 we began to design and manufacture artillery weaponry by ourselves. Over 30 years we have successfully made a large number of weapons, instruments, and vehicles, gradually replacing the Soviet equipment. At the same time, we trained a production force of dedicated scientists and technology experts in comprehensive fields of specialty. We have built up the material and technical bases for design, research, testing, production, and maintenance, are capable of manufacturing different kinds of weapons, and have entered a new stage of research and manufacturing artillery weapons on our own.

Our artillery weapons are no longer composed of mismatched types of guns and vehicles. Today we use sophisticated ammunition, and our artillery reconnaissance and firing calculation instruments are no longer operated by hand. We have developed a cohesive system of artillery and ammunition, accompanied by accessories; reconnaissance, command, communication, survey, and meteorology instruments; and vehicles.

A series of different types of artillery has been formed, and part of the artillery, instruments, and automobiles has been or is being upgraded. Since the 1970s, we have gradually been equipped with antitank and antiaircraft missiles, and new types of missiles are in the development. Different kinds of reconnaissance radar, air reconnaissance systems, laser-range finders, night vision instruments, and fire command systems are in various stages of research, production, and operation. With the development of this equipment, the fighting capability of our artillery troops has been continuously improved. In the various combats we have been involved in since the founding of new China, our artillery troops have played its special role and made important contributions.

Arduous Tasks

In the new historical period, we are faced with the serious challenge of modernizing the design of our artillery weapons.

We are still lacking in certain types of new weapons and we have not been able to form a complete set of equipment. For instance, we still have not met the demand for various missile systems, new types of ammunition, motorized artillery, and advanced electronic and optical reconnaissance instruments, as well as fire command systems. The whole artillery weaponry system is too old. Because of the new technology revolution, artillery weapons of advanced countries are high-tech and high quality, and the distance between the advanced countries and ourselves might be enlarged if we do not do a good job. We are relatively slow in upgrading the equipment of our troops. The antitank, antiaircraft, and neutralizing fire power still cannot meet the basic requirements of modern warfare, especially for antitank and antiaircraft warfare. Further, there is the need to develop different kinds and types of weapons. The technology is getting more and more complicated and more expensive. On the other hand, our level of science and technology is relatively low, our budget very limited, and the contradiction between the need and the possibility is very pronounced.

But at the same time, we must realize that though there are many difficulties, opportunities and favorable conditions do exist. The relaxation of the international situation, the change from the imminence of war to a period of peace has provided us with a favorable environment and valuable time for the modernization of our artillery weapons. Our Party's policy of reform and opening up has provided the opportunity to import advanced technology from abroad, utilize the results of the new technology revolution, reform our system of scientific research and equipment management, improve efficiency in investment, and accelerate development. Our science and technology, especially the development of high technology and its application in the research and production of artillery weapons, as well as our 40 years' experience and technological foundation, have provided the conditions for the development of advanced artillery weapons.

In short, modernization of artillery weapons faces serious situations and arduous tasks, and it will be through a long period of hard work that we will gradually realize modernization. If we have favorable timing and opportunity, and adopt correct policies and strategies, we will be able to succeed and make steady progress. We should start from reality and look toward the future, make an overall plan, and strive to realize the goal of artillery weaponry modernization in a planned and systematic way. Before the end of this century, we should pay attention to the research and manufacturing of key new weapons and equipment, improve and upgrade in a planned way the current weapons and equipment we are using, raise the overall fighting capability of our artillery troops, and lay a good foundation for the realization of all-round modernization in the next century.

Development with Chinese Characteristics

In the last 40 years, the development of artillery weapons has gone down a tortuous road. When reviewing our work, the most important lesson is that the modernization of artillery weapons should take into consideration the actual conditions of our nation and our army, and we should pursue development with Chinese characteristics:

- Persist in and develop the fine tradition of self-reliance and hard work, and make coordinated efforts to overcome difficulties. In the early 1960s, we faced the serious situation of a total foreign technological blockade, Soviet withdrawal of experts, and economic difficulties at home. Our scientists and technicians worked on artillery weapons. There was close coordination between the industrial departments and units that used the equipment, and between the research units and the production units, and we were able to achieve important results in a relatively short period of time. For example, the 63 model of the 107mm rocket gun and the 63 model of 130mm rocket gun took only 5 years to research and manufacture and were quickly used to equip the armed forces. In the new historical period, we should uphold and develop this fine tradition and further raise the quality and level of our scientific and technical troops so as to achieve better results.

- Strengthen model development and testing in development and practice decisionmaking scientifically. The construction of artillery weaponry is complicated, and only through a scientific decisionmaking process can we avoid making serious mistakes. Therefore, we should strengthen testing. We should use scientific methods to predict both requirements for artillery weapons in future anti-aggression wars and our national economic and technical capabilities. On the basis of systematic analysis, we should choose the correct development direction and goals and systems and series, and form practical plans, policies, and measures. Around 1970, under the direct leadership of the Central Military Committee and Marshall Ye Jianying, antitank weapon were made top priority for development. The antitank weapons system and requirements under the division level were clearly defined and intensely researched, and results were soon achieved. In fewer than 10 years, there were breakthroughs in the development of rocket launchers, recoilless guns, antitank guns, and antitank missiles. On the other hand, because there was no clear direction and mistakes were made in the decisionmaking, we took detours in the development of antiaircraft guns and howitzers, and progress was slow. Past experience has shown that artillery troops should make equipment research work a priority, developing test models to determine development direction, equipment systems, tactical technology requirements according to our strategic thinking, and battlefield situation and tactical principles, thus providing choices and possibilities for scientific decisionmaking.
- Shorten the battle line, pay attention to the focal point, have advanced planning for every stage and make advanced artillery weaponry. It has been proven that the results of seeking big and complete projects at an unrealistic speed are often "a lot of research but little equipment." At present, weapons development should be subordinated to the overall national economic

construction, and we should be more careful in planning, stressing the key projects. The development of artillery weapons that it is preferable to have fewer but better products. We should, based on scientific testing, carefully select key projects, concentrate our energy on developing basic models, and produce in appropriate quantity, to equip our forces for fighting capability. At the same time, we should strengthen advanced research, emphasize technological development, and choose a leaping-forward development model in order to shorten the distance between the advanced countries and ourselves.

- Face the world, improve technology through importation, digestion, development, and creation. Our artillery weapons were developed by importing and copying. Now that we are facing the challenge of a new technological revolution, we should further open up to the world and utilize the favorable conditions of opening up and actively to import advanced, appropriate technical equipment and a scientific way of management. In the 1950s, our weapons were based on Soviet artillery weapons. We achieved some progress, but at same time there were some far-reaching negative results. Our artillery weapons should eliminate Soviet-model features but not blindly copy Western models. Our military thinking, strategic policy, and combat principles should be our guides, and we should proceed from the actual conditions of our economy and science and technology levels, to gradually form our own technical style and weapons system. We should take the road of developing weapons research and manufacturing with Chinese characteristics.

DEVELOPMENT OF NUCLEAR WARFARE STRATEGY

Nuclear warfare strategy is a set of policies that deal with preventing or fighting a nuclear war. The policy of trying to prevent an attack by a nuclear weapon from another country by threatening nuclear retaliation is known as the strategy of nuclear deterrence. The goal in deterrence is to always maintain a second strike capability (the ability of a country to respond to a nuclear attack with one of its own) and potentially to strive for first strike status (the ability to completely destroy an enemy's nuclear forces before they could retaliate). During the Cold War, policy and military theorists in nuclear-enabled countries worked out models of what sorts of policies could prevent one from ever being attacked by a nuclear weapon. Different forms of nuclear weapons delivery allow for different types of nuclear strategies. The goals of any strategy are generally to make it difficult for an enemy to launch a pre-emptive strike against the weapon system and difficult to defend against the delivery of the weapon during a potential conflict. Sometimes this has meant keeping the weapon locations hidden, such as deploying them on submarines or rail cars whose locations are very hard for an enemy to track and other times this means protecting them by burying them in hardened bunkers.

Other components of nuclear strategies have included using missile defence (to destroy the missiles before they land) or implementation of civil defence measures (using early-warning systems to evacuate citizens to safe areas before an attack).

Note that weapons which are designed to threaten large populations or to generally deter attacks are known as strategic weapons. Weapons which are designed to actually be used on a battlefield in military situations are known as tactical weapons.

There are critics of the very idea of nuclear strategy for waging nuclear war who have suggested that a nuclear war between two nuclear powers would result in mutual annihilation. From this point of view, the significance of nuclear weapons is purely to deter war because any nuclear war would immediately escalate out of mutual distrust and fear, resulting in mutually assured destruction. This threat of national, if not global, destruction has been a strong motivation for anti-nuclear weapons activism.

Critics from the peace movement and within the military establishment have questioned the usefulness of such weapons in the current military climate. The use of (or threat of use of) such weapons would generally be contrary to the rules of international law applicable in armed conflict, according to an advisory opinion issued by the International Court of Justice in 1996. Perhaps the most controversial idea in nuclear strategy is that nuclear proliferation would be desirable. This view argues that, unlike conventional weapons, nuclear weapons successfully deter all-out war between states, and they are said to have done this during the Cold War between the U.S. and the Soviet Union. Political scientist Kenneth Waltz is the most prominent advocate of this argument.

The threat of potentially suicidal terrorists possessing nuclear weapons (a form of nuclear terrorism) complicates the decision process. The prospect of mutually assured destruction may not deter an enemy who expects to die in the confrontation. Further, if the initial act is from a rogue group instead of a sovereign nation, there is no fixed nation or fixed military targets to retaliate against. It has been argued, especially after the September 11, 2001 attacks, that this complication is the sign of the next age of nuclear strategy, distinct from the relative stability of the Cold War. In 1996, the United States adopted a policy of allowing the targeting of its nuclear weapons at terrorists armed with weapons of mass destruction.

Governance, control, and law

Because of the immense military power they can confer, the political control of nuclear weapons has been a key issue for as long as they have existed; in most countries the use of nuclear force can only be authorized by the head of government or head of state.

In the late 1940s, lack of mutual trust was preventing the United States and the Soviet Union from making ground towards international arms control agreements, but by the 1960s steps were being taken to limit both the proliferation of nuclear weapons to other countries and the environmental effects of nuclear testing. The Partial Test Ban Treaty (1963) restricted all nuclear testing to underground nuclear testing, to prevent contamination from nuclear fallout, while the Nuclear Non-Proliferation Treaty (1968) attempted to place restrictions on the types of activities which signatories could participate in, with the goal of allowing the transference of non-military nuclear technology to member countries without fear of proliferation. In 1957, the International Atomic Energy Agency (IAEA) was established under the mandate of the United Nations in order to encourage the development of the peaceful applications of nuclear technology, provide international safeguards against its misuse, and facilitate the application of safety measures in its use. In 1996, many nations signed the Comprehensive Test Ban Treaty which prohibits all testing of nuclear weapons, which would impose a significant hindrance to their development by any complying country. Due to the strict entry into force criterion of the convention however, it had as of 2011 not entered into force.

Additional treaties and agreements have governed nuclear weapons stockpiles between the countries with the two largest stockpiles, the United States and the Soviet Union, and later between the United States and Russia. These include treaties such as SALT II (never ratified), START I (expired), INF, START II (never ratified), SORT, and New START, as well as non-binding agreements such as SALT I and the Presidential Nuclear Initiatives of 1991. Even when they did not enter into force, these agreements helped limit and later reduce the numbers and types of nuclear weapons between the United States and the Soviet Union/Russia.

Nuclear weapons have also been opposed by agreements between countries. Many nations have been declared Nuclear-Weapon-Free Zones, areas where nuclear weapons production and deployment are prohibited, through the use of treaties. The Treaty of Tlatelolco (1967) prohibited any production or deployment of nuclear weapons in Latin America and the Caribbean, and the Treaty of Pelindaba (1964) prohibits nuclear weapons in many African countries. As recently as 2006 a

Central Asian Nuclear Weapon Free Zone was established amongst the former Soviet republics of Central Asia prohibiting nuclear weapons. In the middle of 1996, the International Court of Justice, the highest court of the United Nations, issued an Advisory Opinion concerned with the "Legality of the Threat or Use of Nuclear Weapons".

The court ruled that the use or threat of use of nuclear weapons would violate various articles of international law, including the Geneva Conventions, the Hague Conventions, the UN Charter, and the Universal Declaration of Human Rights. In view of the unique, destructive characteristics of nuclear weapons, the International Committee of the Red Cross calls on States to ensure that these weapons are never used, irrespective of whether they consider them to be lawful or not.

Additionally, there have been other, specific actions meant to discourage countries from developing nuclear arms. In the wake of the tests by India and Pakistan in 1998, economic sanctions were (temporarily) levied against both countries, though neither were signatories with the Nuclear Non-Proliferation Treaty.

One of the stated *casus belli* for the initiation of the 2003 Iraq War was an accusation by the United States that Iraq was actively pursuing nuclear arms (though this was soon discovered not to be the case as the program had been discontinued). In 1981, Israel had bombed a nuclear reactor being constructed in Osirak, Iraq, in what it called an attempt to halt Iraq's previous nuclear arms ambitions.

Disarmament

Nuclear disarmament refers to both the act of reducing or eliminating nuclear weapons and to the end state of a nuclear-free world, in which nuclear weapons are completely eliminated.

Beginning with the 1963 Partial Test Ban Treaty and continuing through the 1996 Comprehensive Test Ban Treaty, there have been many treaties to limit or reduce nuclear weapons testing and stockpiles. The 1968 Nuclear Non-Proliferation

Treaty has as one of its explicit conditions that all signatories must "pursue negotiations in good faith" towards the long-term goal of "complete disarmament". However, no nuclear state has treated that aspect of the agreement as having binding force.

Only one country—South Africa—has ever fully renounced nuclear weapons they had independently developed. A number of former Soviet republics—Belarus, Kazakhstan, and Ukraine—returned Soviet nuclear arms stationed in their countries to Russia after the collapse of the USSR. Proponents of nuclear disarmament say that it would lessen the probability of nuclear war occurring, especially accidentally. Critics of nuclear disarmament say that it would undermine deterrence and could lead to increased global instability. Various American government officials, who were in office during the Cold War period, have recently been advocating the elimination of nuclear weapons. These officials include Henry Kissinger, George Shultz, Sam Nunn, and William Perry. In January 2010, Lawrence M. Krauss stated that "no issue carries more importance to the long-term health and security of humanity than the effort to reduce, and perhaps one day, rid the world of nuclear weapons".

In the years after the end of the Cold War, there have been numerous campaigns to urge the abolition of nuclear weapons, such as that organized by the Global Zero movement, and the goal of a "world without nuclear weapons" was advocated by United States President Barack Obama in an April 2009 speech in Prague. A CNN poll from April 2010 indicated that the American public was nearly evenly split on the issue.

Controversy

Even before the first nuclear weapons had been developed, scientists involved with the Manhattan Project were divided over the use of the weapon. The role of the two atomic bombings of the country in Japan's surrender and the U.S.'s ethical justification for them has been the subject of scholarly and popular debate for decades. The question of whether nations should have nuclear weapons, or test them, has been continually and nearly universally controversial.

Radioactive fallout from nuclear weapons testing was first drawn to public attention in 1954 when the Castle Bravo hydrogen bomb test at the Pacific Proving Grounds contaminated the crew and catch of the Japanese fishing boat *Lucky Dragon*. One of the fishermen died in Japan seven months later, and the fear of contaminated tuna led to a temporary boycotting of the popular staple in Japan. The incident caused widespread concern around the world, especially regarding the effects of nuclear fallout and atmospheric nuclear testing, and "provided a decisive impetus for the emergence of the anti-nuclear weapons movement in many countries". Peace movements emerged in Japan and in 1954 they converged to form a unified "Japanese Council Against Atomic and Hydrogen Bombs". Japanese opposition to nuclear weapons tests in the Pacific Ocean was widespread, and "an estimated 35 million signatures were collected on petitions calling for bans on nuclear weapons".

In the United Kingdom, the first Aldermaston March organised by the Campaign for Nuclear Disarmament took place at Easter 1958, when several thousand people marched for four days from Trafalgar Square, London, to the Atomic Weapons Research Establishment close to Aldermaston in Berkshire, England, to demonstrate their opposition to nuclear weapons. The Aldermaston marches continued into the late 1960s when tens of thousands of people took part in the four-day marches.

In 1959, a letter in the *Bulletin of Atomic Scientists* was the start of a successful campaign to stop the Atomic Energy Commission dumping radioactive waste in the sea 19 kilometres from Boston. In 1962, Linus Pauling won the Nobel Peace Prize for his work to stop the atmospheric testing of nuclear weapons, and the "Ban the Bomb" movement spread.

In 1963, many countries ratified the Partial Test Ban Treaty prohibiting atmospheric nuclear testing. Radioactive fallout became less of an issue and the anti-nuclear weapons movement went into decline for some years. A resurgence of interest occurred amid European and American fears of nuclear war in the 1980s.

Non-weapons uses

Apart from their use as weapons, nuclear explosives have been tested and used for various non-military uses, and proposed, but not used for large-scale earth moving. When long term health and clean-up costs were included, there was no economic advantage over conventional explosives. Synthetic elements, such as einsteinium and fermium, created by neutron bombardment of uranium and plutonium during thermonuclear explosions, were discovered in the aftermath of the first thermonuclear bomb test.

In 2008 the worldwide presence of new isotopes from atmospheric testing beginning in the 1950s was developed into a reliable way of detecting art forgeries, as all paintings created after that period may contain traces of cesium-137 and strontium-90, isotopes that did not exist in nature before 1945.

Nuclear explosives have also been seriously studied as potential propulsion mechanisms for space travel.

WEAPONS AND EQUIPMENT DEVELOPMENT AND MILITARY SCIENTIFIC THEORY

"Technology determines the tactics." The appearance of large quantities of technical equipment inevitably brings about great transformations in military theory and tactics; this in turn leads to great changes in strategic thinking, patterns of combat, combat style, and military structures:

- Weapons development enhances man's strategic consciousness, deepens his strategic reflections, and increases the emphasis on strategic projections. In today's world, strategic research is extremely dynamic. With the development of strategic rockets and various spacecrafts, as well as the gradual development of energy beam weapons, kinetic energy weapons, and other space weapons systems, war has extended from the surface, air, and sea toward outer space. The areas of man's activities have already extended beyond the earth and moved into space. This has opened up man's field of vision and expanded his modes of thinking. In the wideness of space, the earth is no longer "boundless and limitless," but has become one of the "global villages" in the universe. In the eyes of the strategist, the earth has become small and man's strategic reflection is becoming more profound and his strategic consciousness has been greatly enhanced. Man's heart embraces the whole of the universe. The development of strategic research is even more important than at any time in history and has become an especially important issue for all countries globally. What is coming will be conflicts in space. One of the conflicts will be the military struggle for "control of the high ground in space." The other will be exploitation and use of space, the struggle for the resources of space. For this reason, every country in the world is busily formulating and developing strategic plans. In March 1983, the United States became the first to formulate a "Star Wars Plan." This caused global commotion in strategy research. The Soviet Union responded with "defensive measures" to the "Star Wars Plan." Western Europe came up with the "Eureka Plan." Each of the COMECON countries announced a "Plan for the integrated advancement of science and technology by the year 2000." Japan had its "Policy outline for science and technology;" China had a "Policy for a new technological revolution;" India came out with "Policy statements for new technology;" South Korea had its "Conceptions for long range national growth;" and Yugoslavia had its "National science and technology development strategy." To rank within the world's family of nations, to live and survive in the "global village" in this universe, each nation must come up with ideas for a "grand strategy." "To stand shoulder to shoulder with the giants" one must intensely fix one's eye on the growth of national defence construction and weapons in the next century.

- Modern weapons are not only direct combat strengths between opposing combat opponents, they are also strategic deterrents and tools for international political struggles. The appearance of offensive strategic weapons like missiles, atomic bombs, nuclear-powered submarines, and long-range bombers has caused great changes in military strategy. The research, production, and large stockpiles of strategic weapons are already more than needed to seek out and kill an enemy. It has turned into a tool for political and diplomatic struggle. The large-scale arms race have caused the United States to stockpile over 9,400 nuclear warheads with a total nuclear weight equivalent of over 4 billion tons. The Soviet Union's stockpile of over 8,000 nuclear warheads has a total nuclear weight equivalent of over 5 billion tons. The quantity of nuclear warheads possessed by these two nuclear powers comprises above 97 percent of the global total. Both have the capacity to destroy the other several times over. Living under these conditions, the military strategy of both sides has gone through many changes; strategic ideologies have been revised about every 10 years. However, pressure from the threat that "destroying the enemy doesn't necessarily mean one's own survival" has kept them from crossing the "nuclear threshold" and taking the next step of pressing the button to launch those nuclear missiles. England, France, and China have independently and on their own developed into national nuclear powers. The limited power of these countries is not enough to compete with the capabilities of the United States and the Soviet Union, but they do play a role in the even development of political, economical, and military affairs within the world. This power is entirely a symbol of a country's independence and its existence within the world of politics, economics, military affairs, and science and technology.

In addition to nuclear weapons, the emergence of strategic weapons has definitely caused reforms within the military, changing past combat theories that we must go through war and campaigns to achieve strategic objectives to the possibility that strategic weapons could directly attack the opponent's strategic targets and achieve the strategic objectives. The development of various space weapons has not only intensified military struggles in space, it has also increased ways in which strategic objectives could be directly achieved.

- Today's weapons systems are very mobile. They also have long range, high accuracy, and great power, causing the time and spatial aspects as well as the intensity of war to change greatly. The development of these weapons and the great number of these weapons being deployed within the services have caused the arenas of war to be extended into deep sea and space, the length of war to shorten, and the suddenness, destructiveness, savageness, and mutation to increase unprecedentedly. In the "blitzkrieg" of the German armoured troops during WWII, they could advance only about 30 km daily. Today, under normal circumstances, the Soviets could do 50 km and under nuclear conditions it could reach above 100 km. When the Soviet Union invaded Afghanistan, its push towards Kabul, a distance of 900 km took only 6 days. The time it takes for an intercontinental ballistic missile to travel its whole distance is only slightly more than 30 minutes and there is no more than 20 minutes of early warning for its defence.

During the Falklands War, England's SHEFFIELD class missile destroyer did not even have the opportunity to react before it was hit by Argentina's EXOCET missile. With this short span of time, it is very difficult to react. This has made even greater demands on command and control.

The largeness of the battlefield and the number of troops involved have given rise to immense increases in technical weaponry and specialized technology and have caused even greater problems in the coordination of operations and commands. According to reports, there were only 20 different military specialties during Word War I.

It grew to 160 during World War II, and at present, the number of military technologies and specializations exceed 2,000. During combat, the army, navy, air force, and the other different service branches are all involved at the same time. The types of weapons used are never less than a dozen and usually are in the hundreds. This alone would demand that the commander prepare detailed plans and coordinate his commands well. There must be no mistakes in differentiating missions, allotting time, and coordinating activities. Any small error could lead to major mistakes and even greater disasters.

First strike has always been the combat phase that militarists attach greatest importance to. The success or failure of the first strike impacts the whole battle. In modern combat, because of the short time needed for combat, the phases of combat are no longer clearly delineated. The long range surprise attack or the counterattack during the preliminary period of the combat has become the main combat model for first strike. Thus, every nation has given special attention to studying the first strike phase of a war. The United States emphasizes that "every preparation must be made to win with the first strike." The Soviet Union also believes that "surprise attacks are the most effective combat opening moves to implement in future wars.... Victory can basically be determined in the first phase of a war." This will demand that commanders make complete preparations for first strikes. Intelligence, reconnaissance, personal observations with automatic and rapid analysis, processing and judgment, decisionmaking, formulating careful plans, and even reactions must be quick and accurate because only then could the "first strike win" objective be achieved.

- The extensive use of modern weapons has caused great changes in military structures. Before WWI, the military was basically composed of land forces that included the infantry, artillery, calvary, and navy. Before WWII, there was a great deal of aircraft and tanks in the military, thus the air force, armoured troops and motorized troops came into existence. The air force itself was divided into bomber, fighter, and attack aircraft forces. There were surface vessels, submarines, naval aviation forces and marines in the navy. After WWII, strategic rocket forces, army airborne forces and other service branches were formed. With the development of space technology and the successful development of various spaceflight vehicles as well as the development of various space weapons, the militarization of space will possibly strengthen the military deployment of a new independent military service branch "Space Forces." In 1982, the United States established the Air Force Spaceflight Command (a command comparable to the Strategic Air Force and Tactical Air Force Commands combined), and in 1983, the United States established the Naval Spaceflight Command. In 1985, the two commands and affiliated army commands were combined to form the U.S. Spaceflight Command. Not long after the United States had established the Air Force Spaceflight Command (1982), the Soviet Union appointed Lt. Gen. Sadaluofu as the "Aeronavigation Forces Commander." Some reports have said that "it is possible that the Soviet Union had already established a military spaceflight command like the U.S. Air Force Spaceflight Command and that the aeronavigation force was nothing but a subforce of that command." Various evidence has shown that the growth of the militarization of space has brought about the birth of the "Space Forces." With the advancements made in microelectronics, computers, and artificial intelligence technology, multipurpose robots could soon be used more and more in military applications and in those work areas where the labour is heavy and environmentally dangerous; thus a "robot force" would have to be deployed. The influence of weapons development on military administrative systems and deployment and on the overall structure can be easily seen. At present, the strategic course for overall military development is: a reduction in the overall personnel strength, a rise in the proportion of technical military personnel in the overall structure, a decrease in the proportion of personnel directly involved in combat, and a different scale for the increase in the proportion of logistic personnel (including technical support personnel).

The impact of modern weapons on military theory has been profound and extensive. The various sophisticated tools, means and methods of modern policy decision studies, projection studies, and futures studies have scientifically given impetus to and provided directions for military theories and strategic growth. It has allowed the military to grow scientifically so that it can completely anticipate conflicts and play a better leadership role.

CHINA GROWTH STEALTH FIGHTER MILITARY TECHNOLOGY

The aircraft in the above photo looks at first sight as a complete prototype, but it actually is a very detailed full-scale engineering mock-up. It can be speculated that, after having been used to study the aircraft's internal installations, the mock-up has also received an external finish for presentation purposes. Its real function at this point, however, is probably to buttist in the definition of the required logistic support (i.e., access to the various avionics boxes and on-board systems, ground support equipment like the various ladders and the external power source units, air conditioning units and so on) as well as to study the engines' removal-installation procedures.

Since some time now it has been known that the rapidly-developing Chinese aeronautical industry is studying a new and technologically very advanced combat aircraft, also boasting significant low signature characteristics. This programme is a logical step in China's "Long March" towards full independence in designing, developing and producing combat airplanes of a technological level in line with China's status as the "other" world superpower, on an equal footing as Russia and eventually even the USA.

The scarce information available about this new advanced combat aircraft indicates that two, possibly competing, study groups (both part of the AVIC I Group of aeronautical industries) are or have been working on the subject. One of these groups (601 Insbreastute) originates from Shenyang Airplane Corporation (SAC) which is in charge of the large, twin-engine J-8 fighters in service with the PLAAF (People's Liberation Army Air Force) as well as of licence production of the Su-27SK under the local designation of J-11. The overall configuration of SAC's preliminary design, apparently designated J-13, owes significantly to the American F-A-22, being a tailed delta but with wing and horizontal tailplanes more in line with those of the F-16. The other study group (611 Insbreastute) from Chengdu Airplane Corporation (CAC), has developed the J-12, a concept which follows the less conventional canard layout used with success in the company's J-10.

While previous information (albeit admittedly unconfirmed), gave to the SAC concept the edge, perhaps as a result of the company's experience in large twin-engine fighters, this seems to have since been reversed in favour of the Chengdu design. It is however still not clear whether the designation of J-14 is intended to suggest a successor design to both the J-12 and the J-13, and whether the existence of the J-14 engineering mock-up (clearly based on the J-12) indicates that the type has been selected for development, or the compebreastion is still going on with parallel activities underway on another such mock-up based on the J-13.

While no data is available about the J-14, some speculation can be done in the attempt to extrapolate the aircraft's characteristics and thus the roles it is called to perform. The following considerations are based on what can be seen in the photo, but also involve making some buttumptions on the basis of what is known of the Chinese armed forces' perceived priorities in operational requirements, the domestic industry's approach to combat aircraft design and, finally, the well-know Chinese weaknesses in some technological fields. In addition, the well-developed cooperation with Russian companies, particularly in areas such as powerplant, avionics and possibly computer-based fly-by-wire flight control systems is also taken into consideration.

General Configuration

The J-14 will surely be fitted with a fly-by-wire flight control system and be designed for artificial stability. The Chinese should by now have matured an adequate experience in this field through a number of experimental programmes and application to actual in-service types.

The general configuration of the aircraft is clearly born out from CAC's experience in developing the J-10, with its canard layout and ventral air intake. But while the J-10 is known to be related to the Israeli LAVI, this new and much more ambitious design rather appears to have a definite relationship with the ill-fated Russian 5th generation fighter studied a few years ago, the MiG 1.44 MFI and in fact it shares a number of elements which can doubtless be traced back to the Russian demonstrator. It is thus very probable not to say certain that an agreement has been reached between the Russian and Chinese governments allowing for the transfer of information and technological data as well as consultancy services being provided by RSK MiG and Russian research centres (arguably including the TsAGI aerodynamic research insbreastute) to develop the new Chinese fighter.

The J-14's planform closely matches that of the MiG 1.44, i.e. a canard layout (the canard surface are fully movable) with mid-positioned wing and widely separated twin-vertical surfaces canted outward, which continue under the wing in twin ventral fins, these too being canted outward à la J-10. While not visible in the photo, wind tunnel models show that the 1.44 configuration has been maintained also in the booms protruding from the wing and contributing to support the vertical tailplanes and ventral fins. These booms probably end with radomes covering electronic warfare antennas and possibly also a rearward facing radar, similar to the installation experimented in the Su-37 a few years ago. In the MiG 1.44, the portion of wing between the fuselage-engine pods and the booms is extended rearward past the wing trailing edge and includes a couple of moving surfaces contributing, together with the all-moving canard surfaces, to the longitudinal control of the airplane. It is not yet possible to buttess whether this solution, too has been maintained for the J-14.

But while the overall aerodynamic configuration of the J-14 follows that of the MiG 1.44 demonstrator, a radical redesign has been implemented in the pursuit of a significant reduction in the radar cross-section value. In particular, the aircraft incorporates a pronounced wing-body blending, which was totally lacking in the original Russian design. Further, the air intake, while in the same ventral position under the forward fuselage, has a completely new shape, and by the same token the upper part of the airplane is also completely different and shows towards the rear the protuberances of the engine "pods" which blend with the fuselage and wing roots in a curious reminiscence of the Northrop YF-23. Also, the front fuselage merges down into the upper wing, blending with the separated engine bay bulges while maintaining some relation with the "clbuttical" Su-27 forward fuselage shape. The search for enhanced stealth performance is also apparent in the "flattened" profile of the entire front fuselage section (nearly identical to the Su-32), as well as in the generalised use of serrated doors to cover the landing gear and missile bays.

On the other hand, it remains clear that a canard configuration is hardly the ideal solution from the point of view of a reduced radar signature. Summing up, it would thus seem safe to buttume that the J-14 is a "stealth-optimised" aircraft rather than un uncompromising stealth design à la F-A-22 or (in a different clbutt) the F-35 JSF.

Above the raised front fuselage is located the single-seat pilot chickenpit. This is closed by a single-piece frameless bubble-type transparent canopy which appears technological very demanding under various aspects such as manufacturing process, adequate optical qualities and bird-impact resistance, yet allowing through-ejection. On the other hand, the pilot is provided with superb all-around visibility also due to the position of the chickenpit above the forward fuselage "hump", again a reminiscence of the Su-27.

After Chinese visit Ships, U.S. Officials Hope for Reciprocation

After Chinese visit ships, U.S. officials hope for reciprocation {EXCERPT}, by Allison Batdorff, Stars and Stripes Pacific edition, Friday, June 23, 2006 ANDERSEN AIR FORCE BASE, Guam ˜...

The main landing gear, with single wheels mounted on telescopic legs, retracts outward, with the legs being accommodated in the fuselage side blending into the wing bottom and the wheels into the wing (a similar geometry has been selected for the F-A-22). In order to minimise the volume of the bay occupied by the gear in the retracted position, the telescopic main gear legs are shortened via a pulling bar acting on a lever, similarly to what has been introduced in the Eurofighter TYPHOON. While not clear in the photo, it is possible that the same landing gear leg shortening design has also been selected for the nose twin-wheel element.

Powerplant Installation

In view of the twin-engine layout of the J-14 and its estimated TO weight in air combat configuration (some 25-28 tons with full internal fuel, gun ammunition, 2 x SRAAM and 4 x MRAAM), its engines should give a thrust in the range of 13-14 tons in afterburning mode, so achieving a thrust-to-weight ratio in the order of 1:1. Now it seems difficult to envisage a stateof-the-art Chinese engine, particularly in this thrust clbutt, achieving full production status by the mid of the next decade when the J-14 could reasonably be expected to enter service. Even for the J-10 a Russian engine has been at last preferred. It can thus be buttumed that a Russian engine has been selected for the J-14 as well, and indeed the model which can be seen in the picture to the rear of the right wing of the mock-up has the accessory gearbox mounted above the engine in the traditional Russian style. If, as it is highly probable, this engine is a member of the Saturn-Lyulka AL-31-41 family (but it could also be a prototype of the Chinese Liming LM WS10A in the same thrust clbutt), this would make the type not fully interchangeable with the version selected for the J-10, which has the accessory gearbox located on the engine bottom, Western-style. It is also possible to speculate that the idea is to have the prototypes powered by the lower-thrust AL-31 as used in the J-11-Su-27SK-Su-30MKK, with either an evolved higher-thrust version of AL-31 or a series-production version of the AL-41 being then adopted for the series aircraft.

Coming to the engine-airframe installation, the air intake located in the bottom part of the front fuselage is of the fixed geometry type with no moving ramp, unlike the case with the J-10. This solution has made it possible to eliminate the sharp angles and slots between the moving ramp and in general to provide smooth shapes which reduce radar reflectivity.

The pronounced bulging up of the air intake inner duct helps avoid a direct presentation of the critically reflective engine fan-compressor face to enemy illuminating radar from the forward emisphere. In addition, the bulge is needed to make room for the nose landing gear bay and, even more, for the bottom fuselage weapons bay.

Notwithstanding its fixed geometry, the air intake shows elements which should generate a couple of oblique shock waves before the normal one, thus guaranteeing an adequately efficient dynamic pressure recovery in the supersonic flight regime. The well-shaped bulge along the bottom of the centre fuselage entering the air intake, which forms the upper part of the air intake duct, seems reminiscent of the latest Lockheed Martin's vaunted design for a fixed-ramp, multi-shock air intake planned for use on the production F-35 and already experimented on an F-16.

This peculiar layout, together with the forward-raked air intake lip (already seen in the late 1950s on the F8U-3 CRUSADER III) is clearly intended to generate the oblique shock waves mentioned above.

The location of the air intake under the fuselage is well suited to provide a smooth distortion-free airflow to the engines. From this particular point of view, the hinged bottom lip present in the TYPHOON works even better at extreme angles of attack, but it implies the penalty of a higher radar signature. In more general terms, the choice of a single air intake configuration in a twin-engine airplane may be open to some criticism, in that it is less than ideal to maintain correct working conditions (i.e., smooth undistorted airflow to the remaining engine) in the event of an engine flaming out for whatever reason. The air intake thus establishes a potential single point failure in an otherwise completely redundant twin-engine installation. It can be expected that Thrust Vector Control (TVC) nozzles, probably of the axisymmetric type (despite their not insignificant contribution to overall nuclear signature), will be a standard feature of the J-14 to both enhance manoeuvrability and reduce trim drag in cruise flight.

Armament

Chinese design derived from a Russian model such as the GSh-6-23 23mm installed in the MiG-31 and the Su-24. The gun is installed in the upper right fuselage side, just above the canard surface. The firing port, unlike the F-A-22 is left permanently open, hence generating a not so negligible radar reflection.

The main armament is carried in three weapons bays, whose arrangement looks like virtually a clone of the F-A-22. Two smaller bays are located on the fuselage sides and appear to be tailored to each accommodate a single short-range air-to-air missile, while the large underfuselage bay, closed by twin doors, will probably accept at least four medium-range AAMs. It may be speculated that the J-14 is intended to carry "compressed carriage" clipped-wing versions of the AAMs already in use with the PLAAF, i.e. the PL-8 and the Russian R-73 for short-range dogfights and the R-77 and the indigenous PL-12 for medium-range work. The R-77 is already suitable for carriage in an internal bay in its standard version, being equipped with very small span wings while the lattice tail control fins can be fold forward flush with the missile body.

Underwing store stations are surely foreseen to carry additional weapons and fuel tanks, when there is no need to maintain a high level of stealthness.

Combat Avionics

J-14 is already in full-scale development, the main choices related to the avionics systems should have already been made, at least at the conceptual level. However, the Chinese domestic industry is almost certainly not in a position to supply the advanced avionics required in a sophisticated aircraft like the J-14, and contributions from abroad will be required-from Russia, Israel and arguably even Europe.

The J-14 being intended to enter service in around 2012-2015, it may be expected that the Chinese are aiming at equipping it with a radar with electronically scanning (ASEA) antenna, capable of multiple targets engagements-provided that a source for such a radar could be identified. In the Russian tradition, a pbuttive search and track system based on optronic devices (FLIR with integrated laser rangefinder) is expected to be also installed in a retractable or faired turret. As already mentioned, the dual rear booms could carry, in addition to various pbuttive and-or active defensive systems also a rear-facing radar. Finally, it can be expected that the chickenpit instrumentation for the production version will be based on an Helmet Mounted Display-Sight (HMD-S) totally replacing the HUD, although the latter instrument is clearly visible in the photo. The head-down displays would probably include three or four large Multi Function Displays (MFD), which should have the possibility to present a digital map and a complete tactical situation. A real-time data link is also an expected addition to the fully integrated avionics system to enhance the situation awareness of the pilot, particularly when operating in multiships combat groups to make the most use of the commonly available information from the various platforms.

Bibliography

Ajey Lele: *Strategic Technologies for the Military : Breaking New Frontiers*, Sage, Delhi, 2009.

Amitabh Sikdar: *India and China : Strategic Energy Management and Security*, Manas, Delhi, 2009.

Arend, A.: *International Law and the Use of Force,* London, Routledge, 1993.

Asha Gupta: *Military Rule and Democratization : Changing Perspectives*, Deep & Deep, Delhi, 2003.

Banerjee, Sumanta: *In the Wake of Naxalbari: A History of the Naxalite Movement in India,* Calcutta: Subarnarekha, 1980.

Barber B.R.: *Strong Democracy. Participatory Politics for a New Age.* Berkeley, University of California Press, 1984.

Benjamin, Joseph : *China-Pak Relations : Prospect and Retrospect,* Reference Press, Delhi, 2004.

Bhat, T.P. : *India and China : Trade Complementarities and Competitiveness*, Bookwell, Delhi, 2008.

Bose, S. C., *The Indian Struggle, 1920-1942,* Bombay, Asia Publishing House, 1964.

Bradley, John. *Learning to Glow: A Nuclear Reader.* Tucson: University of Arizona Press, 2000.

Brierly, L.: *The Law of Nations,* New York, Oxford University Press, 1955.

Brooks, Constance : *Disaster Preparedness,* Washington, DC, Association for Research Libraries, 1993.

Budge I: *The New Challenge of Direct Democracy*, Oxford, Polity Press, 1996.

Buszynski, Lezsek: *The future of China-Russia relations.* Lexington: University Press of Kentucky, 2010.

Caf, Dowlah: *Privatization Experience in Bangladesh, 1991-1996.* Washington D.C.: World Bank, 1997.

Caplin, A. and Schotter, A.: *The Foundations of Positive and Normative Economics*, New York, Oxford University Press, 2008.

Chitkara, M.G. : *Indo-Pak Relations Challenges Before New Millennium*, APH, Delhi, 2001.

Clinton, William J. *A National Security Strategy for a New Century*. Washington, DC: Government Printing Office, 1998.

Daniel J.: *Bandits on the Information Superhighway*. O'Reilly & Associates, Inc.: Sebastopol, 1996.

Dasgupta, B.: *The Naxalite Movement*, Bombay: Allied Publishers, 1974.

David Post : *The Rise of Law in Cyberspace*, 48 Stan, L. Rev. 1367, 1996.

Debray, Regis. *Revolution in the Revolution*. New York: Grove Press, Inc., 1993.

Deepak, B R : *India and China : 1904-2004 : A Century of Peace and Conflict*, Manak, Delhi, 2005.

Dixit, Prabla: *Communalism: A Struggle for Power*, New Delhi, Orient Longman, 1981.

Donnan, H. and Wilson, T. M.: *Borders: Frontiers of Identity, Nation and State*, Oxford: Berg, 1999.

Duncan, Francis. *Rickover and the Nuclear Navy: The Discipline of Technology*. Annapolis: Naval Institute Press, 1990.

Dunn, Lewis A., *'India, Pakistan, Iran: A Nuclear Proliferation Chain'*, Colorado: Westview Press, 1977.

Evelyn Goh, *Meeting the China Challenge: The U.S. in Southeast Asian Regional Security Strategies*, DC: East-West Center, 2005.

Friedman, G.: *The Future of War: Power, Technology and American World Dominance in the 21st Century*, N.Y., Random House, 1996.

Gao, Mobo: *The Battle for China's Past: Mao and the Cultural Revolution,* London, Pluto Press, 2008.

Goel, Suresh : *Military, Security and Intelligence Agencies*, MD Publications, Delhi, 2009.

Gul, F. and Pesendorfer, W.: *The Foundations of Positive and Normative Economics*, New York, Oxford University Press 2008.

Hagström, Linus: *Japan's China Policy: A Relational Power Analysis*, London and New York: Routledge, 2005.

Hays, Peter L. and others: *Countering the Proliferation and Use of Weapons of Mass Destruction,* New York, NY: McGraw-Hill, 1998.

Heathcote, T. A.: *The Indian Army – The Garrison of British Imperial India, 1822–1922*. David & Charles. Newton Abbot, Devon. 1974.

Hoffman, Bruce: *Inside Terrorism and Internet Crime*, New York: Columbia University Press, 1998.

Huntington, P. : *The Soldier and the State : The Theory and Politics of Civil-Military Relations*, Natraj Pub, Delhi, 2005.

Huntington, P. : *The Soldier and the State : The Theory and Politics of Civil-Military Relations*, Natraj Pub, Delhi, 2005.

Ian Storey: *ASEAN and the South China Sea: Movement in Lieu of Progress*, Washington, D.C., Jamestown Foundation,2012.

Ikenberry, John G.: *After Victory: Institutions, Strategic Restraint, and the Rebuilding of Order after Major Wars*. Princeton, NJ: Princeton University Press, 2001.

Imtiaz, A.: *State and Foreign Policy: India's Role in South Asia*, New Delhi, Vikas, 1993.

Islam, M. Mufakharul : *Bengal Agriculture 1920-1946: A Quantitative Study*, Cambridge South Asian Studies, Cambridge University Press, 2007.

James Campbell: *Excursions, Adventures and Field-Sports in Ceylon : Its Commercial and Military Importance*, AES, Delhi, 2006.

Janowitz, M.: *The Professional Soldier: A Social and Political Portrait*, N.Y., The Free Press, 1960.

Jha, Prem Shankar : *India and China : The Battle Between Soft and Hard Power*, Penguin Books India, Delhi, 2010.

Joel Moses: *The Computer Age, A Twenty-Year View*.Cambridge, MA, The MIT Press, 1979.

John M. Seidl: *Politics American Style: Race, Environment and Central Cities*, New York, Prentice-Hall, 1972.

Johnston, R.J.: *Geography and Geographers*. London: Edward Arnold, 1991.

Jones, W.H.: *The Government and Politics of Indian Military*, London, Hutchinson, 1971.

Joon Ahn: *The Rise of China and the Future of East Asian Integration*, Asia-Pacific Review, London, Carfax Publishing Company, 2004.

Joshi, Vijay and I.M.D. Little: *India: Macroeconomics and Political Economy, 1964-1991*. Washington, DC: World Bank, 1994.

Kapur, C.K. : *Chinese Military Modernisation*, Manas, Delhi, 2003.

Kelly, John B.: *Britain and the Persian Gulf 1795-1880*, Oxford, Clarendon Press, 1968.

Kumar, Raj : *Weapons and Military Technology*, Sumit Enterprises, Delhi, 2009.

Kunju, N. : *Indo-Pak : Nuclear Cold War*, Reliance, Delhi, 2002.

Laliberte, S. : *Security by Example Defend I.T.* New York, Addison Wesley, 2004.

Lardy, Nicholas R.: *China's Unfinished Economic Revolution.* Washington, DC: Brookings, 1998.

Lieberthal, Kenneth: *Governing China.* New York: WW Norton, 1995.

Link, Albert N.: *Evaluating Economic Damages, A Handbook for Attorneys*, Westport, CT, Quorum Books, 1992.

Magnussen, L., *Evolutionary and Neo-Schumpeterian Approaches to Economics*, Kluwer, Boston, 1994.

Marie Lecomte : *Hindu Kingship, Ethnic Revival, and Maoist Rebellion in Nepal*, Oxford University Press, Delhi, 2009.

Nayyar, K K : *National Security : Military Aspects*, Rupa, Delhi, 2003.

Pierre, Andrew J. *The Global Politics of Arms Sales.* Princeton, N.J., 1982.

Posen, B.R.: *The Sources of Indian Military Doctrine*, Ithaca, 1984, Cornell Univ. Press.

Prabir De: *India and China in an Era of Globalisation : Essays on Economic Cooperation*, Bookwell, Delhi, 2005.

Prasad, Lal Bahadur : *Indian Political System and Law*, New Delhi, Shree, 2005.

Prescott, J.R.V.: *The Geography of Frontiers and Boundaries.* Chicago: Aldine, 1965.

Qureshi, A. Iqbal : *Islam and the Theory of Interest,* Kitab Bhavan, New Delhi, 1994.

Rhodes, Richard, *The Making of the Atomic Bomb*, New York: Simon and Schuster, 1988.

Rita Raj: *Global Encyclopaedia of Military Education and Training*, Global Vision, Delhi, 2010.

Rosen, P.: *Societies and Military Power: India and its Armies*, Ithaca, Cornell University Press, 1996.

Rudolph, Heimanson: *Dictionary of Military*, N.Y.: Oceana Publications, 1967.

Samuel P. Huntington: *The Soldier and the State : The Theory and Politics of Civil-Military Relations*, Natraj Pub, Delhi, 2005.

Shaun Narine, *Explaining ASEAN: Regionalism in Southeast Asia*, Boulder, CO: Lynne Rienner Publishers, 2002.

Shirk, Susan L.: *The Political Logic of Economic Reform in China.* Berkeley: University of California Press, 1993.

Singhal, D. P.: *India and Afghanistan: 1876-1907. A Study in Diplomatic Relations*, St. Lucia, University of Queensland, 1963.

Smith, V. L.: *Papers in Experimental Economics*, Cambridge, Cambridge University Press, 1991.

Strange, Susan: *The Retreat of the State: The Diffusion of Power in the World Economy*, Cambridge: Cambridge University, 1996.

Suresh Goel: *International Encyclopaedia of Military, Security and Intelligence Agencies*, MD Publications, Delhi, 2009.

Sutton, J., *Technology and Defence Market Structure*, MIT Press, Delhi, 1998.

Taylor, F. W.: *The Principles of Scientific Management*, New York, 1917.

Thapa, Deepak : *Understanding the Maoist Movement of Nepal*, Centre for Social Research and Development, Delhi, 2003.

Tietenberg, Tom, *Environmental Economics and Policy,* New York, HarperCollins, 1994

Tinbergen, Jan.: *On the Theory of Economic Policy*; Amsterdam, North-Holland 1952.

Ullman, D. G.: *Making Robust Decisions,* Trafford, 2006.

Vogel, Ezra: *One Step Ahead in China: Guangdong Under Reform.* Cambridge: Harvard University Press, 1989.

Vogel, Steven K.: *Freer Markets, More Rules: Regulatory Reform in Advanced Industrial Countries.* Ithaca: Cornell University Press, 1996.

Wakamiya Yoshibumi, *The Postwar Conservative View of Asia,* Tokyo: LTCB International Library Foundation, 1999.

Whitaker, D. J.: *The Terrorism Reader,* New York: Routledge, 2001.

Wilson, Thomas M., and Hastings Donnan: *A Companion to Border Studies.* Hoboken, NJ: Wiley-Blackwell, 2012.

Woodward, J.: *The Oxford Handbook of Philosophy of Economics,* New York, Oxford University Press, 2009.

Worster, Donald : *Dust Bowl: The Southern Plains in the 1930s,* New York, Oxford University Press, 1979.

Index

G

H

I

K

L

M

N

❑❑❑